Quality of Life of Chinese People in a Changing World

Social Indicators Research Series

Volume 44

This new series aims to provide a public forum for single treatises and collections of papers on social indicators research that are too long to be published in our journal *Social Indicators Research*. Like the journal, the book series deals with statistical assessments of the quality of life from a broad perspective, It welcomes the research on a wide variety of substantive areas, including health, crime, housing, education, family life, leisure activities, transportation, mobility, economics, work, religion and environmental issues. These areas of research will focus on the impact of key issues such as health on the overall quality of life and vice versa. An international review board, consisting of Ruut Veenhoven, Joachim Vogel, Ed Diener, Torbjorn Moum, Mirjam A.G. Sprangers and Wolfgang Glatzer, will ensure the high quality of the series as a whole.

For other titles published in this series, go to
www.springer.com/series/6548

Daniel T.L. Shek

Quality of Life of Chinese People in a Changing World

Previously published in *Social Indicators Research*, Volume 95, No. 3 (2010)

Springer

Prof. Daniel T.L. Shek
The Hong Kong Polytechnic University
China
Daniel.shek@polyu.edu.hk

ISSN: 1387-6570
ISBN: 978-94-007-0223-3

Springer Dordrecht Heidelberg London New York

Library of Congress Control Number: 2010937631

Printed on acid-free paper

Springer is part of Springer Science+Business Media (www.springer.com)

Contents

Soc Indic Res (2010) 95:357–361
DOI 10.1007/s11205-009-9534-6

Introduction: Quality of Life of Chinese People in a Changing World

Daniel T. L. Shek

Accepted: 14 August 2009 / Published online: 6 October 2009

The concept of quality of life (QOL) has attracted much research attention of researchers in different disciplines. Using "quality of life" as the search term, computer search conducted in July 2009 showed that there were 7,972 citations in PsycINFO, 6,383 citations in Sociological Abstracts, 766 citations in Social Work Abstracts, 4,151 citations in ERIC, 12,671 citations in MEDLINE, and 12,738 citations in CINAHL. In contrast, using "quality of life" and "Chinese" as search terms, identical search showed that there were 58, 1, 8, 46, 1,018 and 28 citations in PsycINFO, Sociological Abstracts, Social Work Abstracts, ERIC, MEDLINE and CINAHL, respectively. These figures clearly suggest that existing research studies on quality of life are predominantly conducted in the West and there is a strong need to conduct quality of life research in different Chinese communities (Shek et al. 2005b).

Besides the observation that the number of Chinese quality of life studies is on the low side, there are other reasons why more attention should be devoted to QOL research based on Chinese people. First, because culture plays an important role in the conceptualization and experience of quality of life, the predominance of studies based on non-Chinese participants limits our understanding of the related phenomena in the Chinese culture (Shek 2002; Shek et al. 2005a). For example, while happiness and satisfaction are important components of quality of life in the Western culture, Chinese philosophies such as Confucianism, Buddhism and Taoism emphasize forbearance, endurance and humility. Regarding family quality of life, while communication and emotional expressiveness are strongly emphasized in the West, roles, duties and self-suppression (particularly among the junior members in the family) and interpersonal harmony are virtues upheld in Chinese

D. T. L. Shek (✉)
Department of Applied Social Sciences, The Hong Kong Polytechnic University, Hunghom, Hong Kong
e-mail: daniel.shek@polyu.edu.hk

D. T. L. Shek
Department of Sociology, East China Normal University, Shanghai, China

D. T. L. Shek
Kiang Wu Nursing College of Macau, Macau, China

families. As such, it is important to conduct more QOL studies in the Chinese culture to understand quality of life and its manifestation in a cross-cultural context.

In addition, the size of Chinese population warrants research attention. The World Population Clock showed that the population of China was 1,338,612,968, which was roughly one-fifth of the world's population in 2009. Obviously, data from Chinese people must be collected if any theory is claimed to be universally applicable. This point is important because many Chinese QOL researchers actually borrow Western QOL theoretical frameworks to understand the quality of life of Chinese people based on the assumption that these theories are universally applicable.

Finally, the changing socio-economic and political circumstances of China also suggest the importance of understanding the quality of life of Chinese people. With reference to mainland China, adoption of the open door policy and economic reforms in China since late 1970s has led to fundamental changes in the quality of life of Chinese people. For Hong Kong and Macau, they were returned to China in 1997 and 1999, respectively under the political framework of "one country, two systems". In Taiwan, democratization in the past two decades has fueled the quest for individual freedom and rights particularly among Taiwanese adolescents. In view of such changing socio-economic and political circumstances, it would be important to examine the quality of life of Chinese people in different Chinese contexts.

In their review of quality of life research in the global, Western and Chinese contexts, Shek et al. (2005a) pointed out that despite the abundance of research in the study of quality of life in the global context, several missing gaps and research directions were identified in the existing QOL literature. First, a more holistic understanding of the concept of quality of life with reference to different ecological systems, particularly the family system, should be attempted. Second, in contrast to the vast number of studies on the quality of life of adults with and without special needs, there are comparatively fewer research studies on the quality of life of children and adolescents. Third, comparatively fewer studies have examined the quality of life of persons experiencing economic disadvantage. Fourth, while researchers in different disciplines in different places have examined the concept of quality of life, dialogues among researchers across different professions and places are not widespread. Finally, the debate surrounding whether objective indicators (such as official statistics) or subjective indicators (such as opinion surveys) are sensitive indicators of quality of life still existed.

Against the above background, it is indeed an exciting task for me to serve as the guest editor for this special issue of *Social Indicators Research* entitled "Quality of Life of Chinese People in a Changing World". Most of the papers in this special issue are based on the papers presented at the International Conference on "Human Development and the Environment: Advances in Quality of Life Studies" jointly organized by the Social Welfare Practice and Research Centre and Centre for Quality of Life, Institute of Asia-Pacific Studies, The Chinese University of Hong Kong to commemorate the 60th anniversary of New Asia College.

The first two articles of this special issue are studies on Chinese family quality of life involving different members within a family. In the first article by Yuk King Lau, the impact of work and family conflicts on father–child interactional quality in 556 pairs of working fathers and their school-aged children was examined. The findings showed that fathers' work-to-family conflict was negatively related to the quality of father–child interactions, which in turn adversely affected children's self-esteem. Because quality of father–child interaction has been rarely examined in the Chinese QOL studies, this is a pioneering addition to the literature. In the next paper, Vivian Lou examined the relationship between life satisfaction of older adults and social support from grandchildren in 215 older people in Hong Kong. Results showed that support provided by grandchildren significantly predicted elderly quality of life indexed by life satisfaction after controlling background demographic factors and psychological factors such as attitude towards Chinese tradition and self-rated health status. These two papers clearly illustrate how factors in different systems, particularly family factors, influence individual quality of life. These studies are constructive response to the comment of Shek et al. (2005b) that there are few studies studying Chinese family quality of life.

With reference to the lack of research on Chinese adolescent quality of life, several papers are included in this special issue. In the paper written by Siu and Shek, a series of studies on social problem solving are presented. These studies clearly showed that the Chinese version of the Social Problem-Solving Inventory Revised (C-SPSI-R) demonstrated very good psychometric properties. Results also showed that social problem solving was closely linked to measures of individual quality of life indexed by depression and anxiety as well as family quality of life (overall family functioning and parent-adolescent conflicts). With reference to the comment that there are few Chinese quality of life measures (Shek 2002), this paper is a constructive response.

In the next paper by Lai and Shek, personal (hopelessness, social problem solving, emotional competence) and family (parent–adolescent communication, family functioning) quality of life correlates related to adolescent suicidal ideation were examined in 5,557 Secondary 1 to Secondary 4 students in Hong Kong. Results showed that suicidal ideation was positively related to adolescent hopelessness but negatively related to emotional competence, social problem solving, father–adolescent communication, mother–adolescent communication and family functioning. Again, this paper underscores the intimate relationship between quality of family life and individual quality of life.

In the next paper by Hsi Sheng Wei and Ji Kang Chen, individual, peer and teacher predictors of attachment of students to schools were examined based on data collected from 720 students and 24 teachers. Based on hierarchical linear modeling, findings showed that school grade, peer support, peer victimization, and job satisfaction of the homeroom teachers were related to students' attachment to school. In the next paper, Lee and his associates examined the influence of resilience-related beliefs on children's development in a longitudinal study with three waves of data collection. The study showed that children's resilience beliefs predicted positive child development and the relationship was stronger with growing adversities in children's life.

There are two other papers on adolescent quality of life based on data collected from intervention studies. As the relationships amongst life satisfaction, positive youth development and problem behaviour are under-researched in the existing literature, Rachel Sun and Daniel Shek examined a series of models using structural equation modelling in 7,975 Secondary 1 students. The findings showed that a non-recursive model was found to best fit the data, which suggests that adolescents having higher levels of positive youth development are more satisfied with life and have fewer problem behaviour, with life satisfaction and problem behaviour negatively reinforcing each other. Based on three studies, Daniel Shek examined the perceptions and feelings of students participating in the Project P.A.T.H.S. regarding the program and the perceived benefits of the program via reflective journals in the form of weekly diaries. Results generally showed that the respondents had positive views on the program as well as the instructors and they perceived that they had acquired competencies at the societal, familial, interpersonal and personal levels and their quality of life was promoted after joining the program. The qualitative findings generally suggest that the Project P.A.T.H.S. promotes quality of life amongst the program participants.

In addition to papers on adolescent quality of life, there are three other papers on the quality of life in Chinese adults. In the study by Luk and his associates, responses of 138 teachers in Macau to the Chinese Maslach Burnout Inventory, Chinese Social Problem Solving Inventory and the Body-Mind-Spirit Well-Being Inventory were examined. Results showed that there were significant demographic correlates of burnout, including age, marital status, teaching experiences, education background and satisfaction with income. Besides, social problem solving and body-mind-spirit well-being were negatively associated with emotional exhaustion and depersonalization and positively correlated with personal achievement. As no systematic study of teacher burnout has been conducted in Macau, this is a pioneer attempt.

In the paper by Phoenix Mo and Winnie Mak, the patterns of health promoting behaviors of the general public in Hong Kong was examined in 941 community adults randomly selected via household survey. Results revealed that the respondents adopted healthy life styles, although there were gender and educational differences in different health practices. Results further revealed that stress management and social relations significantly predicted better quality of life for both male and female participants, and preventive health behaviors was a significant predictor of quality of life for female participants only.

In another study, Chak Kie Wong and Vivian Lou examined the welfare recipients' experiences of and attitudes toward the welfare benefit system in Hong Kong using a qualitative methodology based on 19 welfare recipients. The study revealed that welfare recipients showed strong aspirations to exit the welfare benefit system. Unfortunately, they generally had poor quality of life in the process of receiving welfare, with the welfare application process perceived to be painful and strongly stigmatized. In the final study by Chua, Wong and Shek, quality of life in Hong Kong assessed by the Social Development Index (SDI) was described. The current state of social development in Hong Kong based on the SDI-2008 was summarized and the major social, political and economic challenges that were confronted by Hong Kong were identified. The article illustrates the utility of social indicators research such as the SDI in assessing quality of life and assisting related social planning initiatives in Asian communities such as Hong Kong.

With reference to the developments and missing gaps in the QOL literature highlighted in Shek et al. (2005b), this special issue has several unique responses. First, papers examining quality of life with respect to the macro societal conditions (paper by Chua, Wong and Shek), family quality of life (papers by Yuk King Lau and Vivian Lou) and individual quality of life (e.g., papers by Sun and Shek as well as Mo and Mak) are included. The second unique feature of this special issue is that in response to the lack of adolescent quality of life research (e.g. Shek and Lee 2007), several related papers (papers by Siu and Shek, Lai and Shek, Sun and Shek, Shek, and Wei and Chen) are included in this special issue. Third, to clarify our understanding of the linkage between quality of life and economic disadvantage, the paper by Wong and Lou examines the struggles and experiences of welfare recipients. Fourth, papers adopting different methodologies are included in this special collection, including secondary data analyses (paper by Chua, Wong and Shek), survey research (Mo and Mak), weekly diaries (Shek) and focus group methods (Wong and Lou).

As there are several papers authored or co-authored by myself, I have invited several Action Editors to independently handle those papers to uphold the integrity of the peer review system of the journal. These Action Editors included Ching Man Lam, Tak Yan

Lee, Andrew Siu, Rachel Sun, Chak Kie Wong and Sheng Quan Ye. One forceful evidence supporting the integrity of the peer review process is that one paper submitted by my former PhD student (with myself as a co-author) was rejected by an Action Editor.

We would like to take this opportunity to thank those colleagues who have given invaluable assistance in reviewing the papers submitted for possible inclusion in this special issue. They include colleagues from City University of Hong Kong (Chau Kiu Cheung, Sheung Tak Cheng, Sylvia Lai, Sik Hung Ng), Hong Kong Baptist University (Kai Fong Chan), Lingnan University (Alfred Chan), The Chinese University of Hong Kong (Wei Qiao Fan, Ben Law, Ceci Ma, Catalina Ng, Yuk King Lau, Jik Jeon Lee, Angela Shik, Hung Wong, Sheng Quan Ye, Kwong Leung Tang), The Hong Kong Polytechnic University (Andrew Siu, Charles Chan, Cynthia Leung), The University of Hong Kong (Vivian Lou, Sandra Tsang, Samson Tse, Lu Yu), James Cook University, Australia (Matthew Yau), University of British Columbia, Canada (Miu Chung Yan), and University of California, Berkeley (Julian Chun Chung Chow).

Acknowledgement The preparation for this special issue was financially supported by Wofoo Foundation.

References

Shek, D. T. L. (2002). Guest Editor's foreword for the special issue: Research on social work practice in Chinese communities'. *Research on Social Work Practice, 12*, 485–489.

Shek, D. T. L., Chan, Y. K., & Lee, P. (2005a). Quality of life in the global context: A Chinese response. *Social Indicators Research, 71*(1), 1–10.

Shek, D. T. L., Chan, Y. K., & Lee, P. (2005b). Special issue on "Quality of life research in Chinese, Western and global contexts". *Social Indicators Research, 71*(1–3), 1–539.

Shek, D. T. L., & Lee, B. M. (2007). A comprehensive review of quality of life (QOL) research in Hong Kong. *TheScientificWorldJOURNAL: TSW Holistic Health & Medicine, 7*, 1222–1229.

Soc Indic Res (2010) 95:363–376
DOI 10.1007/s11205-009-9535-5

The Impact of Fathers' Work and Family Conflicts on Children's Self-Esteem: The Hong Kong Case

Yuk King Lau

Accepted: 3 May 2009 / Published online: 10 October 2009

Abstract Work and family conflicts are always viewed as issues of human resource management or occupational health. Insufficient attention has been focused on the impact on child development and quality of parenting, especially regarding the impact of a father's work. To examine the impact of work and family conflicts on the quality of father–child interactions in Hong Kong, a cross-sectional survey was conducted. In total, 556 pairs of working fathers and their school-aged children participated in the survey. The findings of the survey indicated that fathers' work-to-family conflicts negatively affected the quality of father–child interactions, which in turn caused harm to children's self-esteem. In addition to work-family conflicts, a low income level of the fathers, a larger number of children in the family, and the presence in the family of children approaching adolescence were significant risk factors to the quality of father–child interactions. The mothers' active parental involvement and the complexity of the fathers' occupation were significant protective factors of the quality of father–child interactions. To facilitate strong family bonding and good quality parenting, possible measures to ensure a healthy work-family balance among working fathers are discussed.

Keywords Working fathers · Work-family conflicts · Children's self-esteem · Hong Kong

1 The Rise of Concern about Work-Family Conflict in the Era of Globalization

Since the industrial revolution, work and family have been conceptualized as two separate spheres (Parson and Bales 1955). Employment policy formulated according to this conceptualization has traditionally paid little attention to the situation of the family or to the impact of work on the family. Interest in the work-family interface was awakened in the 1970s by the increasing number of dual-earner families and single parents in the workforce

Y. K. Lau (✉)
Department of Social Work, The Chinese University of Hong Kong, Shatin, N.T., Hong Kong SAR, China
e-mail: yklau@cuhk.edu.hk

(Greenhaus and Singh 2004). Managing the demands of competing life roles has become a common experience for working populations in both developed and developing countries (Joplin et al. 2003; Yang et al. 2000). Economic restructuring and increased competition due to globalization have contributed to a more demanding work life, a work life that includes increased work-related mobility and work hours, and decreased job security (Wharton and Blair-Loy 2006). Work-family conflict has become a much-investigated topic in contemporary organizational behavior research (Carlson et al. 2000).

Following the global trend, long working hours have been found to be a prominent concern in Hong Kong (Chung et al. 2006; Wharton and Blair-Loy 2006). In the Chinese culture in Hong Kong, work is perceived as instrumental in obtaining the economic means to maintain the family. Commitment to work is a means to an end, and the end is the family's financial security (Redding et al. 1993). According to this family-based work ethic, extra work after official hours or on weekends is an individual sacrifice made for the benefit of the family rather than a sacrifice made by the family for the selfish pursuit of a family member's career (Redding 1993). While there is evidence that there has been a significant reduction in working hours in Hong Kong due to the 2006 implementation of a 5-day working week, it remains common practice for Hong Kong employees to work unpaid overtime and to work late into the evening (Welford 2008). Another study found that Hong Kong employees are more likely to worry about the effects of long working hours on their family and personal life than their United States counterparts (Wharton and Blair-Loy 2006). Thus, work-family conflict has become a common concern both in the West and in Hong Kong.

2 Bi-Dimensionality of the Work-Family Conflict

Greenhaus and Beutell (1985, p. 77) defined the work-family conflict as follows: "It is a form of inter-role conflict in which the role pressures from the work and family domains are mutually noncompliant in some respect. That is, participation in the family role is made difficult by virtue of participation in the work role." Work-family conflict is now recognized as a bidirectional phenomenon (Ayree et al. 1999; Frone 2000). Work-to-family conflict is the interference of a work role in the fulfillment of a family role. Family-to-work conflict is the interference of a family role in the fulfillment of a work role. Results of past studies indicate that the two directions of work-family conflict have different antecedents and consequences (Frone 2000; Greenhaus et al. 2001). Research in both the West and the East has consistently found that work-related variables such as long working hours, a demanding work culture, and weak organizational support are more likely to lead to work-family conflict, while family-related variables such as parental demands are more influential in the case of family-work conflict (Frone et al. 1992; Grandey and Cropanzano 1999; Ngo and Lau 1998). With the increasing work demands in the era of globalization, these results suggest that work-to-family conflict is growing in prominence.

Studies have also indicated that there is a higher percentage of work-to-family conflict, compared with family-to-work conflict, both in the West and in Hong Kong (Ayree et al. 1999; Gutek et al. 1991; Ngo and Lau. 1998). In Hong Kong, the negative spillover effect from work-to-family conflict to family-to-work conflict is significantly greater than that from family-to-work conflict to work-to-family conflict. However, the reciprocal effect between work-to-family conflict and family-to-work conflict is approximately equal in the United States (Ayree et al. 1999). The results indicate the greater prominence of work-to-family conflict in Hong Kong.

3 Consequences of Work-to-Family Conflict

Foreign and local studies consistently prove that work-to-family conflict leads to negative performance on the job and negative personal consequences. In an organization, this conflict is directly associated with staff turnover, absenteeism, a deteriorated commitment to the organization, reduced job satisfaction, and low productivity (Galinsky and Stein 1990; Haar 2004; Kossek and Ozeki 1998, 1999; Netemeyer et al. 1996). At an individual level, it is associated with psychological distress, poor physical health, and reduced life satisfaction (Ayree et al. 1999; Choi 2008; Frone 2000; Grant-Vallone and Donaldson 2001). In considering work-family conflict as a management and occupational health issue, insufficient attention has been paid to the impact on family relation and interactions, especially in regard to the impact of a father's work.

4 The Gender Bias in the Examination of Parental Employment in Families

Given the persistent gender ideology of the care-giving role of mothers, the effect of maternal employment on family, especially on children's development, is a longstanding theme in work and family literature in the West (Perry-Jenkins et al. 2000). Very few studies have examined the effect of paternal employment demands on children or on family relationships (Russell and Bowman 2000). Furthermore, most research has simply assessed parental employment status rather than examining specific aspects of work, such as work overload or work-to-family conflict (Galambos et al. 1995).

Among the small number of studies that have addressed work-stress or the inter-role conflicts of both fathers and mothers, results consistently show that emotional distress arising from conflict and overload due to the competing demands of work and that of family roles is linked to problematic parent–child relations and negative child behaviors (Blau and Grossberg 1992; Bowen 1998; Crouter et al. 1999; Galambos et al. 1995; MacEwen and Barling 1991). Based on the results of their longitudinal studies, Galambos et al. (1995) proposed a model linking parents' work experience and children's behavior. Stress arising from work strain or work-family conflict influences the quality of parenting behavior which then influences the children's behavior. With path analysis on data from a cross-sectional survey that focused specifically on the father's work, Stewart and Barling (1996) found similar results. A father's employment experiences, namely inter-role conflict, job insecurity, and job demands, impacted parenting behavior, which in turn impacted children's behavior. Many studies have found that there are cultural differences in the consequences of work-family conflicts (Wang et al. 2004). Therefore, the extent to which Stewart and Barling's (1996) model and its previous results apply to Hong Kong has to be examined. A cross sectional survey was conducted in December 2006.

5 Theoretical Framework

With a focus specifically on the father's work, Stewart and Barling's (1996) indirect effect model was taken as the conceptual framework with an expanded scope. As Stewart and Barling (1996) mentioned, previous studies mostly concentrated on negative parenting behaviors such as punishment and rejection. Similarly, for child development, the previous studies mostly focused on child behavior, and specifically on problem behavior (Cooksey et al. 1997; Galambos et al. 1995; MacEwen and Barling 1991; Parcel and Menaghan 1993,

1994a). The over-attention on negative parenting behaviors and child outcomes reflects an assumption that work and family are necessarily enemies.

Gottfried and Gottfried (2006) pointed out that when research is framed to focus on stress and negative outcomes, then attention is not paid to the positive and adaptive function of parental and dual-earner employment with regard to parenting and child development. For instance, the level of parents' income affects parenting (Voydanoff 1987) and a higher level benefits the family with enhanced material well-being (Roehling and Bultman 2002). Positive socialization from an occupation with high complexity is also associated with better quality of parenting, and in turn more positive child outcomes in terms of behavior and the formation of personal values (Cooksey et al. 1997; Parcel and Menaghan 1994b; Ryu and Mortimer 1996). To capture both the negative impact and positive function of fathers' work situations, more inclusive and neutral indicators of parenting behaviors and child development were adopted in this study. Children's self-esteem was used as an indicator of their development. Children's perceptions on the quality of parenting and the parent–child relationship were used as the indicators of the quality of father–child interactions. It was hypothesized that: (1) The quality of father–child interactions would positively affect children's self-esteem. (2) Work-to-family conflict that the fathers experienced would negatively affect the quality of father–child interactions. (3) Greater occupational complexity would positively affect the quality of father–child interactions. (4) A higher income level of the fathers would positively affect the quality of father–child interactions.

Taking a family adaptation perspective rather than an adverse perspective on work-family interactions, Gottfried and Gottfried (2006) further proposed that a balance of factors and family adaption should be taken into consideration. These factors include the level of the other parent's parental involvement, the developmental level and gender of both parents and children, the number of children in the family, as and the impact of alternative family forms. These factors were included as control variables in the study.

6 Methods

The survey was part of a comprehensive survey of parents' work situations, with an emphasis on the antecedents of work-family conflict and its impact on child development. The target population of the survey was primary 4 to secondary 3 students (Grade 4 to Grade 9) and their parents. The procedures used for sampling were as follows: In November 2006, eight primary schools and seven secondary schools were randomly selected from the school list posted on the website of the Education Bureau. International schools were excluded. An invitation to participate in the survey was then sent to the selected schools. An alternative school was randomly selected from the list to replace a school which declined to participate. In total, 51 primary schools and 43 secondary schools were contacted in the sampling process. After the schools consented to participate, they were asked to select two classes from each of the selected grades for the survey. Thus, the participating schools were in fact self-selected samples and the participating class was not randomly sampled. Both situations limited the representativeness of the samples in this study.

Questionnaires for parents were distributed and collected through the participating students. With parental consent, the students filled in the children questionnaire in class and these were collected by our research assistant immediately after their completion. In total, 556 working fathers and 981 working mothers participated in the survey, together with their children. With the aim of studying the effect of fathers' family-work situations in this paper, the following discussion will focus on the data concerning working fathers and their children.

6.1 Variables and Measurement in the Fathers' Questionnaire

Work and family conflict was measured using the "Multidimensional Measure of Work-family Conflict" (Carlson et al. 2000). This consists of six subscales, which are categorized according to two domains: work interference with family and family interference with work. The three subscales on work interference with family were adopted for this study: (1) time constraints, (2) emotional constraints, and (3) incompatible behavior patterns learned from work settings. Each subscale originally had ten items. However, for this study, each set of ten subscale items was summarized into three items per subscale to reduce the total length of the questionnaire. Examples of the items include: "My work keeps me from my family activities more than I would like"; "I am often so emotionally drained when I get home from work that it prevents me from participating in family life", and "Behavior that is effective and necessary for me at work would be counterproductive at home". The scores of the answers were captured on a five-point Likert scale ranged from (1) strongly disagree to (5) strongly agree. The original internal consistencies of the subscales were .87, .85, and .78, respectively. Principle component analyses indicated that the first two dimensions were closely related in Hong Kong and the subscale on behavioral interference was not perceived as a distinct dimension. Excluding the three items on behavioral interference, a combined index on time constraints and emotional constraints was used for the analyses in this study. The combined scale had a Cronbach's alpha of .90, indicating good reliability.

Occupational complexity: Following the measurement used in the previous studies (Cooksey et al. 1997; Parcel and Menaghan 1993), occupational categories (from managerial and administrative positions to unskilled positions) were used to indicate the level of occupational complexity. The categories were recoded into dummy variables in the process of data analysis. Three categories of occupations, managerial and administrative positions, professional positions, and art and crafts were assigned a value of 1 to indicate a high level of complexity. Occupations in other categories such as clerical positions and unskilled positions were assigned a value of 0.

Fathers' income: the fathers' average monthly income was used to indicate their level of earnings. The scores of the answers were in an ordinal order ranged from (1) less than HK$5,000 to (9) more than HK$60,000. Two dummy variables were constructed for the correlation and regression analyses. The first dummy variable was an income level less than HK$10,000 per month. The second dummy variable was an income level higher than HK$30,000 per month.

Demographic data: The participating fathers were asked to provide the exact number of years of their age (e.g., 35). Their educational level was measured using an ordinal scale: (1) no education, (2) primary education, (3) Grade 7-Grade 9, (4) Grade 10-Grade 12, (5) matriculation, and (6) tertiary or above. Taking the senior high education level as the reference category, the answers were recoded into two dummy variables. The first variable was an education level of junior high or lower. The second dummy was an education level of tertiary or above.

6.2 Variables and Measurement in the Students' Questionnaire

Children's self-esteem: Harter's (1985) "Self-perception profile for children" was used to measure three dimensions of the children's self-esteem: (1) scholastic competence, (2) social competence, and (3) behavior/conduct. There were six items for each sub-scale. The scores for the answers ranged from 1 to 4, with the higher score indicating a higher sense of competence. The internal consistencies of the original subscales ranged from .78 to .86. Cronbach's alpha of the subscales in this study were .691, .648, and .764, respectively.

Parent–child relationship was measured by the "Parent–Child Affection Scale" (Amato and Booth 1995). This is a four-item scale. In the pilot test, the overlapping meanings of the items in their Chinese version were identified. Two items were subsequently dropped. The scores for the answers ranged from 1 to 5, with the higher score indicating a higher sense of emotional bonding. The original reliability of the scale was .70. The Cronbach's alpha of the revised scale in this study was .86 for the father–child relationship.

The quality of parenting was measured using a self-constructed scale. Making reference to literature on quality of parenting (Arnold et al. 1993; Mantzicopoulos and Oh-Hwang 1998), the self-constructed scale measured the parent's emotional stability, availability, consistency in parental rule enforcement, knowledge about children, provision of stimulating activities, and interaction with the child. The students had to indicate whether the item was applicable to their parents or not (1 = applicable, 0 = not applicable). A pilot test and factor analysis were conducted to improve its psychometric properties. The final scale consisted of 13 items with a Cronbach's alpha of .79.

Mother's parental involvement: Ahrons and Wallisch (1987) Parental Involvement Scale was adopted to measure the mother's parental involvement. The scale consisted of 14 items on both physical care and emotional care. The involvement level was measured on a five-point scale that ranged from never (1) to very often (5). The reliability of the scale in previous studies ranged from .88 to .95. The Cronbach's alpha of the scale in this study was .86.

Demographic data of the students: students had to indicate their *age*, *gender, number of siblings,* and *parents' marital status* (intact marriage, divorced/separated, or widowed). The marital statuses were regrouped into a dummy variable: marriage remained intact (1) or not (0). Gender was also recoded as a dummy variable (1 for male, 0 for female). *Number of children in the family* was computed from number of siblings plus one (the responding student).

7 Results of the Study

7.1 Demographic Background of the Participants

The mean age of the participating fathers was 45.71. Concerning the fathers' educational levels, 40.6% (226) of them had an education level of junior high or lower, 38.1% (212) had an education level of senior high, and 20.3% (113) had attained tertiary education or above. Regarding their occupational categories, 38.7% (215) of them were in categories with high occupational complexity (managers, administrators, professionals, or craftsmen). As for individual income, 24.1% (134) of the fathers earned a monthly income below HK$10,000, which was the mean individual monthly income in 2006; 38.8% (216) had a monthly income in the range HK$10,000–19,999; 14.2% (124) had a monthly income in the range HK$20,000–29,999; and 21.6% (120) had a monthly income over HK$30,000.

The participating students were aged between eight and 18 years old, with a mean age of 11.75. Among the students, 52.5% (292) were female. Regarding the parents' marital status, 5.6% (31) of the parents were separated, divorced, or widowed. According to the children's perception, most of the mothers had fair to good parental involvement. Results of the *t*-test showed that there was no significant difference between mothers who were in full-time employment and those who were not in regard to their parental involvement. Mean and standard deviation of the demographic variables and other variables are summarized in Table 1. Correlations among the variables are also summarized in Table 1. In the data analysis process, listwise deletion was used for missing data (Schafer and Graham, 2002). Only complete cases were used for the analyses.

7.2 Path Analyses on the Mediating Effect of Parent–Child Interactions on the Impact of Parents' Work and Family Conflict on Children

Path analyses were conducted through a series of standard multiple regression analyses. In the first series of regression analyses, the three dimensions of children's self-esteem were regressed on all the other variables. Table 2 presents the regression models. The results showed that the father–child relationship significantly predicted all three dimensions of children's self-esteem ($\beta = .24$, $P < .001$; $\beta = .21$, $P < .01$, $\beta = .16$, $P < .05$). The quality of fathering was a significant predictor in children's academic competence and behavior/conduct ($\beta = .23$, $P < .001$; $\beta = .23$, $P < .01$). Being male predicted a higher sense of scholastic competence for the student ($\beta = -.23, P < .001$). The parents having an intact marriage predicted a more positive self-appraisal by the student of his or her behavior/conduct ($\beta = .111, p = .05$; $\beta = .114, p = .05$). Work-family conflict had no direct effect on children's self-esteem. The identified significance of the quality of father–child interactions on children's self-esteem confirmed the first hypothesis of the study (see Table 3).

In the second series of regression analyses, the quality of fathering and the father–child relationship were regressed on the rest of the variables, respectively. The mothers' parental involvement was found to be the strongest predictor of both dimensions of father–child interactions ($\beta = .38$, $P < .001$; $\beta = .23$, $P < .001$). Unexpectedly, they were negatively predicted by a paternal education level of tertiary or above ($\beta = -.12, P < .04$; $\beta = -.14$, $P < .05$). Although the coefficient value is small, work-to-family conflict negatively predicted the quality of the working fathers' parenting and the father–child relationship ($\beta = -.09, P < .05$; $\beta = -.09, P < .05$). The results confirmed hypothesis 2 of the study. The father's occupational complexity, reflected by its occupation category, positively predicted the father–child relationship ($\beta = .16$, $P < .01$), but it had no significance in the quality of fathering. Hypothesis 3 of the study was partially confirmed.

The relationship of the quality of father–child interactions with the fathers' income is interesting. The fathers' monthly income did not have any significant effect on the father–child relationship. The quality of fathering was negatively predicted by a paternal monthly income level less than HK$10,000 ($\beta = -.15$, $P < .01$). However, for working fathers with a monthly income of HK$10,000 to HK$20,000 as the standard, a higher income level made no difference to their quality of parenting.

In addition to the above findings, two more significant predictors were identified in the analyses. The number of children in the family negatively predicted the quality of fathering ($\beta = -.12$, $P < .05$), and the student's age negatively predicted the father–child relationship ($\beta = -.17$, $P < .05$).

8 Discussion and Recommendations

The above results support the applicability of Stewart and Barling's (1996) indirect effect model in Hong Kong. Fathers' work-to-family conflict negatively affects the quality of

Table 1 Descriptive statistics and inter-correlations of the variables

	M	SD	1	2	3	4	5	6	7	8	9	10	11	12	13	14	15	16
1. SchC	15.52	3.47																
2. SocC	16.24	3.32	.36***															
3. BeC	17.34	3.41	.39***	.32***														
4. QF	5.14	2.35	.40***	.27***	.32***													
5. FCR	8.05	1.86	.37***	.29***	.35***	.65***												
6. WFC	18.59	4.92	−.08	−.07	−.01	−.13**	−.09*											
7. <10,000	.24	.43	−.10*	−.02	−.06	−.21***	−.14**	.12**										
8. >30,000	.22	.42	.16***	.09*	.08	.18***	.14***	−.03	−.29***									
9. OCA	.39	.49	.16***	.09*	.08	.21***	.20***	−.03	−.30***	.46***								
10. MaInvo	3.56	.76	.28***	−.17***	.28***	.43***	.35***	−.08	−.18***	.24***	.25***							
11. FaAge	45.71	5.61	−.08	−.02	−.01	−.11*	−.09*	−.05	.17***	−.02	−.12**	−.14**						
12. <JH	.41	.49	−.09*	−.03	.02	−.12**	−.11*	.06	.32***	−.37***	−.39***	−.17***	.10*					
13. >tertiary	.21	.40	.15***	.05	.03	.12**	.10*	−.06	−.27***	.59***	.52***	.22***	−.07	−.42***				
14. No.Ch	2.23	1.05	−.11*	−.01	−.08	−.15***	−.12**	.05	.09*	−.03	−.13**	−.15***	.14**	.24***	−.11*			
15. InMar	.93	.25	.03	.00	.09	.04	−.01	−.06	−.07	.07	.11**	.11*	.04	−.18***	.05	.04		
16. StGen	.47	.50	−.13**	−.08	−.12*	−.08	−.10***	−.03	.03	−.06	−.01	−.12**	.03	.07	−.02	.03	.04	
17. StAge	11.75	1.94	−.13**	−.00	−.11*	−.24***	−.24***	−.03	.20***	−.22***	−.22***	−.31***	.21***	.15***	−.19***	.21***	−.03	05

SchC scholastic competence, *SocC* social competence, *BeC* behavior/conduct, *QF* quality of fathering, *FCR* father–child relationship, *WFC* work-family conflict, *<10,000* father earned less than HK$10,000 a month, *>30,000* father earned more than HK$30,000 a month, *OCA* occupational complexity and autonomy, *MaInvo* mother's' parental involvement, *FaAge* father's age, *<JH* father's education level junior high or below, *>tertiary* father's education level tertiary or above, *No.Ch* number of children in the family, *InMar* parents' marriage intact, *StGen* student's gender, *StAge* student's age

* $P < .05$, ** $P < .01$, *** $P < .001$

Table 2 Results of regression analyses on significant predictors of children's self-esteem

	Scholastic competence		Social competence		Behavior/ conduct	
	B	*β*	*B*	*β*	*B*	*β*
Quality of fathering	.36	.23***	.21	.15	.34	.23**
Father–child relationship	.46	.24***	.39	.21**	.29	.16*
Mother's parental involvement	.57	.12*	.31	.07	.29	.07
Work-to-family conflict	−.03	−.04	.01	.02	.04	.05
Father's age	.01	.01	−.02	−.03	.05	.08
Father's education level junior high or below	.27	.04	.00	.00	.68	.09
Father's education tertiary or above	.66	.07	−.09	−.01	.06	.01
Father earned less than HK$10,000 per month	.13	.02	.72	.09	.24	.03
Father earned more than HK$30,000 per month	.75	.09	.34	.04	.33	.04
Parents' marriage intact	.18	.01	.27	.02	2.02	.12*
Father's occupation complexity	−.49	−.07	.13	.02	−.06	−.01
Student's gender ($M = 1$, $F = 0$)	1.69	.23***	−.14	−.02	−.48	−.07
Student's age	.03	.02	.22	.12	−.14	−.07
No. of children in the family	−.17	−.04	.14	.02	.14	.04
Constant		6.85**		8.08**		8.45**
R^2		.29		.12		.19
Adjusted R^2		.26		.08		.15
F		9.07***		3.00***		4.97***
df		14, 31		14, 31		14, 31

* $P < .05$, ** $P < .01$, *** $P < .001$

father–child interactions, in turn causing harm to children's self-esteem through this negative impact. A low level of monthly income is also harmful to the quality of fathering in terms of emotional stability, availability, knowledge about children, and provision of stimulating activities. However, a higher income level does not have the expected positive effect on the quality of fathering and the father–child relationship. The results suggest that an adequate income is necessary to facilitate good quality fathering. Nevertheless, high earnings add little extra benefit to the quality of the father–child relationship. Despite the harmful effect on the quality of fathering, a low level of paternal income does not have a negative impact on the children's perception of the father–child relationship. Children's understanding and acceptance of the father's limitations in his earning capability and parenting may be a possible protective factor. To capture a more complete picture, children's belief and understanding should be included in future studies.

An unexpected finding is the negative association between fathers having a tertiary education or above and the quality of father–child interactions. In reference to the correlations among variables in Table 1, an education level of tertiary or above is correlated with prestigious occupation categories that are high in occupational complexity ($r = .52$, $P < .001$) and a higher level of parental involvement of the mothers ($r = 22$, $P < .001$). They are the two significant protective factors of the quality of father–child interactions in the model. After controlling the effects of these two protective factors, an education level of tertiary or above is a risk factor rather than a resource. This contradicts the human

Table 3 Results of regression analyses on significant predictors of quality of fathering and father–child relationship

	Quality of fathering		Father–child relationship	
	B	β	B	β
Work-to-family conflict	−.04	−.09*	−.04	−.09*
Mother's parental involvement	1.14	.38***	.56	.23***
Father's education level tertiary or above	−.71	−.12*	−.64	−.14*
Father's occupation complexity	.40	.09	.59	.16**
Father earned less than HK$10,000 per month	−.82	−.15**	−.31	−.07
Father earned more than HK$30,000 per month	.31	.06	−.15	−.04
Father's education level junior high or below	−.08	−.02	.01	.00
Parent's marriage intact	−.07	−.01	−.64	−.07
Student's gender ($M = 1$, $F = 0$)	−.04	−.01	−.31	−.08
Student's age	−.05	.04	−.17	−.17**
No. of children in the family	−.29	−.12*	−.12	−.08
Father's age	−.01	−.02	.01	.02
Constant		3.87*		9.43***
R^2		.28		.19
Adjusted R^2		.26		.16
F		11.78***		7.05***
df		12, 36		12, 37

* $P < .05$, ** $P < .01$, *** $P < .001$

capital perspective that a higher education normally contributes to a better quality of parenting and in turn a better parent–child relationship (Davis-Kean 2005). Taking the social context of Hong Kong into consideration, educated parents generally place high expectations on their children in terms of their academic performance and social achievement. Having a highly educated father may be a source of stress for children and adolescents in Hong Kong. This interpretation is subject to further verification in future studies.

As mentioned in the previous paragraphs, the mother's active parental involvement is a protective factor of children's self-esteem in their scholastic competence and the strongest protective factor of a good quality father–child interaction. An active maternal involvement with children in physical and emotional care may lower the children's expectations of the availability and involvement of their fathers in these aspects. The results also reflect the mothers' important bridging and facilitating role in father–child interactions. In this sense, supporting the mother's parental involvement will be very beneficial to both the fathers and the children. However, the lack of significant difference between the parental participation of mothers with full-time employment and those without reminds us about the possible role overload of working mothers in Hong Kong. There is evidence on the persistent gender division of labor in dual-earner families in Hong Kong (Chan 2008; Lau et al. 2006). Supporting the mother's parental involvement without simultaneous effort in facilitating the father's parental involvement will further reinforce the gender division of labor in these families. Family-friendly work policies should be advocated to facilitate active parental involvement by working fathers and prevent role overload of both working fathers and working mothers.

Another protective factor is occupational complexity, which facilitates the fathers' quality of parenting. Occupational complexity is mostly indicated by high-ranking or prestigious occupation categories in this study. In addition to the positive socialization from work experiences, the positive impact may be due to a status enhancement effect provided by the occupation status (Parasuraman and Greenhaus 2002). This finding provides support for Gottfried and Gottfried's (2006) proposal on an expanded scope of work-family studies to address the positive and adaptive function of parental employment. The specific work situations that are beneficial to the parenting competence of the workers in Hong Kong and the mechanism by which the two variables are linked have to be carefully scrutinized in future studies.

The results also draw our attention to working fathers with a larger number of children, with children approaching adolescence, and children in families in forms other than intact families. Consistent with the results of previous studies, a larger number of children in the family constrains fathers' nurture and stimulation of children (Parcel and Menaghan 1993). Children's approaching adolescence has been found to be a risk factor to the father–child relationship. This impact deserves special attention as there is evidence that father-adolescent conflict, relative to mother-adolescent conflict, exerts a stronger influence on adolescent well-being in Hong Kong (Shek 1998). Though playing no significant role in the quality of the father–child interaction, the non-intact marital status of their parents robs children of self-esteem in their behavior/conduct. Together with a low income level and work-to-family conflict, these risk factors may pile up stress and present special parenting challenges to working fathers.

Integrating all the findings, providing a family-friendly work environment such as reasonable working hours and workload, flexible work schedule, and adequate organizational support will be beneficial to all working parents. Previous local studies have identified that organizational support and family-friendly work policies help to relieve conflict (Foley et al. 2005; Hill et al. 2004). The implementation of the 5-day working week in 2006 and the advocacy of family-friendly employment policies in recent years are positive moves in facilitating a good work-life balance among Hong Kong employees. The enriching effect of occupational complexity on parental competence suggests that an important dimension of family-sensitive management is the provision of a stimulating and growth-enhancing environment for employees, especially for those in low-income employment. Special support such as income support, income protection, and parental support should be given to working fathers with a low income, a larger number of children, children approaching adolescence, or a broken marriage. Parental support in the form of parent education or peer group learning in the workplace is another family-friendly policy that would be particularly beneficial for these working fathers.

Despite the insightful findings of the study, it is important to note that the study had several limitations. Although an attempt was made to construct a comprehensive model for the study, the model left out many significant variables as reflected by the moderate adjusted R^2 values of the model. Further expansion of the model is necessary. Regarding the measurement tools, a self-constructed scale rather than a validated scale was adopted for the measurement of the quality of fathering. Furthermore, modifications had been made in many of the measurement scales. The impact of the modifications on the psychometric properties of the scale had not been examined in detail. Further validation of these scales is therefore necessary. Moreover, there was a high percentage of missing data for some of the variables. This had a negative effect on the quality of the data and reduced the number of usable cases for the analyses. Lastly, the failure to achieve random sampling limited the generalizability of the findings. Their generalizability has to be further verified with systematic and representative studies.

Acknowledgment The author would like to express her sincere gratitude to the Boys' and Girls' Club Association of Hong Kong for granting permission to use the data from the study "The Impact of Parents' Work Situations on Children's Development."

References

Ahrons, C. R., & Wallisch, L. (1987). Parenting in binuclear families: Relationships between biological and stepparents. In K. Palsey & M. Ihinger-Tallman (Eds.), *Remarriage and stepparents: Current research and theory* (pp. 225–256). New York: Guilford Press.

Amato, P. R., & Booth, A. (1995). A prospective study of divorce and parent–child relationships. *Journal of Marriage and the Family, 58*(2), 356–365.

Arnold, D. S., O'Leary, S. O., Wolff, L. S., & Acker, M. M. (1993). The parenting scale: A measure of dysfunctional parenting in discipline situations. *Psychological Assessment, 5*(2), 137–144.

Ayree, S., Fields, D., & Luk, V. (1999a). A cross-cultural test of a model of the work-family interface. *Journal of Management, 25*(4), 491–511.

Ayree, S., Luk, V., Leung, A., & Lo, S. (1999b). Role stressors, interrole conflict, and well-being: The moderating influence of spousal support and coping behaviors among employed parents in Hong Kong. *Journal of Vocational Behavior, 54*(2), 259–278.

Blau, F. D., & Grossberg, A. J. (1992). Maternal labor supply and children's cognitive development. *The Review of Economics and Statistics, 74*(3), 474–481.

Bowen, G. L. (1998). Effects of leader support in the work unit on the relationship between work spillover and family adaptation. *Journal of Family and Economic Issues, 19*(1), 25–52.

Carlson, D. S., Kacmar, K. M., & Williams, L. (2000). Construction and initial validation of a multidimensional measure of work-family conflict. *Journal of Vocational Behavior, 56*(2), 249–276.

Chan, A. H. N. (2008). The dynamics of motherhood performance: Hong Kong's middle class working mothers on- and off-line. *Sociological Research Online, 23*(4). Retrieved from http://www.socresonline.org.uk/13/4/4.html on 16-4-09.

Choi, J. (2008). Work and family demands and life stress among Chinese employees: The mediating effect of work-family conflict. *The International Journal of Human Resource Management, 19*(5), 878–895.

Chung, T. Y., Pang, K. L., & Chan, S. L. (2006). *Survey on Hong Kong working people and work-life balance 2006*. Hong Kong: Hong Kong University Public Opinion Research Center. (In Chinese).

Cooksey, E. C., Menaghan, E. G., & Jekielek, S. M. (1997). Life course effects of work and family circumstances on children. *Social Forces, 76*(2), 637–667.

Crouter, A. C., Bumpus, M. F., Maguire, M. C., & McHale, S. M. (1999). Linking parents' work pressure and adolescents' well-being: Insights into dynamics in dual-earner families. *Developmental Psychology, 35*(6), 1453–1461.

Davis-Kean, P. E. (2005). The influence of parent education and family income on child achievement—The indirect role of parent expectations and home environment. *Journal of Family Psychology, 19*(2), 294–304.

Foley, S., Ngo, H. Y., & Liu, S. (2005). The effects of work stressors, perceived organizational support, and gender on work-family conflict in Hong Kong. *Asia Pacific Journal of Management, 22*(3), 237–256.

Frone, M. R. (2000). Work-family conflict and employee psychiatric disorders: The national comorbidity survey. *Journal of Applied Psychology, 85*(6), 888–895.

Frone, M. R., Russell, M., & Cooper, M. L. (1992). Antecedents and outcomes of work-family conflict: Testing a model of the work-family interface. *Journal of Applied Psychology, 77*(1), 65–78.

Galambos, N. L., Sears, H. A., Almeida, D. M., & Kolaric, G. C. (1995). Parents' work overload and problem behavior in young adolescents. *Journal of Research on Adolescence, 5*(2), 201–223.

Galinsky, E., & Stein, P. J. (1990). The impact of human resources policies on employees: Balancing work/family life. *Journal of Family Issues, 11*(4), 368–383.

Gottfried, A. E., & Gottfried, A. W. (2006). A long-term investigation of the role maternal and dual-earner employment in children's development. *American Behavioral Scientist, 49*(10), 1310–1327.

Grandey, A. A., & Cropanzano, R. (1999). The conservation of resources model applied to work-family conflict and strain. *Journal of Vocational Behavior, 54*(2), 350–370.

Grant-Vallone, E. J., & Donaldson, S. I. (2001). Consequences of work-family conflict on employee well-being over time. *Work & Stress, 15*(3), 214–226.

Greenhaus, J. H., & Beutell, N. J. (1985). Sources of conflict between work and family roles. *Academy of Management Review, 10*(1), 76–88.

Greenhaus, J. H., Parasuraman, S., & Collins, K. M. (2001). Career involvement and family involvement as moderators of relationships between work-family conflict and withdrawal from a profession. *Journal of Occupational Health Psychology, 6*(2), 91–100.

Greenhaus, J. H., & Singh, R. (2004). Work-family relationships. In C. D. Spielberger (Ed.), *Encyclopedia of applied psychology* (pp. 687–698). San Diego: Elsevier.

Gutek, B. A., Searle, S., & Klepa, L. (1991). Rational versus gender role explanations for work-family conflict. *Journal of Applied Psychology, 76*(4), 560–568.

Haar, J. M. (2004). Work-family conflict and turnover intention: Exploring the moderation effects of perceived work-family support. *New Zealand Journal of Psychology, 33*(1), 35–39.

Harter, S. (1985). *Manual for the self-perception profile for children.* USA: University of Denver.

Hill, J. H., Yang, C. M., Hawkins, A. J., & Ferris, M. (2004). A cross cultural test of the work-family interface in 48 countries. *Journal of Marriage and Family, 66*(5), 1300–1316.

Joplin, J. R. W., Shaffer, M. A., Francesco, A. M., & Lau, T. (2003). The macro-environment and work-family conflict: Development of a cross cultural comparative framework. *International Journal of Cross Cultural Management, 3*(3), 305–328.

Kossek, E. E., & Ozeki, C. (1998). Work-family conflict, policies, and job-life satisfaction relationship: A review and directions for organizational behavior-human resources research. *Journal of Applied Psychology, 83*(2), 139–149.

Kossek, E. E., & Ozeki, C. (1999). Bridging the work-family policy and productivity gap: A literature review. *Community, Work and Family, 2*(1), 7–32.

Lau, Y. K., Ma, J. L. C., & Chan, Y. K. (2006). ''Labour force participation of married women in Hong Kong: A feminist perspective. *Journal of Comparative Family Studies, 37*(1), 93–112.

MacEwen, K. E., & Barling, J. (1991). Effects of maternal employment experiences on children's behavior via mood, cognitive difficulties and parenting behavior. *Journal of Marriage and the Family, 53*(3), 635–644.

Mantzicopoulos, P. Y., & Oh-Hwang, Y. (1998). The relationship of psychological maturity to parenting quality and intellectual ability for American and Korean Adolescents. *Contemporary Educational Psychology, 23*(2), 195–206.

Netemeyer, R. G., Boles, J. S., & McMurrian, R. (1996). Development and validation of work-family conflict and family-work conflict scales. *Journal of Applied Psychology, 81*(4), 400–410.

Ngo, H., & Lau, C. (1998). Interferences between work and family among male and female executives in Hong Kong. *Research and Practice in Human Resource Management, 6*(1), 17–34.

Parasuraman, S., & Greenhaus, J. H. (2002). Toward reducing some critical gaps in work-family research. *Human Resources Management Review, 12*(3), 299–312.

Parcel, T. L., & Menaghan, E. G. (1993). Family social capital and children's behavior problems. *Social Psychology Quarterly, 56*(2), 120–135.

Parcel, T. L., & Menaghan, E. G. (1994a). Early parental work, family social capital, and early childhood outcomes. *American Journal of Sociology, 99*(4), 972–1009.

Parcel, T. L., & Menaghan, E. G. (1994b). *Parents' jobs and children's lives.* New York: Aldine de Gruyter.

Parson, T., & Bales, R. F. (1955). *Family, socialization and interaction process.* Glencoe, IL: Free Press.

Perry-Jenkins, M., Repetti, R. L., & Crouter, A. C. (2000). Work and family in the 1990s. *Journal of Marriage and the Family, 62*(4), 981–998.

Redding, S. G. (1993). *The spirit of Chinese capitalism.* New York: de Gruyter.

Redding, S. G., Norman, A., & Schlander, A. (1993). The nature of individual attachment to the organization: A review of East Asian variations. In H. C. Triandis, M. D. Dunnette, & L. M. Hough (Eds.), *Handbook of industrial and organizational psychology* (Vol. 4, pp. 647–688). Palo Alto, CA: Consulting Psychologists Press.

Roehling, P. V., & Bultman, M. (2002). Does absence make the heart grow fonder? Work-related travel and marital satisfaction. *Sex Roles, 46*(9/10), 279–293.

Russell, G., & Bowman, L. (2000). *Work and family—current thinking, research and practice (Prepared for the Department of Family and Community Service as a background paper for the National Families Strategy).* Australia: Macquarie Research Limited, Macquarie University.

Ryu, S., & Mortimer, J. T. (1996). The "occupational linkage hypothesis" applied to occupation value formation in adolescence. In J. T. Mortimer & M. D. Finch (Eds.), *Adolescents, work, and family: An intergenerational development analysis.* Thousand Oaks, CA: Sage.

Schafer, J. L., & Graham, J. W. (2002). Missing data: Our view of the state of art. *Psychological Methods, 7*(2), 147–177.

Shek, D. T. L. (1998). A longitudinal study of the relations between parent-adolescent conflict and adolescent psychological well-being. *The Journal of Genetic Psychology, 159*(1), 53–67.
Stewart, W., & Barling, J. (1996). Fathers' work experience effect children's behavior via-job-related affect and parenting behaviors. *Journal of Organizational Behavior, 17*(3), 221–232.
Voydanoff, P. (1987). *Work and family life*. Beverly Hill: Sage.
Wang, P., Lawler, J. J., Walumbwa, F. O., & Shi, K. (2004). Work-family conflict and job withdrawal intentions: The moderating effect of cultural differences. *International Journal of Stress Management, 11*(4), 392–412.
Welford, R. (2008). *Work life balance in Hong Kong: Survey results*. Hong Kong: The University of Hong Kong and CSR Asia.
Wharton, A. S., & Blair-Loy, M. (2006). Long work hours and family life—A cross-national study of employees' concern. *Journal of Family Issues, 27*(3), 415–436.
Yang, N. N., Chen, C. C., Choi, J. P., & Zou, Y. M. (2000). Sources of work-family conflict: A Sino-U.S. comparison of the effects of work and family demands. *Academy of Management Journal, 43*(1), 113–123.

Soc Indic Res (2010) 95:377–391
DOI 10.1007/s11205-009-9526-6

Life Satisfaction of Older Adults in Hong Kong: The Role of Social Support from Grandchildren

Vivian W. Q. Lou

Accepted: 5 April 2009 / Published online: 9 October 2009

Abstract This study explores the relationship between the life satisfaction of older adults and the social support from grandchildren in Hong Kong. Two hundred and fifteen older people (from the ages of 64 to 101, mean age 79.3), whose youngest grandchild was aged 12 or older, were recruited from elderly service agencies to participate in the study. Face-to-face interviews were conducted by trained interviewers using a standardized questionnaire, which included the Life Satisfaction Scale for Chinese, the Lubben Social Network Scale, the Chinese Tradition Scale, grandchildren social support measures, self-rated health, self-rated financial adequacy, and demographic variables. Hierarchical regression showed that the life satisfaction of older adults benefitted significantly from the social support from grandchildren (R^2 change = .05, $F_{\text{change}} = 7.15, p < .001$); while controlling demographic characteristics, general social support, attitude towards Chinese tradition, self-rated health, and self-rated financial adequacy. The total explained variance was 51%. Emotional support and appraisal support from grandchildren were identified as significant contributing factors. The policy and practice implications for active aging policies are discussed in a Chinese context.

Keywords Life satisfaction · Older adults · Adolescent and/or adult grandchildren · Social support

1 Introduction

It was argued that, regardless of the physical condition of an individual's life, life satisfaction, which refers to the subjective evaluation of a person's life, plays a significant role in indicating the quality of life. According to a review by Diener et al. (1999), in general, a person with a higher level of subjective well-being has a positive attitude toward life, is economically self-sufficient, is healthy, and has higher job morale. Social support was also

V. W. Q. Lou (✉)
Department of Social Work & Social Administration, The University of Hong Kong, Pokfulam Road, Hong Kong
e-mail: wlou@hku.hk

argued to significantly contribute to life satisfaction (Bishop et al. 2006). However, studies mostly focus on family support and/or peer support from people at peer level, and neglect to incorporate variables from intergenerational interaction (Gow, et al. 2007; Kang et al. 2003; Yeung and Fung 2007). Chinese elders in the current generation have been exposed to a high-context cultural tradition; which emphasizes family, hierarchy, and intergeneration relations (Chow 2004; Lou 2005). For example, while factors associated with quality of life focused more on health and functioning aspects of life in western literature, the Chinese literature focused more on the social and relational aspects of life (Chan et al. 2000; Lau et al. 1998; Silverman et al. 2000). Studies on the life satisfaction of Chinese elders also showed that the fulfillment of social and relational needs was a significant aspect of life satisfaction (Lou et al. 2008a); while support from family members, including children and grandchildren, could have a moderating effect on physical illness and psychological distress (Song and Chi 2001). Population aging provides opportunities for a large proportion of older adults to live to an age where they have adolescent and/or adult grandchildren, an age at which the effects of intergenerational relations was found to be both rewarding and stressful (Lou and Chi 2008). Therefore, it would be worthwhile to explore the relationship between the support of grandchildren and life satisfaction in older adults to expand the scope of research from a two-generational scope to a cross-generational scope. This study aims to examine the role of social support from adolescent and/or adult grandchildren and its effect on the life satisfaction of older adults.

2 Life Satisfaction and Associated Factors

The life satisfaction of older adults was found to be associated with factors that are embedded at both personal and interpersonal levels. At the personal level, higher levels of life satisfaction were associated with health status, financial status, and socio-economic status. Elderly people's physical health status influenced their daily lives, people with poor health have limited competence to be involved in social activities, frequent medical consultation visits, and/or unexpected health changes that might cause hospitalization; all of which lead to barriers in achieving life expectations (Stolar et al. 1992). Recent studies have found that subjective evaluations of health can be significant predictors of life satisfaction among older adults (Varshney 2008). People with more wealth were believed to have a greater ability to achieve life goals, which was reported to provide higher levels of life satisfaction (Lipovcan et al. 2007). Socio-economic characteristics were also found to be related to life satisfaction (Fernandez-Ballesteros et al. 2001).

Studies of life satisfaction and/or quality of life among Chinese elders suggest that there are cultural influences on the factors associated with life satisfaction. The contributing forces of global life satisfaction for Chinese elders can be categorized into two factors—social and relational needs factors and basic needs factors (Lou et al. 2008a). The current generation of elders in China, including Hong Kong, experienced a great many hardships earlier in life; such as the Second World War, Civil war, and changes of governance, to name a few. Basic needs such as food, housing, and transportation; and related aspects such as health and financial status remain extremely important for them. Besides basic needs factors, social and relational needs factors also play an important role in contributing to global life satisfaction (Lou et al. 2008a). A longitudinal study on life satisfaction among older Hong Kong people revealed that various aspects of social support, including size of support network, emotional support, and quality of support, were significant contributing factors (Chou and Chi 1999). An inclination towards Chinese tradition, such as intergenerational exchange, was also identified to make a unique contribution to the life satisfaction of Chinese older people (Lou et al. 2008b). Recent western studies on intergenerational exchanges also argued that consideration needs to be paid to both the positive and negative sides of the intergenerational exchange, in which the former would be associated with resilience and successful aging, while the latter could be troublesome to the individual (Lowenstein et al. 2007).

3 Incorporating Social Support from Grandchildren into Social Support Research

Social support can be argued to have both direct and indirect effects on the subjective well-being of older adults. On the one hand, social support can fulfill the basic needs for social companionship of older adults, provide emotional bonds between older adults and others, and serve as an information channel for individuals. On the other hand, the literature points out that social support can moderate the negative impact caused by ill-health, crisis, and environmental demands (Alloway and Bebbington 1987; Cohen and Mckay 1984; Hobfoll and Stokes 1988).

Social support for older adults is conceptualized as coming from three main sources—family, friends, and/or significant others (Lubben and Gironda 2003). Support from the current generation of grandchildren has not been well studied. Traditionally, Chinese older adults stand at the top of the hierarchical layer of the relationship, both in the family and in society. Naturally, grandparents are symbolically associated with wisdom and power, which deserve legitimate high status in the family and in society. This high status was established and maintained through moral and practical mechanisms, such as filial piety and intergenerational exchange (Chow 2004; Mjelde-Mossey et al. 2005). Active involvement in and contribution to family well-being through various means such as socializing with grandchildren, helping with household chores, and providing financial help to children was found to have positive impact on sense of happiness of Chinese elders (e.g. Luo et al. 2008).

However, the modernization process has challenged the understanding and practice of filial piety in intergenerational relations (Brian and Logan 2001). A recent study found that the younger generation in Hong Kong agreed least with filial piety values, compared with those from Mainland China. The emphasis on individual autonomy, which was influenced by the West, was purported as being one of the possible reasons that had led to a priority shift from family to individual needs (Kwan et al. 2003). Under such circumstances, it would be worth exploring whether support from grandchildren could make unique contributions to the life satisfaction of older adults in Hong Kong, a context that contains influences from both Chinese tradition and western culture.

Grandparenthood experiences were affected by the life course transitions of both the grandparent's and the grandchildren's generations, and the particular social context within which they are embedded (Brian and Logan 2001; Crosnoe and Elder 2002). While studies on grandparents taking care of young children have often focused on the stressful aspect of being surrogate parents, literature from adolescent grandchildren's and adult grandchildren's perspectives shows mutual emotional bonds between grandparents and grandchildren (Sheehan and Petrovic 2008). Grandparents also experienced learning opportunities such as new computer technology (i.e. e-mail), new values, and connecting with new activities while communicating with adolescent and/or adult grandchildren (Lou and Chi 2008; Storm et al. 1999). Thus, this paper focused on the effect of social support from adolescent and/or adult grandchildren on the life satisfaction of older people in Hong Kong.

4 Theoretical Framework

Even though there is a lack of consensus regarding the operationalization of social support, there is some agreement that social support is a multidimensional concept (Hupcey 1998). In general, there are three constructs of social support which consist of support networks, supportive behaviors, and a subjective appraisal of support (Cohen 1992). In regard to social support networks, it would be unwise to only focus on grandchildren, while ignoring the general concept that includes family and friends. Hence, the present study treats social support networks as a control variable (Lubben and Gironda 2004). In addition, the network size of grandchildren is an uncontrollable factor (i.e. the number of grandchildren an older adult has). Hence, this construct was not further developed for the purpose of examining social support from grandchildren in the present study.

In line with the supportive behavioral construct, it was argued that individuals were not only satisfied by receiving support from others, but also by giving support in a reciprocal relationship (Lubben and Gironda 2004; Vaux 1988). The motivations behind this vary from family/social obligations, to self-interest or altruism. However, the association between this type of reciprocal behavioral and subjective well-being was also inconclusive. Reciprocal support exchange between the older person and his/her spouse, children, and friends was associated with a higher quality of life and better mental health among older Korean and Chinese people, respectively (Kim et al. 2000; Luo et al. 2008). However, other studies found that the extent and pattern of exchange with the older person varies when s/he communicates with spouse, children, or friends (Ingersoll-Dayton and Antonucci 1988). To our best knowledge, the support exchange between grandparents and adolescent and/or adult grandchildren has not been well explored in the literature. In the context of grandparent-grandchildren relationships, even though adolescent and/or adult grandchildren place less demands on providing daily care, grandparents still feel stress when they are required to be a role model and to provide advice (Lou and Chi 2008). Grandparents sometimes have to take up the role of being a source of help in shielding grandchildren from the likelihood of developing psychological distress in adolescence and young adulthood (Ruiz and Silverstein 2007). In this regard, the present study explored the effect of reciprocal support between grandparents and grandchildren on the life satisfaction of the grandparents. Reciprocal support was operationalized by exchange behaviors between grandchildren and grandparents—whether grandchildren and grandparents would consult the other party when they have important decisions to make (Ingersoll-Dayton and Antonucci 1988).

In regard to the subjective appraisal of support, it was revealed that social support could provide a person with positive emotions, and the recognition of self-worth and self-esteem (Cohen 1992; Lubben and Gironda 2004; Vaux 1988). A study by Krause and Kyriakos (1990) found that emotional support is provided to older adults more frequently than any other kind of assistance. Grandparents were perceived as a special source of attachment targets by adolescent grandchildren and also adult grandchildren (Crosnoe and Elder 2002; Taylor et al. 2005). This dimension is operationalized by perceived emotional support from adolescent and/or adult grandchildren in the present study. In late life, social support was argued to boost feelings of personal worth, self control, and self-esteem when support was provided by involvement in important roles in their life (Krause and Borawski-Clark 1994). As discussed in previous parts of the paper, the grandparent link to hierarchical status in the family and kinship continuity is quite important for older adults in Chinese culture. It is believed that support from grandchildren would bring a sense of self-worth, self control, and self-esteem to grandparents in Hong Kong. In this study, this was operationalized by the perceived positive consequences of being grandparents at both the personal (i.e. life meaning, self-worth, and self-acceptance) and interpersonal (i.e. positive relationships with others) level (Lou and Chi 2008).

In summary, this paper conceptualizes social support from adolescent and/or adult grandchildren into three dimensions: emotional support, reciprocal support, and appraisal support. It is hypothesized that social support from adolescent and/or adult grandchildren contributes to the life satisfaction of older adults, while other demographic and psychological factors are taken into consideration.

Based on the previous discussion on life satisfaction and its associated factors, the association between social support from grandchildren and the life satisfaction of Chinese older people in Hong Kong will be examined by controlling two other categories of variables. The first category refers to demographic characteristics such as age, gender, level of education, marital status, and living arrangement. The second category refers to variables that indicate health, wealth, social support in general, and perceptions about tradition. The literature argues that variables belonging to either category might be associated with the life satisfaction of older people in one way or another (Chou and Chi 1999; Lou et al. 2008a, b). Controlling the effects of the captioned variables helps to manifest the distinct effect of grandchildren's social support on the life satisfaction of grandparents.

5 Methods

This study utilized data from face-to-face interview surveys conducted in Hong Kong. Trained interviewers were recruited from undergraduate students from one university in Hong Kong. They conducted face-to-face interviews with a standardized questionnaire. The interviewers visited residential homes and senior centers that had agreed to participate. After obtaining verbal consent from qualified subjects, the interviewer invited the respondent to a private room or a quiet corner to carry out the interview. Each interview lasted about 30 min. Ethical approval was granted by the ethical review committee of The Chinese University of Hong Kong.

6 Sampling

The sample was recruited from members living in residential homes and community centers in Hong Kong by using multi-stage sampling. First, strata sampling was used to select 90 service units from a list of elderly residential homes and senior centers in Hong Kong. Two strata were used, which were the nature of services (residential or community-based service) and geographic areas (Hong Kong Island, Kowloon, or the New Territory). Fifteen service units were randomly selected in each of the six categories (e.g. community centers in Hong Kong Island, residential homes in the New Territory, etc.). Invitation letters, together with a brief introduction of the study which included the purpose and significance of the research, were sent to the administrators of each selected service unit. From the 90 letters sent out, 17 declined to participate, and 21 were invalid due to renovation, temporary suspension of visiting due to a flu epidemic, and invalid address due to relocation. The overall success rate was 75%.

The second step was to screen for qualified subjects by adopting quota sampling. A trained interviewer visited each center or residential home which agreed to participate in the study. At the elderly centers, the interviewer walked to the common area of the center and randomly approached older people to ask whether they had a youngest grandchild aged 12 or older. Those who self-reported that they did were invited for an interview; those who had difficulties with communication and/or those who self-reported that they did not have were not invited. Of those who were invited, only those who gave consent were interviewed using the standardized questionnaire. Within each residential home or senior center, six respondents were set as the maximum number of participants that could be interviewed to ensure that the sample of the current study came from various geographic areas.

7 Measures

7.1 Life Satisfaction

The dependent variable life satisfaction was measured by the Life Satisfaction Scale for Chinese (Lou et al. 2008a). This is an eight-item scale that measures domain-specific life satisfaction for Chinese older adults. The eight domains included were family relationships, intergenerational communication, friendship, partner, food/meals, finance, housing, and health. The response alternatives consisted of satisfied or dissatisfied. The scale score is the sum of the item score, with higher scores associated with higher life satisfaction. Besides overall life satisfaction, two sub-scale scores could be built to measure life satisfaction with social needs and life satisfaction with basic needs. The reliability of the total scale and the two sub-scales were satisfactory as indicated by Cronbach's alpha equal to .90, .89, and .81, respectively.

7.2 Social Support

The Lubben Social Network Scale (LSNS) was used to measure social network support among older adults and validated among Hong Kong Chinese (Chi and Boey 1993; Lubben 1988). This is a ten-item scale that measures social network support from family, friends, and interdependent relations. Some of the response alternatives consisted of the number of family or friend networks people had (none, one, two, three or four, five to eight, and more than nine); or frequency of contact (less than once a month, once a month, several times a month, once a week, several times a week, and daily). The score ranged from 0 to 50, with higher scores associated with better social support. The reliability of the total score was satisfactory, as indicated by Cronbach's alpha equal to 0.78.

7.3 Chinese Tradition

The Chinese Tradition Scale (CTS) was used to measure Chinese tradition among older adults (Mjelde-Mossey et al. 2005). The CTS is a 9-item instrument designed to measure family tradition tendencies among the elderly at both a cognitive and behavioral level. It is designed to assess a general tendency towards family tradition, but could also explore two other components—reliance on children for financial needs, and reciprocal support for emotional and instrumental needs. The scale score is computed by summing the item responses ($1 = \text{Yes}$, $0 = \text{No/Not Applicable}$), with a theoretical range from 0 to 9. Higher scores are associated with higher levels of inclination to tradition. The reliability of the total score was satisfactory as indicated by Cronbach's alpha equal to 0.77.

7.4 Social Support from Adolescent and/or adult Grandchildren

Social support from adolescent and/or adult grandchildren was measured by three groups of variables: emotional support, reciprocal support, and appraisal support. Emotional support was measured by a single item question: "How frequently do you feel that your grandchildren provide you emotional support?" on a 5-point Likert scale (not at all to always). Reciprocal support was measured by two items: "When you have an important decision to make, would you discuss it with your grandchildren?" on a Yes/No response format; and "When your grandchildren have an important decision to make, would they approach you for discussion?" on a Yes/No response format. Those who reported 'yes' for both questions were grouped into a reciprocal support group; and the remaining respondents were grouped into a non-reciprocal support group. Appraisal support was measured by a 7-item scale regarding the positive consequences brought from relationships with grandchildren; such as meaningfulness, family continuity, new perceptions, new knowledge, new life energy, more acceptances of self and positive relations with others. The response alternatives were a 5-point Likert scale based on the frequency with which they felt the emotion (not at all to always). The reliability of the appraisal support was satisfactory, as indicated by Cronbach's alpha equal to 0.76.

7.5 Self-Rated Health

Self-rated health was assessed by a single item question: "How would you rate your overall health at the present time?" on a 5-point scale (poor, fair, good, very good, excellent). Self-rated health is a popular area of study among variables which assess health conditions for older adults, including the Chinese population (Bjorner et al. 1996; Chi and Boey 1993).

7.6 Self-Rated Financial Adequacy

Self-rated financial adequacy was measured by a single item question: "Do you think that you have enough money to cover your daily expenses?" on a 3-point scale (adequate, just enough, inadequate). This scale is widely used to measure the financial status of the elderly and has satisfactory reliability and validity among elderly Chinese people (Chou and Chi 1999).

7.7 Demographic Variables

The demographic measures included sex, age (in years), level of education (no formal education, formal education), marital status (currently married, currently not married), religious affiliation (Yes/No), and living arrangement.

8 Analytical Method

Descriptive analysis was conducted to explore respondents' level of life satisfaction and social support from grandchildren. Then hierarchical regression was computed to test for factors affecting life satisfaction. Three models were tested in which the first model only included demographic data. The second included demographic variables, social network support, and inclination to tradition. The third model included social support from grandchildren on top of the second model. The data were analyzed using SPSS (SPSS 2002).

9 Results

9.1 Sample Characteristics

A total of 215 respondents were successfully interviewed. Among them, 77.2% were female; the ages ranged from 64 to 101, with a mean age of 79.3 years old. About half of the respondents said they did not receive any formal education. During the time of the survey, about half (43.7%) were married; and about forty percent (38.6%) lived with family members. The number of adolescent and/or adult grandchildren respondents reported ranged from 1 to 29, with a mean of 6.7 grandchildren. About half of the respondents said they had religious affiliations such as Buddhism, Christianity, Catholicism, Daoism, and traditional Chinese beliefs. The characteristics of the respondents are listed in Table 1.

9.2 Life Satisfaction

On life satisfaction, the respondents scored a mean of 19.36, with a standard deviation of 3.80. While various domains were explored, the results showed that about half of the respondents felt satisfied with various facets of life, with the highest satisfaction rate associated with communication with their children and grandchildren (58.6%) and the

Table 1 Characteristics of respondents

	Frequency (%)
Sex	
Male	49 (22.8)
Female	166 (77.2)
Age (M = 79.3, SD = 6.9)	
60–69	18 (8.4)
70–79	95 (44.2)
80 or above	102 (47.4)
Formal education	
Yes	112 (52.1)
No	103 (47.9)
Marital status	
Currently married	94 (43.7)
Currently not married	121 (56.3)
Religious affiliation[a]	
Yes	115 (53.5)
No	100 (46.5)
Living arrangement	
Alone	24 (11.2)
With family/friends	83 (38.6)
In residential homes	108 (50.2)
Number of grandchildren[b] (M = 6.7, SD = 4.5)	
1–3	53 (25.9)
4–6	64 (31.2)
7 or above	88 (42.9)

[a] Chinese traditional religion, Christian, Catholic, Muslim, and Taoism

[b] Valid case = 205

Table 2 Life satisfaction of the respondents

	Feel satisfied (%)
Family relationships	124 (57.7)
Communications with children/grandchildren	126 (58.6)
Friendships	117 (54.4)
Living partner	87 (40.5)
Food/meal	116 (54.0)
Finances	104 (48.4)
Health	92 (42.8)
Housing	122 (56.7)

lowest satisfaction associated with their living partner (40.5%). Detailed distributions were presented in Table 2.

9.3 Social Support

9.3.1 Social Network Support

According to the Lubben Social Network Support scale, the respondents obtained a mean of 21.79, with a standardized deviation of 10.26.

9.3.2 Social Support from Adolescent and/or adult Grandchildren

Emotional support: 91 (42.3%) had at least one grandchild that s/he felt close to and with whom they could share and seek help. 107 (49.8%) of the respondents sometimes or frequently felt that her/his grandchildren provided emotional support.

Reciprocal support: 60 (27.9%) of the respondents reported that they would approach their grandchildren to discuss important decisions in their life. Reciprocally, 57 (26.5%) of the respondents said their grandchildren would approach them for an important discussion. In sum, 22.8% of the respondents were treated as reciprocal group; while the remaining 77.2% was treated as non-reciprocal group.

Appraisal support: Within a theoretical range of 1 to 35, the mean score obtained by the respondents was 22.06, with a standardized deviation of 5.48. More than half of the respondents agreed that being a grandparent was meaningful: they felt the continuity of the family kinship, and they became more self-confident (Table 3).

Table 3 Appraisal support from grandchildren perceived by the respondents

	Feel satisfied (%)
Connect with new knowledge and skills	59 (27.4)
Learn new knowledge (computer, e-mail, etc.)	37 (17.2)
Life became more energetic	86 (40.0)
Became more self-confident	108 (50.2)
Became more self-accepting	94 (43.7)
Finds being grandparent meaningful	121 (56.2)
Feels family kinship being continued	118 (54.9)

9.4 Relationship Between Social Support from Adolescent and/or adult Grandchildren and Life Satisfaction

Three models were tested by adopting a hierarchical regression. In the first model, only demographic characteristics were entered including age, gender, level of education, marital status, and religious affiliation. The model explained 13% of the variance ($F = 4.97$, $p < .01$). Variables that made significant contributions to explain life satisfaction were not living alone and not living in residential homes. In other words, those respondents who lived with family members were more satisfied as compared to those living alone or living in residential homes. In the second model, variables that were identified as making significant contributions to the life satisfaction of older adults in Hong Kong were entered. These included social network support, inclination to Chinese tradition, self-rated health, and self-rated financial adequacy. After controlling for demographic variables, the model explained 47% of the variance ($F_{change} = 33.68$, $p < .001$). Those respondents, who reported having higher levels of social network support and higher levels of inclination to Chinese tradition, a comparatively healthier and comparatively wealthier life than others, reported a higher level of life satisfaction. However, the previous variables that significantly contributed to life satisfaction in model one (e.g. living alone and living at a residential home) became insignificant; while the level of education became significant. Those with a lower level of education reported a higher level of life satisfaction. In the third model, variables indicating social support from adolescent and/or adult grandchildren (e.g. emotional support, reciprocal support, and appraisal support) were entered. The whole model explained 51% of the variance; therefore, social support from adolescent and/or adult grandchildren was significant, while controlling for all of the contributions of other variables ($F_{change} = 7.15$, $p < .001$). Those respondents who received more emotional support and appraisal support from adolescent and/or adult grandchildren were more likely to have higher levels of life satisfaction as compared to others. Those respondents who experienced reciprocal support were more likely to have lower levels of life satisfaction as compared to those who did not experience reciprocal support with their grandchildren ($t = -2.49$, $p < .01$) (Table 4).

10 Discussion

The results of the present study showed that social support from adolescent and/or adult grandchildren played a significant role in contributing to the life satisfaction of older adults in Hong Kong. This effect was identified while the contributions of demographic and other psychological factors were controlled.

Grandparents who had a lower level of education, a higher level of social support network, an inclination to Chinese tradition, better self-rated health, and a greater sense of having adequate financial resources were found to have higher level of life satisfaction in the present study. In general, these findings were consistent with the literature showing a general observation on subjective well-being internationally (Diener et al. 1999); and the specific observation that the current generation of elders in Hong Kong are highly concerned about wealth and health, and still benefit from attachment to Chinese family tradition (Chou and Chi 1999; Mjelde-Mossey et al. 2005). The findings on the relationship between level of education and life satisfaction were also consistent with the literature by adopting the same life satisfaction measure in the Chinese population (Lou et al. 2008a, b). There are two possible explanations for this. The positive relationship between the level of education and subjective well-being was argued to be confounded by occupational status

Table 4 Hierarchical regression of life satisfaction

	Model 1			Model 2			Model 3		
	B	SE	Beta	B	SE	Beta	B	SE	Beta
Living alone	−1.79	0.82	−0.15*	−0.01	0.67	−0.001	0.27	0.66	0.02
Living in residential home	−3.08	0.63	−0.41***	−0.99	0.55	−0.13	−0.62	0.53	−0.08
Formal education	−0.16	0.32	−0.04	−0.62	0.25	−0.14*	−0.56	0.24	−0.13*
LSNS				0.09	0.03	0.25**	0.07	0.03	0.20**
Chinese tradition				0.54	0.09	0.35***	0.51	0.09	0.33***
Self-rated health				0.50	0.22	0.12*	0.41	0.22	0.10[a]
Self-rated financial adequacy				1.01	0.23	0.24***	0.96	0.22	0.23***
Support from grandchildren									
Emotional support							0.43	0.17	0.14*
Reciprocal support							−1.15	0.46	−0.13**
Appraisal support							0.09	0.05	0.13*
	Adjusted $R^2 = .13$ ($p < .0001$)			Adjusted $R^2 = .47$, $R^2_{change} = .34$ ($p < .0001$)			Adjusted $R^2 = .51$, $R^2_{change} = .05$ ($p < .0001$)		

* $p < .05$; ** $p < .01$; *** $p < .001$

[a] $p = .06$

and income. For older adults, the importance of occupational status and income had been gradually declining throughout their life. Without a pension system for the majority of older people in Hong Kong, a continuous linkage between previous occupation and income with the level of education was weak. In addition, more highly educated people might be more susceptible to feeling frustrated due to their unmet expectations in life (Chou et al. 2006; Diener et al. 1999).

The findings on the relationship between the three dimensions of grandchildren's, social support, and life satisfaction supported the notion that the positive side of the grandchildren support could be a resilient resource for successful aging; while the negative side of grandchildren support could be a burden for grandparents (Lowenstein et al. 2007). On the one hand, the effect of emotional support and appraisal support from grandchildren on their grandparents' life satisfaction was found to be positive. These findings provide evidence and support for the positive side of intergenerational interaction by expanding the sources of social support from two generation to cross-generation. On the other hand, reciprocal support between grandparents and adolescent and/or adult grandchildren showed an adverse effect on the life satisfaction of grandparents. This finding seemed to suggest a negative side to social support, which will be discussed in detail later.

The contribution of emotional support from adolescent and/or adult grandchildren seemed to suggest that the grandparent-adolescent and/or adult grandchildren relationship provides opportunities to fulfill companionship needs for both parties, which was consistent with the literature (Crosnoe and Elder 2002; Taylor et al. 2005). Both sides are mutually attached and the grandparents feel supported while interacting with their grandchildren. The significance of appraisal support from grandchildren on the life satisfaction of grandparents indicated both the practical and symbolic function of grandchildren's support. At a symbolic level, the meaning of being a grandparent seemed positive and important for older adults (Krause and Borawski-Clark 1994). In addition, a sense of family kinship and continuity relates to a feeling of hope about the future for senior family members (Chow 2004; Lou and Chi 2008). At a practical level, the learning opportunities provided by communicating with grandchildren seemed to bring energy and a new dimension to the 'old' life of grandparents (Lou and Chi 2008; Storm et al. 1999). Considering the family-oriented life of older adults of the current generation in Hong Kong, it is understandable that being connected to grandchildren plays a significant role in their life satisfaction.

The negative contribution to life satisfaction made by reciprocal support between grandparents and grandchildren seems to suggest that grandparent-grandchildren relationships, like any other relationships, have both a positive and negative side. This finding supported the notion that the negative side of the grandchildren-grandparent interaction could be burdensome to the older adults (Lowenstein et al. 2007). Seeking advice from grandchildren violates the social role expectations of both older adults and grandchildren from a developmental and a cultural perspective. Grandparents, due to their seniority, should play a more authoritative and resourceful role from a cultural perspective. Seeking advice from the younger generation might reflect that they have limited resources at their peer level and their own children's level. Along with the developmental perspective, grandchildren are regarded as occupying a lower level in the family hierarchy. Grandparents are not expected to seek 'advice' from younger generations on life challenges. Hence, it is understandable that grandparents would feel anxious when they need to seek advice from grandchildren who are adolescents and older on important decisions. Adolescent and/or adult grandchildren may not have sufficient knowledge relating to the main concerns of older people, such as health and living arrangements, and they may not be able to provide valuable advices on how to deal with these issues in daily lives. On the other hand, adolescents and/or adults treasure autonomy and they would be more likely to seek help from peers and parents (Crosnoe and Elder 2002). When grandchildren need to consult their grandparents for important decisions, grandparents might feel pressure from their responsibilities (Lou and Chi 2008). Hence, the reciprocal help seeking between grandchildren aged adolescent or above and grandparents tended to be negative instead of positive.

The findings of the present study could generate at least three policy and practice implications for the active aging framework in the Chinese Hong Kong context. First, while more and more older people are able to live to an age where they have adolescent and/or adult grandchildren, policies in Hong Kong that emphasize 'strengthening the family' should take into consideration intergenerational dynamics, especially grandparent-grandchildren dyads, in order to become more comprehensive (The HKSAR Government, 2008). Second, while we refer to support from grandchildren, it is important to differentiate between positive and negative aspect of support. The findings of this study seem to suggest that emotional and appraisal support from grandchildren play a positive role in achieving life satisfaction, and should be promoted. In particular, emotional and appraisal support could be resilience sources for those elderly people with limited resources in other aspects; such as those with less traditional family beliefs, lower self-rated health and financial adequacy, and poor social support from family and friends. On the contrary, reciprocal support gained by consulting each other for important decisions in life seemed to play a negative role that was troublesome to grandparents. It could be associated with both age-inappropriate expectations and cultural-specific role expectations towards grandparents and grandchildren. Last but not the least, while physical distance was not found to be a major barrier for intergenerational relationships, grandchildren support could be better achieved in a context with positive attitudes towards both sides (Taylor et al. 2005). Consequently, efforts which are targeted at advocating positive attitude toward older people in Hong Kong are advocated.

The present study has several limitations. First, even though a multi-stage sampling procedure was adopted to enhance the diversity of the sample, it was a non-representative sample. In addition, although the interviewer was instructed to randomly approach older people at selected centers, this approach was not able to adequately control selection bias on a practical level. Moreover, elderly people with communication difficulties were excluded. Any attempt at generalization of the findings should be done with caution. Second, the global measure of grandchildren support failed to differentiate between adolescent grandchildren and adult grandchildren. Further studies are recommended to test whether both positive and negative aspect of supports are present among adolescent grandchildren, adult grandchildren, or both. However, there is always conflict between the bottom-up or up-bottom measurement approach. While we chose to measure support from a grandchild at a specific age, we neglected the fact that many of the older people have more than one grandchild at different ages at a certain time. While we chose to measure support from a global perspective, we fell into the inadequacy of targeting grandchildren at specific developmental stages. Last but not the least, the operationalization of social support between grandparents and grandchildren focused on the frequency of support. Future studies could focus on both frequency and intensity to further explore the conceptualization of social support.

Acknowledgement This research project is supported by a Direct Grant of The Chinese University of Hong Kong. Ref. No. 2020824.

References

Alloway, R., & Bebbington, P. (1987). The buffer theory of social support—A review of the literature. *Psychological Medicine, 17*, 91–108.

Bishop, A. J., Martin, P., & Poon, L. (2006). Happiness and congruence in older adulthood: A structural model of life satisfaction. *Aging and Mental Health, 10*, 445–453.

Bjorner, J. B., Kristensen, T. S., Orth-Gomér, K., Tibblin, G., Sullivan, M., & Westerholm, P. (1996). *Self-rated health: A useful concept in research, prevention, and clinical medicine*. Stockholm: Swedish Council for Planning and Coordination of Research.

Brian, J. S., & Logan, J. (2001). Intergenerational relations: A comparison between Chinese and American families. *Journal of Sociology, 2*, 85–95 (in Chinese).

Chan, C. M. A., Phillips, D. R., Chi, I., Ho, S., Cheng, S. T., & Cheung, J. (2000). *The study of the quality of life of elderly residents in the community in Hong Kong*. Report submitted to the Health and Welfare Bureau, Hong Kong Government.

Chi, I., & Boey, K. W. (1993). Hong Kong validation of measuring instruments of mental health status of the elderly. *Clinical Gerontologist, 13*, 35–52.

Chou, K. L., & Chi, I. (1999). Determinants of life satisfaction in Hong Kong Chinese elderly: A longitudinal study. *Aging and Mental Health, 3*, 328–335.

Chou, K. L., Chow, N. W. S., & Chi, I. (2006). Economic status of the elderly in Hong Kong. *International Social Work, 49*, 218–232.

Chow, N. W. S. (2004). Asian value and aged care. *Geriatrics and Gerontology International, 4*, 521–525.

Cohen, S. (1992). Stress, social support and disorder. In H. O. F. Veiel & U. Baumann (Eds.), *The meaning and measurement of social support* (pp. 109–124). New York: Hemisphere.

Cohen, S., & Mckay, G. (1984). Social support, stress, and the buffering hypothesis: A theoretical analysis. *Handbook of Psychology and Health, 4*, 253–267.

Crosnoe, R., & Elder, G. H., Jr. (2002). Life course transitions, the generational stake, and grandparent-grandchild relationships. *Journal of Marriage and Family, 64*, 1089–1096.

Diener, E., Suh, E. M., Lucas, R. E., & Smith, H. L. (1999). Subjective well-being: Three decades of progress. *Psychological Bulletin, 125*, 276–302.

Fernandez-Ballesteros, R., Zamarron, M. D., & Ruiz, M. A. (2001). The contribution of socio-demographic and psychological factors to life satisfaction. *Ageing and Society, 21*, 25–43.
Gow, A. J., Pattie, A., Whiteman, M. C., Whalley, L. J., & Deary, I. J. (2007). Social support and successful aging: Investigating the relationship between lifetime cognitive change and life satisfaction. *Journal of Individual Differences, 28*, 103–115.
Hobfoll, S. E., & Stokes, J. P. (1988). The process and mechanics of social support. In S. W. Duck (Ed.), *Handbook of personal relationships* (pp. 497–517). New York: John Wiley and Sons Ltd.
Hupcey, J. (1998). Clarifying the social support theory-research linkage. *Journal of Advanced Nursing, 27*, 1231–1241.
Ingersoll-Dayton, B., & Antonucci, T. C. (1988). Reciprocal and nonreciprocal social support: Contrasting sides of intimate relationships. *Journal of Gerontology, 43*, S65–S73.
Kang, S. M., Shaver, P. R., Sue, S., Min, K. H., & Jing, H. B. (2003). Culture-specific patterns in the prediction of life satisfaction: Roles of emotion, relationship quality, and self-esteem. *Personality and Social Psychology Bulletin, 29*, 1596–1608.
Kim, H., Hisata, M., Kai, I., & Lee, S. K. (2000). Social support exchange and quality of life among the Korean elderly. *Journal of Cross-Cultural Gerontology, 15*, 331–347.
Krause, N., & Borawski-Clark, E. (1994). Clarifying the functions of social support in later life. *Research on Aging, 16*, 251–279.
Krause, N., & Kyriakos, S. M. (1990). Measuring social support among older adults. *International Journal of Aging and Human Development, 30*, 37–53.
Kwan, A. Y. H., Cheung, J. C. K., & Ng, S. H. (2003). *Revisit of filial piety concept among the young, the adult, and the old in Beijing, Guangzhou, Hong Kong, Nanjing, Shanghai, Xia, and Xian*. Hong Kong: Department of Applied Social Studies, City University of Hong Kong.
Lau, A., Chi, I., & McKenna, K. (1998). Self-perceived quality of life of Chinese elderly people in Hong Kong. *Occupational Therapy International, 5*, 118–139.
Lipovcan, L. K., Brkljacić, T., & Sakić, V. (2007). Monthly income and subjective well-being of Croatian citizens. *Croatian Medical Journal, 48*, 727–733.
Lou, V. W. Q. (2005, November). *Grandparenting roles played by older people in Hong Kong*. Paper presented at the 13th Annual Congress of Gerontology, Hong Kong Association of Gerontology, Hong Kong.
Lou, V. W. Q., & Chi, I. (2008). Measure grandparenthood stress and reward: Developing a scale based on perceptions by grandparents with adolescent grandchildren in Hong Kong. *Geriatrics and Gerontology International., 8*, 291–299.
Lou, V. W. Q., Chi, I., & Mjelde-Mossey, L. A. (2008a). Development and validation of a life satisfaction scale for Chinese elders. *International Journal of Ageing and Human Development, 67*, 149–170.
Lou, V. W. Q., Chi, I., & Mjelde-Mossey, L. A. (2008b). *Faithful to tradition and life satisfaction among Chinese Elders*. Paper presented at the Gerontological Society of America's 61st Annual Scientific Meeting, Maryland, USA.
Lowenstein, A., Katz, R., & Gur-Yaish, N. (2007). Reciprocity in parent–child exchange and life satisfaction among the elderly: A cross-national perspective. *Journal of Social Issues, 63*, 865–883.
Lubben, J. E. (1988). Assessing social networks among elderly populations. *Family and Community Health, 11*(3), 42–52.
Lubben, J., & Gironda, M. (2003). Centrality of social ties to the health and well-being of older adults. In B. Berkman & L. Harootyan (Eds.), *Social work and health care in an aging society*. New York: Springer Publishing Company.
Lubben, J., & Gironda, M. (2004). Measuring social networks and assessing their benefits. In C. Phillipson, G. Allan, & D. A. Morgan (Eds.), *Social networks and social exclusion: Sociological and policy perspectives* (pp. 20–34). Aldershot: Ashgate.
Luo, Y. M., Hu, H., & Zhu, Z. H. (2008). Correlation between intergeneration social support and subject well-being of the elderly in Hunan province. *Chinese Journal of Clinical Psychology, 16*, 173–175 (in Chinese).
Mjelde-Mossey, L. A., Chi, I., & Lou, V. W. Q. (2005). Assessing tradition in Chinese elders living in a changing social environment: Implications for social work practice. *Journal of Human Behavior in the Social Environment, 11*, 41–57.
Ruiz, S., & Silverstein, M. (2007). Relationships with grandparents and the emotional well-being of late adolescent and young adult grandchildren. *Journal of Social Issues, 63*, 793–808.
Sheehan, N., & Petrovic, K. (2008). Grandparents and their adult grandchildren: Recurring themes from the literature. *Marriage & Family Review, 44*, 99–124.
Silverman, P., Hecht, L., & McMillin, J. D. (2000). Modeling life satisfaction among the aged: A comparison of Chinese and Americans. *Journal of Cross Cultural Gerontology, 15*, 289–305.

Song, X. M., & Chi, I. (2001). The role of social support in the relationship between physical health strain and depression of elderly Chinese. In I. Chi, N. Chappell, & J. Lubben (Eds.), *Elderly Chinese in Pacific Rim countries—Social support and integration* (pp. 189–200). Hong Kong: Hong Kong University Press.

SPSS, Inc. (2002). *Statistical package for the social sciences, 11.0*. Chicago, Illinois: Author.

Stolar, G. E., MacEntee, M. I., & Hill, P. (1992). Seniors' assessment of their health and life satisfaction: The case for contextual evaluation. *International Journal of Aging and Human Development, 35*, 305–317.

Storm, R. D., Strom, S. K., Wang, C. M., Shen, Y. L., Griswold, D., Chan, H. S., et al. (1999). Grandparents in the United States and the Republic of China: A comparison of generations and culture. *International Journal of Aging and Human Development, 49*, 279–317.

Taylor, A., Robila, M., & Lee, H. S. (2005). Distance, Contact, and Intergenerational Relationships: Grandparents and adult grandchildren from an international perspective. *Journal of Adult Development, 12*, 33–41.

Varshney, S. (2008). Predictors of successful aging: Associations between social network patterns, life satisfaction, depression, subjective health and leisure time activity for older adults in India. *Dissertation Abstracts International: Section B The Sciences and Engineering*, 68, 7681.

Vaux, A. (1988). *Social support: Theory, research, and intervention*. New York: Praeger.

Yeung, G. T. Y., & Fung, H. H. (2007). Social support and life satisfaction among Hong Kong Chinese older adults: Family first? *European Journal of Ageing, 4*, 219–227.

Soc Indic Res (2010) 95:393–406
DOI 10.1007/s11205-009-9527-5

Social Problem Solving as a Predictor of Well-being in Adolescents and Young Adults

Andrew M. H. Siu · Daniel T. L. Shek

Accepted: 5 April 2009 / Published online: 2 October 2009

Abstract Social problem solving is the cognitive-affective-behavioral process by which people attempt to resolve real-life problems in a social environment, and is of key importance in the management of emotions and well-being. This paper reviews a series of studies on social problem solving conducted by the authors. First, we developed and validated the Chinese version of the Social Problem-Solving Inventory Revised (C-SPSI-R) which demonstrated very good psychometric properties. Second, we identified the scope of stressful social situations faced by young adults and their self-efficacy in facing such situations ($N = 179$). Young adults were generally confident about their basic social skills but found it much more stressful to relate to family members, handle conflicts, handle negative behaviors from others, self-disclose to others, and to express love. Third, in two separate studies, we found that social problem solving was closely linked to measures of depression ($n = 200$), anxiety ($n = 235$), and family well-being ($N = 1462$). Measures of anxiety and depression were found to be significantly related to aspects of social problem solving in expected directions and expected strength. In another study, higher parental social problem solving behavior and lower avoidance behavior were found to be related to indicators of family well-being, including better overall family functioning, and fewer parent–adolescent conflicts.

Keywords Social problem solving · Depression · Anxiety · Family functioning · Well-being

A. M. H. Siu (✉)
Department of Rehabilitation Sciences, Hong Kong Polytechnic University, Hunghom, Hong Kong, People's Republic of China
e-mail: rsandsiu@inet.polyu.edu.hk

D. T. L. Shek
Department of Applied Social Sciences, The Hong Kong Polytechnic University, Hunghom, Hong Kong, People's Republic of China

1 Introduction

The quality of interpersonal relationships is a key determinant of the well-being of individuals in modern societies (Feeney and Noller 1996). In everyday life, we need to maintain bonding with our family or friends, to work cooperatively with colleagues or peers, and to handle differences and conflicts among others. Successful coping in social situations and in interpersonal relationships is dependent upon the timely application of a social skills repertoire, including verbal and nonverbal skills, social problem solving abilities, and self-management skills (Corrigan et al. 1992).

Social problem solving is the cognitive-affective-behavioral process by which people attempt to resolve problems they experience in real-life social environments (D'Zurilla et al. 1996). The social problem solving model proposed by D'Zurilla and Nezu (1990) is a major update of the traditional information-processing model, which defines problem solving as a series of cognitive skills relating to problem identification, goal setting, finding suitable solutions, and evaluating problem-solving outcomes (Logan 1989). Effective problem solving is postulated to be dependent not just on the effective application of rational problem-solving skills, but also on a positive orientation towards problem solving (problem orientation) and the management of behavioral styles like impulsiveness and acting-out behavior, or procrastination and avoidance. Social problem solving can be seen as a major intrapersonal and interpersonal process that leads to quality relationships and an enhanced quality of life (Felce and Perry 1995; Wallander et al. 2001).

Training in social problem solving is commonly used in remedial programs in schools and in the treatment of a wide variety of psychiatric disorders. In child and adolescent research, social problem solving and empathy are both commonly regarded as favorable outcomes of child development (Moore et al. 2001). Training in social problem solving is a critical element in programs for promoting the quality of social relationships (Shure 1997) and the management of anger and aggressive behavior (Frey et al. 2000) in children and adolescents. More recent programs have combined empathy and training in social problem solving with the aim of promoting social competence and the prevention of aggression (Frey et al. 2000). In psychiatry, training in social problem solving skills has been used in treatment of anxiety disorders (Albano et al. 1995), depression (Nezu 1986a), and suicidal tendencies (Clum et al. 1996).

A number of studies have shown that social problem solving ability, either by itself, or together with social support, can reduce or minimize the impact of life stress on individuals (Dubow and Tisak 1989; Dubow et al. 1991; D'Zurilla and Sheedy 1991; Goodman et al. 1995). Social problem solving abilities are found to moderate the relationship between negative life stress and measures of distress such as hopelessness (Bonner and Rich 1988), anxiety (Nezu 1986a), depressive symptoms (Nezu 1986b), and behavioral and academic adjustment (Kang and Lee 1992).

To put the assessment and management of social problem solving deficits in context, it is necessary for therapists to ask the client to review their problem solving experience on personal issues, difficulties in interpersonal relationship, or problematic social situations (as in the instructions of Social Problem Solving Inventory Revised). However, the scope of problematic social situations is wide, and clients often find it hard to conceptualize what these social situations would include. It would therefore be of interest to understand the scope of stressful social situations and the self-efficacy in handling these social situations, so that we could provide a context for assessment and management of social problem solving deficits.

It would also be interesting to establish how social problem solving as a form of personal competence and personal quality of life is related to the quality of family life. In family research, training in problem-solving skills has long been identified as an effective intervention for managing parent–child relationship and conflicts (Guevremont and Foster 1993; Robin and Foster 1984). Social problem solving can be employed as an important individual resource in the renegotiation of family resources, and of parent–child interpersonal boundaries and mutual expectations. Unfortunately, despite the potential contribution of social problem solving (i.e. individual quality of life) to parenting and family functioning (i.e. family quality of life), only a few studies have closely examined the relationship between individual social problem solving and indicators of family quality of life such as family functioning and parent–child relational qualities (Kennedy et al. 1988). Some initial evidence has shown that aggression in adolescents is related to differences in social problem-solving strategies between parents and adolescents (Jaffe and D'Zurilla 2003), and that social problem solving is an important resource for families experiencing the stress of caring for a disabled child (Goldberg 1998).

Although problem-solving training is widely recognized in the literature as an important intervention in parent–adolescent conflicts, there are very few studies of the role of social problem solving in the family dynamics of Chinese populations. In the existing literature, there are very few studies on the relationship between social problem solving skills and family well-being or functioning in Chinese populations. In the previous studies, we proposed that the social problem solving abilities of parent and child may be a valuable resource in resolving family harmony problems and parent–adolescent conflicts in Chinese families. There are several reasons for this. First, Chinese people often try to uphold the Confucian ideal of maintaining interpersonal harmony but tend to neglect the importance of interpersonal communication and problem solving that can lead to harmonious outcomes (Shek and Chan 1998). Second, Chinese people emphasize the importance of emotional control, maintenance of politeness, and avoidance of aggressive persuasion techniques in conflict negotiation (Shenkar and Ronen 1987). As a result, Chinese people are much more likely to use avoidance, compromise, and tolerance when handling conflicts, rather than applying the problem-solving strategies of conflict management (Allison 1997; Kirkbride et al. 1991). Third, the hierarchical nature of Chinese families can be a major barrier to the application of problem-solving skills in family relationships. Chinese children are often expected to respect and listen to their parents' advice (and not to talk back) rather than solve problems together with their parents (Graber et al. 1996). Having conflicts with one's parents is socially unacceptable, as it allegedly makes the parents "lose face" (mianzi) (Ting-Toomey 1988). Due to these social norms and attitudes, individual social problem solving abilities are not strongly encouraged in Chinese culture. On the other hand, the application of social problem solving skills in families is hypothesized to have a positive impact on family well-being and to contribute to the resolution of parent–adolescent conflicts.

This paper critically reviews a series of studies on social problem solving conducted by the authors. The major objective of this paper is to examine how far social problem solving is related to indicators of mental health and well-being. First, we review the evidence on the psychometric properties of two instruments, the Chinese Social Problem-Solving Inventory Revised (C-SPSI-R). Second, we perceive a need to define the scope of stressful situations which requires social problem solving for clinical practice. We present a recent study on the scope of stressful social situations faced by young adults and their self-efficacy in facing such situations ($N = 179$). Third, we review two studies which aim to examine the relationship between social problem solving and depression ($n = 200$), anxiety ($n = 235$), and family well-being ($N = 1462$). Lastly, this paper reviews the links between social problem solving and well-being and suggests directions for further research.

2 Study 1: The Measurement of Social Problem Solving

The lack of standardized instruments in Chinese was one of the barriers to the study of social problem solving in Chinese populations. The C-SPSI-R was translated from the Social Problem-Solving Inventory Revised (SPSI-R; D'Zurilla 1986), which is one of the popular self-report measures of social problem solving. The current version of the SPSI-R has 52 items (D'Zurilla and Maydeu-Olivares 1995; Maydeu-Olivares and D'Zurilla 1996), and has five subscales which measure Positive Problem Orientation (PPO), Negative Problem Orientation (NPO), Rational Problem Solving (RPS), Avoidance Style (AS), and Impulsiveness/Carelessness Style (ICS).

The PPO subscale represents the constructive orientation toward problem solving, such as the optimism that problems can be solved, self-efficacy in solving problems successfully, and a willingness to commit to solving problems. The NPO subscale assesses motivational factors that inhibit problem solving, such as pessimism about ability to solve problems, and the tendency to easily become frustrated and upset when confronted with problems. The RPS subscale assesses the degree to which a person systematically uses rational problem-solving principles and strategies. The ICS subscale evaluates a deficient problem-solving pattern that is narrow, impulsive, careless, hurried, and incomplete. The final subscale, the AS subscale, assesses another defective problem-solving pattern characterized by procrastination, inaction, or dependency.

Siu (2003) translated the SPSI-R into Chinese and conducted studies on the psychometric properties of the full and short forms of the C-SPSI. Using a sample of 352 adolescents and young adults, Siu and Shek (2005a) reported that both the full and short forms of the C-SPSI had a five-factor structure that was largely consistent with the structure of the original English SPSI-R. The C-SPSI-R subscales were found to be internally consistent and had a good test–retest reliability. Based on the expert panel review of content validity and exploratory factor analysis, a 25-item short form of the C-SPSI-R was developed.

Confirmatory factor analyses of the short form were performed to compare how far the data fitted three models, including a five-factor model obtained from a pilot study ($N = 352$) of the C-SPSI-R short form (Siu and Shek 2005a), the groupings of items in the SPSI-R, and an alternative five-factor hierarchical model (i.e., one secondary factor and five primary factors). The results showed that the five-factor model from the pilot study (GFI = .93, AGFI = .92, RMSEA = .05 and CFI = .90) had a much better fit with the data than the other two. The C-SPSI-R subscales also demonstrated good internal consistency, with α ranging from .65 to .80 ($\alpha = .81$ for AS, .73 for NPO, .69 for RPS, .65 for ICS, and .68 for PPO). The correlations among the five subscales were largely consistent with expectation. There were significant positive correlations ($r = .47$) among the positive subscales (PPO and RPS), and among the negative subscales (r among NPO, ICS, and AS ranges from .52 to .71). There were significant negative correlations between negative and positive subscales (r ranges from $-.08$ to $-.19$).

3 Study 2: Efficacy of Young Adults in Handling Stressful Social Situations

This study investigated the self-efficacy of Hong Kong young adults (aged 18–30) in handling stressful social situations. Stage 1 of the study used an open-ended questionnaire to collect social situations perceived as stressful by the young adult respondents. A total of 238 situations were collected from 54 young adults. Content analysis was conducted on the situations collected, and the 238 situations were reduced to 36 stressful social situations and categorized into the three logical factors of social skills (11 items), interpersonal relationships (IR: 18 items), and social situations (SS: 7 items). Factor analysis of the 11 questions on social skills comprised two factors, which were labeled basic social skills (BS) and advanced social skills (AS). The two factors accounted for 55.65% of the variance, and the factor loadings were significant (ranging from .44 to .93) (Table 1). For the sections on interpersonal relationships and social situations, both sections were found to be unidimensional, and the single factor in each analysis accounted for 59.31 and 42.34% of the variances respectively. In addition, all the factor loadings were significant and ranged from .44 to .82. The internal consistency of items under the four factors ranged from very good to excellent (Cronbach's α ranged from .83 to .93) On the whole, the results of factor and reliability analysis showed that the 36-item questionnaire had four stable factors (BS, AS, IR, SS) that could be used in subsequent analysis. These 36 situations were used as the items in the online survey questionnaire in Stage 2.

In Stage 2, a convenient sample of 179 Hong Kong young adults completed the 36-item questionnaire online that was used to carry out the survey. The self-efficacy in handling different social skills and social situations is listed in Table 2 in order of rank. Among the interpersonal relationship items, young adults had a higher self-efficacy in handling relationships with friends but had the lowest efficacy in relating to family members. As far as the social skills (BS and AS) items were concerned, young adults were found to be generally most confident of their basic social skills. This was followed by their confidence in giving assertive responses, but they were less confident when handling conflicts and the

Table 1 Rotated factor solution of the self-efficacy in social skills section of the questionnaire

Items		Factor[a]	
		1	2
q6	Maintain conversation with others	*.93*	−.05
q5	Have appropriate topics to discuss with others	*.85*	.05
q7	Start/have conversation with unfamiliar people	*.73*	−.04
q8	Express own's feeling freely	*.68*	.06
q9	Reveal own's privacy to others	*.54*	−.01
q10	Express different opinions	*.49*	.35
q13	Refusing others' inappropriate requests	−.17	*.91*
q15	Give appropriate response when people have disrespectful criticism on you	−.02	*.78*
q12	Make requests to others	.17	*.62*
q14	Give appropriate response when people show their praise and respect to you	.21	*.54*
q11	Make complaints on others	.27	*.44*
	$\alpha =$	.88	.83

Note: Maximum likelihood extraction and oblique rotation was used. The solution accounts for 55.6% of the variance

[a] The highest factor loading for each item is italicised. Factor 1 = Basic Social Skills (BS); Factor 2 = Advanced Social Skill (AS)

Table 2 Self-efficacy in handling stressful social situations, as perceived by young adults

Rank	Items[a]	Subscale[a]	M	SD
1	Have appropriate topics to discuss with others	BS	6.85	.75
2	Develop friendship with people	IR	6.82	.83
3	Maintain friendship	IR	6.79	.89
4	Adapt to new learning and work environment	IR	6.77	.73
5	Make new friends	IR	6.70	.77
6	Maintain conversation with others	BS	6.61	.66
7	Have good relationship with boss, colleagues, and clients	SS	6.57	.76
8	Make friends with people from different cultures and backgrounds	IR	6.54	.94
9	Give appropriate response when people show their praise and respect to you	AS	6.49	.65
10	Express different opinions	BS	6.48	.72
11	Gain satisfaction/sense of success from work or studying	SS	6.41	.13
12	Participate in a new social group	IR	6.39	.73
13	Show confidence in social situation	IR	6.37	.96
14	Establish good communication with colleagues and supervisors	IR	6.35	.76
15	Express one's own feelings freely	BS	6.32	.85
16	Maintain an intimate relationship with partner	IR	6.30	.29
17	Build up an intimate relationship with partner	IR	6.29	.26
18	Handle divergent opinions	IR	6.25	.70
19	Refuse inappropriate requests of others	AS	6.15	.97
20	Give appropriate response when people make a disrespectful criticism of you	AS	6.15	.66
21	Prevent emotion from affecting daily life	IR	6.15	.76
22	Strike a good balance when allocating time for family, friends, partner, study, and work	SS	6.11	.03
23	Participate in social activities voluntarily	IR	6.08	.13
24	Show family members that you care about them	IR	6.03	.03
25	Start/have conversation with unfamiliar people or strangers	BS	5.98	.00
26	Handle financial dispute with friends	SS	5.93	.81
27	Make requests of others	BS	5.78	.61
28	Handle financial difficulties arising from payment for tuition	SS	5.72	.89
29	Work with/live with difficult people	SS	5.68	.97
30	Handle being misunderstood	IR	5.67	.81
31	Make complaints about others	AS	5.54	.71
32	Handle conflicts with colleagues and supervisors	IR	5.54	.97
33	Handle family conflicts	IR	5.54	.89
34	Handle isolation by others	SS	5.23	.52
35	Reveal one's own personal life to others when appropriate	BS	5.03	.97
36	Express love to the one you admire	IR	4.94	.52

BS basic social skills, *AS* advanced social skills, *IR* interpersonal relationship, *SS* social situations

[a] The items were in Chinese, and this is a translated and abridged version of the original items

negative behaviors of others. The two most difficult situations among the social situations (SS) items were to "reveal one's personal life to others" and to "express love to the one you admire."

Results of the Friedman tests showed that there were significant differences in rank between the four groups of items (basic social skills, advanced social skills, interpersonal relationships, social situations) ($\chi^2 = 11.08$, $p = .011$). Further pairwise comparisons between combinations of the four groups of items were conducted using the Wilcoxon Signed Ranks Test (with Bonferroni corrections). The groups of items in the BS domains ($Z = 2.84$, $p = .004$) and the IR domains ($Z = 2.96$, $p = .004$) occupied significantly higher ranks than the SS items. This meant that the participants were generally more confident in basic social skills and handling interpersonal relationships than in handling some specific social situations.

The female participants ($M = 6.37$, $SD = 1.14$) had a self-efficacy in handling interpersonal relationships that was significantly higher than that of their male counterparts ($M = 5.93$, $SD = 1.55$) ($t = 2.16, p = 0.03$), but this better performance was not reflected in the other sections of the questionnaire. Results of independent t tests showed that the female participants had a higher self-efficacy than male participants when answering question 21 ($t = -2.32$, $p = 0.02$), question 24 ($t = -3.35$, $p < 0.001$), and question 27 ($t = -2.31$, $p = 0.02$), which are related to building or maintaining friendships. This higher self-efficacy was also demonstrated when answering question 22 ($t = -2.01$, $p = 0.05$) and question 28 ($t = -3.35$, $p < 0.001$) both of which are related to participating in social activities and when answering question 29 ($t = -2.11, p = 0.04$), which is related to handling peers at work.

On the whole, there were no significant differences in self-efficacy in handling stressful social situations or in the frequency of facing them between the participants who were students and those who were employed. Neither did age significantly correlate with self-efficacy in handling stressful social situations. Education had a low but significant positive correlation with self-efficacy in handling interpersonal relationships ($r = 0.15, p = 0.04$).

4 Study 3: The Relationship between Social Problem Solving and Depression or Anxiety

A convenient sample ($n = 235$) was recruited from the Secondary 1 to Secondary 3 (Grades 7–9) classes of three secondary schools in different geographical districts of Hong Kong. The age of the participants ranged from 11 to 15, with a mean of 13.18 ($SD = 1.15$). There were slightly more females (55.7%) than males (44.3%) in the sample. There were no significant differences in age among the schools.

The first part of the study explored the relationship between social problem solving and depression (Siu and Shek 2005a), and 200 participants completed the C-BDI and the C-SPSI-R concurrently. The results of correlational analysis (with Bonferroni corrections) showed that the C BDI scores were significantly related to four subscales of the C-SPSI-R (see Table 3). While the negative subscales of ICS, AS, and NPO showed a significant positive correlation with depression, the PPO subscale produced a significant negative correlation with depression. On the other hand, there was no significant relationship between the RPS subscale and depression. These findings replicated those reported by D'Zurilla et al. (1996). This implies that depression is related to the motivational and behavioral aspects of problem solving, rather than to skills competence in rational problem solving (Chang and D'Zurilla 1996).

In the second part of the study ($n = 235$), the participants completed both the State-Trait Anxiety Inventory (STAI) and the C-SPSI-R. The STAI scales (state and trait scales) had significant correlations with all the C-SPSI-R subscales, except the ICS subscale.

Table 3 Correlations between C-SPSI-R and measures of depression and anxiety

C-SPSI-R subscales	C-BDI ($N = 200$)	STAI: state ($N = 235$)	STAI: trait ($N = 235$)
Positive problem orientation	−.31**	−.20**	−.31**
Negative problem orientation	.66**	.29**	.49**
Impulsiveness/carelessness style	.23**	.00	.09
Avoidance style	.67**	.23**	.42**
Rational problem solving	−.05	−.16*	−.14*

Note: *C-BDI* Chinese beck's depression inventory I, *STAI* Chinese state-trait anxiety inventory
* $p < .05$, ** $p < .01$

In general, the trait scale of the STAI had higher correlations (r = ranges from |.14| to.|49| with the C-SPSI-R subscales than the state scale (r ranges from |.16| to |.29|). The results also indicated that the impulsiveness/carelessness style of problem solving was not related to anxiety. However, there is a moderate to strong relationship between anxiety and problem orientation and avoidance style, while the relationship between anxiety and rational problem solving is relatively weaker. Again, these relationships replicated overseas findings on relationships between anxiety and social problem solving (Nezu 1986a).

5 Study 4: Social Problem Solving and Family Well-being

This study explored the relationship between social problem solving and measures of family well-being in adolescents and their families. A convenient sample of 1,462 participants was recruited from 11 high schools in Hong Kong. The age of the participants ranged from 11 to 17, with a mean of 13.78 ($SD = 1.13$). There were more females (59.5%) than males (40.5%) in the sample. The participants completed three instruments concurrently, including the C-SPSI-R, the Chinese Family Assessment Instrument (C-FAI), and the Conflict Behavior Checklist (CBQ-20 Child version).

The C-FAI is one of the first generic instruments developed to measure family functioning in Chinese populations (Shek 2002). The 33-item C-FAI has five subscales of mutuality, communication, conflict and harmony, parental concern, and parental control. In a series of validation studies (Shek 2002; Siu and Shek 2005b), the C-FAI was found to have a high internal consistency ($\alpha > .90$) and high test–retest reliability ($r > .84$), and its scores permitted the differentiation of clinical samples participating in family interventions and non-clinical samples. The CBQ-20 is used to measure the perceived level of conflict and negative communication between participants and their parents (Foster and Robin 1989). Shek (1997, 1998) showed that the Chinese version of the CBQ-20 had good psychometric properties.

In the study, the social problem solving of adolescents was hypothesized to be related to family functioning. The C-SPSI-R total score had positive correlations with all five subscales of the C-FAI (Table 4). In particular, the AS subscale had significant negative correlations (r ranges from −.22 to −.31) with all five subscales of the C-FAI. This indicated that the use of avoidance strategies is associated with a decrease in family functioning indexed by the different subscales of the C-FAI. The NPO subscale had low negative correlations with all the C-FAI subscales, which indicated that family functioning decreases with an increase in negative problem orientation. The PPO subscale had

Table 4 Correlation coefficients between the five subscales of the C-SPSI-R short form and measures of family functioning (CFAI)

C-FAI subscales	C-SPSI-R short form					
	AS	NPO	RPS	ICS	PPO	C-SPSI-R Total
Mutuality	−.28**	−.18**	.11**	−.09**	.19**	.29**
Communication	−.26**	−.19**	.12**	−.07**	.21**	.29**
Conflict and harmony	−.31**	−.16**	.04	−.14**	.16**	.28**
Parental concern	−.27**	−.12**	.07**	−.16**	.15**	.26**
Parental control	−.22**	−.16**	.03	−.15**	.12**	.24**

Note: *AS* avoidance style, *RPS* rational problem solving, *NPO* negative problem orientation, *ICS* impulsiveness/carelessness style, *PPO* positive problem orientation

* $p < .05$, ** $p < .01$

significant positive correlations (r ranging from .12 to .21) with all five C-FAI subscales, indicating that an increase in positive problem orientation was associated with an increase in the five aspects of family functioning.

The second objective of this paper is to ascertain how far the social problem solving abilities of parents and adolescents contribute to conflicts. It is hypothesized that higher problem-solving abilities of both parties contributes to fewer parent–adolescent conflicts. The perceived social problem solving abilities of parents and the perceived social problem solving abilities of adolescents (in five subscales of the C-SPSI-R) were used to predict the level and intensity of conflict (measured by the CBQ-20). The results of multiple regression analyses showed that the social problem solving abilities of parents and adolescents could predict between 23 and 33% of the variance in the conflict in the four parent–adolescent dyads (Table 5). It was noted that the percentage of variance explained in parent–daughter conflicts (the R^2 are .30 and .33) was much higher than that of parent–son conflicts (the R^2 here are .24 and .23). The social problem solving abilities of the parents were the most important predictor in all four dyads. The second most important predictor was the avoidance style of adolescents, which was a significant predictor for three

Table 5 Comparison of the important predictors of parent–adolescent conflicts across the four dyads

Predictor variables	Conflicts between dyads[a]			
	Mother–son	Mother–daughter	Father–son	Father–daughter
Adolescents				
Avoidance style	.22***	.18***	.09	.17***
Negative problem orientation	−.07	.08*	−.00	.04
Rational problem solving	.08	−.01	.01	.05
Impulsiveness/careless style	−.02	.03	.06	.02
Positive problem orientation	−.10*	−.02	−.05	−.03
Parents				
Social problem solving	−.41***	−.44***	−.42***	.49***
R^2	.24	.30	.23	.33

[a] Standardized regression coefficients (β) were reported, and regression coefficients that were significant were indicated by: * $p < .05$, ** $p < .01$, *** $p < .001$

of the four dyads (the exception being the father–son dyad). It was also interesting to see that the negative problem orientation of daughters and the positive problem orientation of sons were significant predictors of mother–adolescent conflicts.

6 Discussion

The development of the C-SPSI-R is a significant step in facilitating research on the social problem solving of Chinese populations. The results of validation studies, including the evaluation of content validity, reliability studies, and exploratory and confirmatory factor analyses, provide strong evidence supporting the psychometric properties of the instrument. The 25-item short form of the C-SPSI-R has a stable five-factor model that is largely consistent with previous findings based on the English version of the SPSI-R (Maydeu-Olivares and D'Zurilla 1995; Maydeu-Olivares and D'Zurilla 1996). The consistent factor structure across cultures and different samples provides support for the social problem-solving theory.

The study of stressful social situations (Study 2) is important in identifying the scope of social problems faced by young adults in daily life. As few studies have examined the scope of stressful social situations in adults and their self-efficacy in handling such situations, this study fills the gap in the literature. It is particularly useful to examine the perceptions of young adults, as many of them are in transition from a student way of life to full-time employment. Good social adjustment in the workplace is crucial to job satisfaction and overall well-being. Young adults are generally confident with their basic social skills in making friends, but find it much more stressful to handle conflict among family members or among friends, to express assertive responses, to handle negative feedback, criticism, or negative behavior from others, and hardest of all to self-disclose to others and to express love.

The ranking of the 36 stressful social situations generally aligns with clinical experience in social skills training (Csoti 1999), such as that it is harder to make an assertive response (in other words, to handle negative behaviors from others) than to acquire basic social skills (like possessing topics to initiate conversations with others). Young adults find that it is easier to relate to friends and peers, than to family members or people at work. They are probably quite hesitant in some behaviors related to building intimate relationships, dating, or couple relationships, which are the key developmental tasks in early adulthood. It takes time for them to gain experience from practicing these skills and to learn to handle these situations effectively. These findings are consistent with the features of the Chinese culture that Chinese people are not trained to be assertive and expressive in emotions.

The study on the relationships between social problem solving and measures of anxiety and depression replicates previous overseas findings. On the whole, it is observed from these studies that negative problem orientation and avoidance behavior are strongly related to depression and anxiety. While the impulsiveness–carelessness style of problem solving was found to be related to depression, anxiety is not associated with an impulsive–careless style of problem solving.

For the positive C-SPSI-R subscales, high positive problem orientation had is associated with lower depression and anxiety scores. A finding that differs slightly from those of overseas studies is that rational problem-solving skills can be independent of and depression levels in Chinese populations. This means that having good rational problem-solving skills is not adequate for the management of depression. Motivational (problem orientation) and behavioral (e.g., avoidance) factors may greatly limit the success of social problem solving even when a person has adequate rational problem-solving skills. Furthermore, rational problem solving tends to contribute a little to the management of anxiety, as a low but significant correlation was found.

In the last study (Study 4), the findings generally support the hypothesis that social problem solving is related to family well-being, including measures of overall family functioning and of the level of parent–adolescent conflicts. The negative problem-solving subscales of the AS, NPO, and ICS are associated with lower family functioning measured by the CFAI, while the positive subscales of the PPO and RPS are associated with higher family functioning. The C-SPSI-R total scores of adolescents are all significantly related to aspects of family functioning.

When the social problem solving scores of parents and adolescents are used to predict the level of parent–adolescent conflict, the overall social problem solving scores of parents and the avoidance behavior of adolescents are the best predictors of conflict. In mother–adolescent conflicts, a daughter's negative problem orientation and a son's positive problem orientation are additional and significant predictors of conflict. The results imply that the social problem solving abilities of parents are much more important than those of adolescents. This result may come about because parents are likely to be much more experienced and skilful in solving social problems than adolescents, and they can make a greater impact on relationships and conflict than their children can. Parents still retain a great deal of power within Chinese families, and their positive problem–solving efforts are the key determinant of the quality of the relationship in parent–child relationships. If parents are unwilling to face issues and conflicts rationally or have a positive attitude toward problem solving, it can be very hard for the adolescent to resolve the conflict by their own efforts. The alternative explanation is that adolescents who have more conflicts with their parents tend more to attribute the conflict situation to their parents' social problem solving ability and give them lower rating, that is, a reverse causal relationship. This explanation could be further verified in future studies by replacing the perceived social problem solving of parents by the adolescents with the parents' own self-rating.

On the whole, the results reiterate the popularity of avoidance strategies in coping with conflicts in Chinese families, particularly among adolescents. Lastly, it is important to note that social problem solving is probably only one of the many interpersonal competencies that are important in conflict management in families and that it accounts for around 20–30% of the variation in parent–adolescent conflicts. Other abilities like empathy or prosocial reasoning may also be important factors contributing to the quality of family relationships and well-being.

The four studies reviewed in this paper together represent an overview of current developments in social problem solving research on the local scene. The development and validation of the C-SPSI-R is a major step toward establishing a line of research in social problem solving. We also find the scope of "social problems," as defined by D'Zurilla's model of social problem solving, to be rather wide, as it includes aspects like personal issues, interpersonal issues, and specific life events or social situations. The second study reviewed in this paper focuses on refining the scope of social problems by examining the variety of stressful social situations experienced by young adults. The study adopts an empirical approach, collecting stressful social situations using an open-ended questionnaire. The study also provides important information on the ranking of the difficulties experienced by the young adults in coping with the 36 social situations. These situations can further be used to develop assessments of social problem solving performance or in connection with the planning of the curriculum for social skills training for young adults.

The third and fourth studies provide evidence supporting links between social problem solving and family well-being. The two studies highlight evidence that social problem solving is one of the key interpersonal competences that contributes to the well-being of individuals. Positive problem solving orientation and behavior are significantly linked to lower levels of both anxiety and depression. In the family context, social problem solving scores are significantly related to all aspects of family functioning. In particular, the social problem solving of parents and the avoidance behavior of adolescents are the most important determinants of parent–adolescent conflict. The clarification of these linkages underscores the theoretical importance of the role of social problem solving in individual well-being. Most of the linkages between social problem solving and indicators of individual well-being, like anxiety, depression, family functioning, and parent–adolescent conflicts are in the expected directions and of the expected strength. This confirms the role of social problem solving in individual well-being.

Although the present series of studies clarifies the relationships between social problem solving and different indicators of well-being, there are still many areas for potential research. First, the C-SPSI-R assesses social problem solving tendencies using a self-report format instead of actual social problem solving performance in simulated situations or using reviews of previous experience. There is a need to further explore the agreement between the C-SPSI-R and measures of social problem solving performance, and to investigate how actual performance may be related to well-being. Second, the evidence from existing research often relates social problem solving to negative emotions like depression or anxiety, or to family conflicts, as social problem solving is theorized to moderate the impact of stress on individuals. While this enables the comparison of these results with overseas studies, there is a need to adopt more indexes of well-being and quality-of-life measures in future studies. Third, most of the existing studies of social problem solving are cross-sectional studies, and such studies can establish an association between social problem solving and well-being indicators. Research data from panel studies that follow up the development of social problem solving over time may provide important evidence for causal links between social problem solving and well-being. As the associations between these variables are confirmed, it is time for researchers to hypothesize and test causal models using methods like structural equation modeling. Lastly, greater effort needs to put in to examining the effectiveness of training in social problem solving and the impact of this training on well-being on the local scene. It would be interesting to investigate how social problem solving in education could prepare students to face problems and self-manage in the course of their academic study, or to investigate how young adults can better prepare themselves for the challenges of interpersonal relationships in the workplace through training in social problem solving.

References

Albano, A. M., Marten, P. A., Holt, C. S., & Heimberg, R. G. (1995). Cognitive-behavioral group treatment for social phobia in adolescents: A preliminary study. *Journal of Nervous and Mental Disease, 183*, 649–656.

Allison, R. E. (1997).The concept of harmony in Chuang Tzu. In S. H. Liu & R. E. Allison (Eds.), *Harmony and strife: Contemporary perspectives, east and west* (pp. 169–186). The Hong Kong: Chinese University Press.

Bonner, R. L., & Rich, A. R. (1988). Negative life stress, social problem-solving self-appraisal, and hopelessness: Implications for suicide research. *Cognitive Therapy and Research, 12*, 549–556.

Chang, E. C., & D'Zurilla, T. J. (1996). Relations between problem orientation and optimism, pessimism, and trait affectivity. *Behavior Research and Therapy, 34*, 185–194.

Clum, G. A., Yang, B., Febbraro, G. A., & Canfield, D. L. (1996). An investigation of the validity of the SPSI and SPSI-R in differentiating high-suicidal from depressed, low-suicidal college students. *Journal of Psychopathology and Behavioral Assessment, 18*, 119–132.

Corrigan, P. W., Schade, M. L., & Liberman, R. P. (1992). Social skills training. In R. P. Liberman (Ed.), *Handbook of psychiatric rehabilitation*. New York: Macmillan.

Csoti, M. (1999). *People skills for young adults*. London: Jessica Kingsley.

D'Zurilla, T. J. (1986). *Problem-solving therapy: A social competence approach to clinical intervention*. New York: Springer.

D'Zurilla, T. J., & Maydeu-Olivares, A. (1995). Conceptual and methodological issues in social problem-solving assessment. *Behavior Therapy, 26*, 409–432.

D'Zurilla, T. J., & Nezu, A. M. (1990). Development and preliminary evaluation of the social problem-solving inventory. *Psychological Assessment, 2*, 156–163.

D'Zurilla, T. J., Nezu, A. M., & Maydeu-Olivares, A. (1996). *Manual for the social problem-solving inventory—revised (SPSI-R)*. Tonawanda, NY: Multi-Health Systems.

D'Zurilla, T. J., & Sheedy, C. F. (1991). Relation between social problem-solving ability and subsequent level of psychological stress in college students. *Journal of Personality and Social Psychology, 61*, 841–846.

Dubow, E. F., & Tisak, J. (1989). The relation between stressful life events and adjustment in elementary school children: The role of social support and social problem-solving skills. *Child Development, 60*, 1412–1423.

Dubow, E. F., Tisak, J., Causey, D., & Hryshko, A. (1991). A two-year longitudinal study of stressful life events, social support, and social problem-solving skills: Contributions to children's behavioral and academic adjustment. *Child Development, 62*, 583–599.

Feeney, J. A., & Noller, P. (1996). *Adult attachment*. Newcastle, UK: Sage.

Felce, D., & Perry, J. (1995). Quality of life: Its definition and measurement. *Research in Developmental Disabilities, 16*, 51–74.

Foster, S. L., & Robin, A. L. (1989). Parent-adolescent conflict. In E. J. Mash (Ed.), *Treatment of childhood disorders* (pp. 493–528). New York: Guilford Press.

Frey, K. S., Hirschstein, M. K., & Guzzo, B. A. (2000). Second step: Preventing aggression by promoting social competence. *Journal of Emotional and Behavioral Disorders, 8*, 102–112.

Frye, A. A., & Goodman, S. H. (2000). Which social problem solving components buffer depression in adolescent girls? *Cognitive Therapy and Research, 24*, 637–650.

Goldberg, A. J. S. (1998). Family problem solving: A resource and potential target for intervention in families of children with Down's syndrome. *Dissertation Abstracts International Section B: The Sciences and Engineering, 59*(4-B), 1913.

Goodman, S. H., Gravitt, G. W., & Kaslow, N. J. (1995). Social problem solving: A moderator of the relation between negative life stress and depression symptoms in children. *Journal of Abnormal Child Psychology, 23*, 473–485.

Graber, J. A. E., Brooks-Gunn, J. E., & Petersen, A. C. E. (1996). *Transitions through adolescence: Interpersonal domains and context*. Mahwah, NJ: Lawrence Erlbaum.

Guevremont, D. C., & Foster, S. L. (1993). Impact of social problem-solving training on aggressive boys: Skill acquisition, behavior change, and generalization. *Journal of Abnormal Child Psychology, 21*, 13–27.

Jaffe, W. B., & D'Zurilla, T. J. (2003). Adolescent problem solving, parent problem solving, and externalizing behavior in adolescents. *Behavior Therapy, 34*, 295–311.

Kang, S. H., & Lee, J. Y. (1992). Stress-buffering effects of social support and social problem solving skills in the adjustment of children. *Korean Journal of Child Studies, 13*, 175–188.

Kennedy, M. G., Felner, R. D., Cauce, A., & Primavera, J. (1988). Social problem solving and adjustment in adolescence: The influence of moral reasoning level, scoring alternatives, and family climate. *Journal of Clinical Child Psychology, 17*, 73–83.

Kirkbride, P. S., Tang, S. F., & Westwood, R. I. (1991). Chinese conflict preferences and negotiating behaviour: Cultural and psychological influences. *Organization Studies, 12*, 365–386.

Logan, G. D. (1989). Automaticity and cognitive control. In J. A. Bargh & J. S. Uleman (Eds.), *Unintended thought* (pp. 52–74). New York: Guilford Press.

Maydeu-Olivares, A., & D'Zurilla, T. J. (1995). A factor analysis of the social problem-solving inventory using polychoric correlations. *European Journal of Psychological Assessment, 11*, 98–107.

Maydeu-Olivares, A., & D'Zurilla, T. J. (1996). A factor-analytic study of the social problem-solving inventory: An integration of theory and data. *Cognitive Therapy and Research, 20*, 115–133.

Moore, K. A., Evans, V. J., Brooks, G., & Roth, J. (2001). What are good child outcomes? In A. Thornton (Ed.), *The well-being of children and families: Research and data needs* (pp. 59–84). Ann Arbor, MI: University of Michigan Press.

Nezu, A. M. (1986a). Negative life stress and anxiety: Problem solving as a moderator variable. *Psychological Reports, 58*, 279–283.

Nezu, A. M. (1986b). Social problem solving as a moderating variable between negative life stress and depressive symptoms. *Cognitive Therapy and Research, 10*, 489–498.

Robin, A. L., & Foster, S. L. (1984). Problem-solving communication training: A behavioral-family systems approach to parent-adolescent conflict. *Advances in Child Behavioral Analysis and Therapy, 3*, 195–240.

Shek, D. T. L. (1997). Family environment and adolescent psychological well-being, school adjustment, and problem behavior: A pioneer study in a Chinese context. *Journal of Genetic Psychology, 158*, 113–128.

Shek, D. T. L. (1998). A longitudinal study of the relations of parent-adolescent conflict to adolescent psychological well-being. *Journal of Genetic Psychology, 159*, 53–67.

Shek, D. T. L. (2002). Assessment of family functioning Chinese adolescents: The Chinese family assessment instrument. In N. N. Singh, T. Ollendick, & A. N. Singh (Eds.), *International perspectives on child and adolescent mental health* (pp. 297–316). Amsterdam, Netherlands: Elsevier.

Shek, D. T. L., & Chan, L. K. (1998). Perceptions of a happy family amongst Chinese adolescents and their parents. *Journal of Youth Studies, 1*, 178–189.

Shenkar, O., & Ronen, S. (1987). The cultural context of negotiations: The implications of Chinese interpersonal norms. *Journal of Applied Behavioral Science, 23*, 263–275.

Shure, M. (1997). Interpersonal cognitive problem solving: Primary prevention of early high-risk behaviors in the preschool and primary years. In G. Albee & T. Gullotta (Eds.), *Primary prevention works* (pp. 167–188). Thousand Oaks, CA: Sage.

Siu, A. M. H. (2003). Interpersonal competence, family functioning, and parent-adolescent conflicts. *Dissertation Abstracts International Section A: Humanities and Social Sciences, 63*(10-A), 3733.

Siu, A. M. H., & Shek, D. T. L. (2005a). The Chinese version of the social problem-solving inventory: Some initial results on reliability and validity. *Journal of Clinical Psychology, 61*, 347–360.

Siu, A. M. H., & Shek, D. T. L. (2005b). Psychometric properties of the Chinese family assessment instrument in Chinese adolescents in Hong Kong. *Adolescence, 40*, 817–830.

Ting-Toomey, S. (1988). Intercultural conflict styles: A face-negotiation theory. In Y. Y. Kim & W. B. Gudykunst (Eds.), *Theories in intercultural communication* (pp. 215–235). Beverly Hills, CA: Sage).

Wallander, J. L., Schmitt, M., & Koot, H. M. (2001). Quality of life measurement in children and adolescents: Issues, instruments and applications. *Journal of Clinical Psychology, 57*, 571–585.

Soc Indic Res (2010) 95:407–419
DOI 10.1007/s11205-009-9528-4

Personal and Family Correlates of Suicidal Ideation Among Chinese Adolescents in Hong Kong

Sylvia Y. C. Lai Kwok · Daniel T. L. Shek

Received: 29 November 2008 / Accepted: 26 February 2009 / Published online: 6 October 2009

Abstract Based on the family ecological model, personal (hopelessness, social problem solving, emotional competence) and family (parent-adolescent communication, family functioning) quality of life measures related to adolescent suicidal ideation were examined in 5,557 Secondary 1 to Secondary 4 students in Hong Kong. Results showed that suicidal ideation was positively related to adolescent hopelessness but negatively related to emotional competence, social problem solving, father–adolescent communication, mother–adolescent communication and family functioning. Multiple regression analyses showed that hopelessness was the most important predictor of adolescent suicidal ideation, followed by mother–adolescent communication, family functioning, social problem solving, father–adolescent communication, and emotional competence. Path analyses with and without direct effects showed that hopelessness mediated the effect of personal and family correlates on adolescent suicidal ideation. Theoretical and practice implications of the findings are discussed.

Keywords Suicidal ideation · Hopelessness · Social problem solving · Emotional competence · Family functioning · Parent-adolescent communication

1 Introduction

Although there are different views on the definitions of quality of life, there is a general agreement among researchers (e.g., Felce and Perry 1995; Wallander et al. 2001) that the concept is a multidimensional one, including material well-being (finance, income, housing quality, and transport), physical well-being (health, fitness, mobility, and personal safety), social well-being (personal relationships and community involvement), emotional well-being (positive affect, mental health, fulfillment, satisfaction, faith/belief, and self-esteem),

S. Y. C. Lai Kwok (✉)
Department of Applied Social Studies, City University of Hong Kong, Hong Kong, China
e-mail: scyckwok@cityu.edu.hk

D. T. L. Shek
Department of Applied Social Sciences, The Hong Kong Polytechnic University, Hong Kong, China

and productive well-being (competence and productivity). With particular reference to mental health, different indicators, such as psychological symptoms, suicide, and suicidal ideation have been used. Although suicidal ideation has commonly been used by researchers to examine quality of life among adolescents, few researchers have examined both its personal and family correlates.

Depending on the theoretical standpoint taken, personal and family correlates of adolescent suicidal ideation are weighted differently. For instance, the cognitive–emotive–behavioral theory stresses the importance of hopelessness, emotional competence, and social problem-solving in influencing suicidal ideation (Ellis and Bernard 2006). In contrast, family-centered theories emphasize the impact of family processes on suicidal ideation, for example, family functioning and parent–adolescent communication (Beavers et al. 1990; Epstein et al. 1993; Olson et al. 1989). From a family ecological perspective (Belsky et al. 1984; Bronfenbrenner 1979), human behaviors are influenced by both individual and contextual factors such as the family. Hence, there is reason to say that both personal and family factors have impact on adolescent suicidal ideation.

With reference to the concept of quality of life (Felce and Perry 1995; Wallander et al. 2001), personal quality of life indicators such as hopelessness, social problem-solving, and emotional competence, contribute to personal adjustment, such as suicidal ideation. Similarly, it is expected that family quality of life indicators (such as parent–adolescent relational qualities and family functioning) would influence adolescent psychological well-being (Shek 2008), and therefore are likely to have an impact on the emergence of suicidal ideation.

Several studies point towards a relationship of individual quality of life measures and suicidal ideation. For instance, a significant relationship between hopelessness and suicidality has been obtained (e.g., Cukrowicz et al. 2004; Rutter and Behrendt 2004), with hopelessness as the best predictor of suicidal ideation among student and adolescent samples suffering from bipolar disorder (Hallfors et al. 2006; Rucklidge 2006). Another individual factor, a person's emotional competence, has been related to depression and mental health (Miner and Coleman 2001; Znoj and Lude 2002), and a lack of social problem-solving ability seems to be closely linked with suicidal behavior (e.g., Carris et al. 1998; Yang and Clum 1996).

A number of studies suggest that different family quality of life measures might also be related to adolescent suicidal ideation. Previous studies found a link between parent–adolescent communication and adolescent psychological well-being (Landman-Peeters et al. 2005; Shek et al. 2006). Research further indicates that adolescent suicidal ideation is related to family dysfunction, family discord, poor family environment, family rigidity, family conflicts, and low levels of family cohesion and support (Esposito and Clum 2003; Lee et al. 2006).

There are several limitations intrinsic to the existing studies regarding the relationships among personal correlates, family correlates, and suicidal ideation in the existing literature. First, the studies on the relationship among different measures of personal (e.g., social problem-solving) and family quality of life (e.g., family functioning) with adolescent suicidal ideation (Fremouw et al. 1993; Mitchell and Rosenthal 1992) are inconclusive. Second, few studies have included both personal, as well as family quality of life measures, in a single study. From a family ecological perspective, it would be important to include both personal and family quality of life measures in a single study to assess their relative contribution to adolescent suicidal ideation.

Third, the sample size in the existing studies was either too small or limited to a homogenous subsample. Fourth, most of the measuring instruments for the studies conducted in Hong Kong were adapted from the West, which may not be able to capture the essence of the Chinese culture. Fifth, there is a predominance of Western studies regarding the relationship between the personal or family quality of life measures and adolescent suicidal ideation. A survey of the PsycINFO in January 2009 with the search term "suicidal ideation" showed that while there were 4,804 citations, there were only 53 citations when the search terms "suicidal ideation" and "Chinese" were used. As Chinese people constitute roughly one-fifth of the world's population (Shek 2006), my study is an important contribution to fill the gap.

Finally, as there are inconsistent findings on the mediating role of hopelessness on the relationship between personal and family quality of life and adolescent suicidal ideation, further research should be attempted. Hopelessness was found to be a mediating variable between depression and suicide intent (e.g., Weishaar and Beck 1992), between early negative life events and suicidal behavior (e.g., Yang and Clum 2000), and between anxiety and suicidal behavior (Thompson et al. 2005). Studies also showed that hopelessness mediated the relationship between problem-solving deficits and suicidal ideation (Dixon et al. 1994; Miros 2000) and Pinto and Whisman (1996) supported a mediating model in which hopelessness contributed to negative affect, which ultimately influenced suicidal ideation. However, the mediating role of hopelessness was not fully supported in other studies (e.g., Levy et al. 1995).

Against the above background, several research questions were addressed in this study. These include: (1) What is the relationship between the personal quality of life (hopelessness, emotional competence, and social problem-solving) measures and Chinese adolescent suicidal ideation in Hong Kong? Based on the predictions of the rational–emotive–behavioral theory and previous research findings (Ellis and Bernard 2006; Stewart et al. 2005; Znoj and Lude 2002), it was hypothesized that: (a) hopelessness would have a positive relationship with suicidal ideation (Hypothesis 1); (b) emotional competence would have a negative relationship with suicidal ideation (Hypothesis 2); and (c) social problem-solving would have a negative relationship with suicidal ideation (Hypothesis 3). (2) What is the relationship between the family quality of life (parent–adolescent communication and perceived family functioning) measures and Chinese adolescent suicidal ideation in Hong Kong? Based on the predictions of family theories and previous research findings (Walsh 1993; Epstein et al. 1993; Shek et al. 2006), it was hypothesized that parent–adolescent communication would have a negative relationship with suicidal ideation (Hypothesis 4), and perceived family functioning would have a negative relationship with suicidal ideation (Hypothesis 5). (3) What is the relative importance of the personal and family correlates in predicting Chinese adolescent suicidal ideation in Hong Kong? Since there were no previous studies in this aspect, the hypothesis could not be formulated. (4) What is the role of hopelessness in the relationship between the personal and family quality of life and suicidal ideation? Based on the previous research findings (Miros 2000; Thompson et al. 2005), it was predicted that hopelessness would mediate the relationship between the personal and family quality of life and suicidal ideation (Hypothesis 6).

2 Method

2.1 Participants and Procedures

A cross-sectional survey was conducted and secondary schools were approached by convenience sampling with the help of agencies providing school social work service. Of the 68 schools (out of a total of 426 secondary schools in Hong Kong) that were contacted, 42 schools (including self-financed, subvented, and government schools) from Hong Kong Island, Kowloon, and the New Territories agreed to join the study. The response rate was 62%, which is comparable with similar local and international studies on suicidal ideation and behavior (Cheung et al. 2006; Lynch et al. 2006). By the end of the survey period, a total of 5,557 valid questionnaires had been collected. With reference to the total secondary student population in Hong Kong at the time the study was conducted (328,573 students), the sample size used (2%) can be regarded as adequate. There were slightly more males (53.1%) than females (46.9%) in the sample, which reflects the distribution among the general population. The participants were evenly distributed among different forms (25.8% in Secondary 1; 24.7% in Secondary 2; 24.4% in Secondary 3; and 25.1% in Secondary 4). The age of the respondents varied from 11 to 18 years, with an overall mean of 13.87 years (SD = 1.47).

School, parental, and participant consent were obtained prior to data collection. During the survey, a school social worker, a teacher or a research assistant was present to give a short briefing on the general aims and the confidentiality of the study. They were present throughout the whole administration process to answer queries raised by the participants. Briefing the participants and filling out the questionnaires took around 40 min.

2.2 Measures of Personal Quality of Life

2.2.1 Assessment of Emotional Competence

Emotional competence was assessed using the Chinese Emotional Intelligence Scale in a short form (C-EIS-R) developed by Chan (2003). The instrument was adapted from the English 33-item EIS originally developed by Schutte et al. (1998). The short form of the 12-item C-EIS-R has four empirical subscales to represent four dimensions of emotional intelligence: self-management of emotions, social skills, empathy, and utilization of emotions. Respondents indicate their agreement to each of the 12 statements using a five-point scale ranging from 1 (strongly agree) to 5 (strongly disagree). A higher score indicates better emotional competence. The scale was found to be internally consistent in this study (alpha = .79).

2.2.2 Assessment of Social Problem-Solving

Social problem-solving was assessed using the Chinese version of the Social Problem Solving Inventory in a short form (C-SPSI-R) developed by Siu and Shek (2005b). The instrument was adapted from the 52-item Social Problem-Solving Inventory Revised (SPSI-R) (D'Zurilla et al. 1996). A validation study was conducted locally with 352 secondary school students (Siu and Shek 2005b). The short form of the 25-item C-SPSI-R had a five-factor structure that was largely consistent with the original English SPSI-R. However, the three-factor model of the C-SPSI (Siu and Shek 2005b) was used in this study because the internal consistency of the three subscales was good. The three subscales are negative problem orientation (NPO), rational problem-solving (RPS), and impulsiveness/carelessness style (ICS). For each of the 25 items, the respondents were requested to choose an answer on a five-point Likert scale ranging from "Not at all true of me" to "Extremely true of me". Half of the test items indicate a constructive orientation toward problem solving, while the other half indicates a dysfunctional or inhibitive orientation. The items are presented in a random order. A higher score indicates better social competence. There were findings showing that the related measures were valid and reliable (Siu and Shek 2005b). Reliability analyses showed that this abridged version of C-SPSI-R was reliable in this study (alpha = .83).

2.2.3 Assessment of Hopelessness

Hopelessness was assessed using the Hopelessness subscale of the Chinese Hopelessness Scale (C-HOPE) developed by Shek (1993). The original English scale was devised by Beck et al. (1974). The subscale has ten items and the respondents were asked to choose an answer from a four-point Likert scale ranging from "strongly agree" to "strongly disagree". A higher score indicates a higher degree of hopelessness. According to Shek and Lee's study (2005), the scale possessed adequate construct validity. The scale was demonstrated to be internally consistent in this study (alpha = .88).

2.2.4 Assessment of Suicidal Ideation

Adolescent suicidal ideation was assessed using the 13-item Suicidal Ideation Sub-Scale (C-SIS) of the Suicidal Risk Scale for Hong Kong students developed locally by Tse and Bagley (2002). For each item, respondents were required to choose an answer from a four-point Likert scale ranging from "strongly agree" to "strongly disagree". A higher score indicates a higher level of suicidal ideation. A previous validation study (Tse and Bagley 2002) showed that the C-SIS has high reliability and validity. Reliability analyses showed that the scale had high reliability in this study (alpha = .93).

2.3 Measures of Family Quality of Life

2.3.1 Assessment of Parent–Adolescent Communication

Parent–adolescent communication was assessed using the father–adolescent communication scale (FACS) and mother–adolescent communication scale (MACS) developed by Shek et al. (2006). Each instrument contains 25 items that are identical across both versions, and differ only with respect to the target person (i.e., mother or father). A higher FACS or MACS score indicates a higher level of quality of parent–adolescent communication. In Shek et al.'s (2006) study, it was reported that the two measures were able to discriminate adolescents with good parental communication from those with a bad one. Reliability analyses showed that the FACS and MACS had high reliability (alpha = .93 and .94, respectively) in this study.

2.3.2 Assessment of Family Functioning

Family functioning was assessed using the Chinese Family Assessment Instrument (C-FAI), which is one of the first indigenous instrument designed to measure family functioning in Chinese families (Shek 2000). For each question, respondents were required to choose an answer from a five-point Likert scale ranging from "strongly agree" to "strongly disagree". There are five subscales: mutuality, communication, conflict and harmony, parental concern, and parental control. A higher score in the five subscales indicates a higher level of family functioning. Two large-sample validation studies were conducted (Siu and Shek 2005a; Shek 2002), which provided strong support for the psychometric properties of the scale. The scale was demonstrated to have high reliability in this study (alpha = .93).

3 Results

Pearson correlation analyses with Bonferroni-corrected alpha levels were performed (Table 1). Results showed that while hopelessness was positively related to adolescent suicidal ideation, emotional competence and social problem-solving were negatively related to adolescent suicidal ideation. These findings provided support for Hypotheses 1, 2, and 3. Furthermore, both father–adolescent communication and mother–adolescent communication were negatively related to adolescent suicidal ideation, whereas perceived family functioning was negatively related to adolescent suicidal ideation, thus providing support for Hypotheses 4 and 5.

The direct effects models (personal and family correlates as predictors and adolescent suicidal ideation as dependent variable) were estimated using standard regression analyses (Table 2). As indicated by R^2, both personal and family quality of life measures predicted 51% of the variance in adolescent suicidal ideation. It was found that hopelessness was the most important predictor, followed by mother–adolescent communication, family functioning, social problem-solving and father–adolescent communication, while emotional competence was the least important. Father–adolescent communication and emotional competence were less significant than the other correlates ($p < .01$).

Standard regression analyses were also performed by entering the personal and family correlates as predictors and hopelessness as a dependent variable. Then hopelessness was also entered as a predictor of adolescent suicidal ideation. Path analyses showed that while all the personal and family correlates were found to exert direct effects on adolescent suicidal ideation, they were also indirectly related to suicidal ideation via hopelessness (Table 2). This supported Hypothesis 6 that the impact of the personal and family correlates was mediated by hopelessness. When all the low direct-effect links (with beta coefficients <.5) were deleted in a follow-up analysis, hopelessness (beta = .68, $p < .001$) predicted 47% of the variance in adolescent suicidal ideation. These findings suggest that

Table 1 Correlations between emotional competence, social problem solving, hopelessness, father–adolescent communication, mother–adolescent communication, family functioning and adolescent suicidal ideation

	Emotional competence	Social problem solving	Hopelessness	Father–adolescent communication	Mother–adolescent communication	Family functioning
Suicidal ideation	−.19*	−.37*	.68*	−.36*	−.42*	−.46*

* $p < .0017$ (Bonferroni-corrected alpha level)

Table 2 Direct effects models of adolescent suicidal ideation and hopelessness

	Emotional competence	Social problem solving	Hopelessness	Father–adolescent communication	Mother–adolescent communication	Family functioning	R^2	Adj. R^2
Suicidal ideation	−.03**	−.06***	.57***	−.05**	−.10***	−.06***	.51	.51
Hopelessness	−.05**	−.30***	NA	−.12***	−.17***	−.19***	.35	.35

** $p < .01$, *** $p < .001$

Table 3 Decomposition of direct and indirect effects of the personal and family correlates on adolescent suicidal ideation

	Direct effect	Indirect effect	Total effect
Emotional competence	−.03	−.029	−.059
Social problem solving	−.06	−.17	−.230
Father adolescent communication	−.05	−.068	−.118
Mother adolescent communication	−.10	−.097	−.197
Family functioning	−.06	−.108	−.168

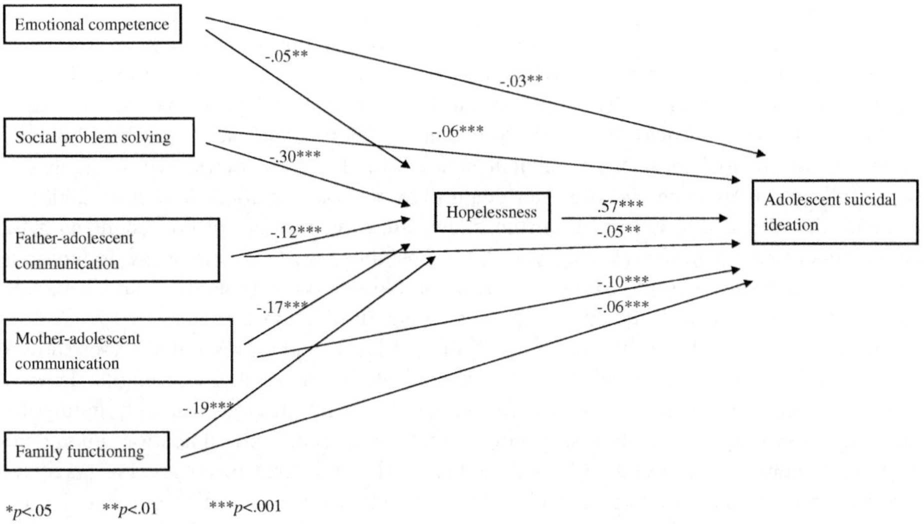

Fig. 1 Direct and indirect effects model on adolescent suicidal ideation

the predictor variables influenced the outcome variable mainly through adolescent hopelessness and the direct effect was weak.

Decomposition of the direct and indirect effects of the personal and family correlates showed that social problem-solving had the greatest total effect on adolescent suicidal ideation, followed by mother–adolescent communication, family functioning, and father–adolescent communication, while emotional competence had the smallest total effect (Table 3; Fig. 1).

4 Discussion

In response to the limitations in the related literature, there are several unique features of the present study. First, Chinese adolescents were recruited in this study. Second, a large sample based on Secondary 1 to Secondary 4 students was used ($N = 5,557$). Third, indigenously developed and validated measures of hopelessness, emotional competence, social problem-solving, parent–adolescent communication, family functioning, and suicidal ideation were used. Fourth, the relative importance of the personal and family correlates on adolescent suicidal ideation, as well as the mediating effect of hopelessness on the linkage between the personal and family correlates and adolescent suicidal ideation, was examined by testing the direct effects models and the mediating model.

For the personal quality of life measures, both correlation and regression analyses showed that a lower level of emotional competence was related to a higher level of adolescent suicidal ideation. This corroborates the previous finding that there was less suicidal ideation among those who could handle other people's emotions well and had good social skills (Ciarrochi et al. 2002). Since these people had greater social support and more intimate relationships with others, it would help to protect them from depression and suicidal ideation (Kalafat 1997).

Results also showed that a lower level of social problem-solving skills was related to a higher level of adolescent suicidal ideation. This is consistent with previous findings that adolescents who had inadequate problem-solving skills were at increased risk for suicidal thoughts and behaviors (e.g., Kingsbury et al. 1999; Thompson et al. 2005). Moreover, results showed that a higher level of hopelessness was associated with a higher level of adolescent suicidal ideation. This observation is consistent with previous literature (e.g., Hallfors et al. 2006; Rucklidge 2006; Smith et al. 2006). Adolescents feeling hopeless might regard suicidal ideation or suicidal behavior as the only alternative available and wrongfully put their hopes on life after death (Tse and Bagley 2002; Yip et al. 2006).

From the above discussion, it can be shown that the results are consistent with the cognitive–emotive–behavioral theory, which postulates that hopelessness (cognition), emotional competence (emotion), and social problem-solving (cognition and behavior) have impact on adolescent quality of life (i.e., suicidal ideation).

For the family quality of life measures, both correlation and regression analyses showed that a lower level of parent–adolescent communication was related to a higher level of adolescent suicidal ideation. This observation is in line with previous research finding that there was less frequent and less satisfying parent–adolescent communication among suicidal adolescents (Everall et al. 2006). Results also showed that a lower level of perceived healthy family functioning was associated with a higher level of adolescent suicidal ideation. This is in line with both local and overseas findings (Fotti et al. 2006; Stewart et al. 2005). Since family is a shelter that provides concern and emotional support for most adolescents in Hong Kong where mutuality, communication, harmony, and parental concern in the family are valued and treasured by the adolescents, this may contribute to a decrease in adolescent suicidal ideation.

Hence, the above results are consistent with the predictions of different family theories, including Beavers model, Circumplex model, and McMaster model (Walsh 1993), that parent–adolescent communication and family functioning are determinants of adolescent quality of life (i.e., suicidal ideation).

In general, the results show that all personal and family correlates were important predictors of adolescent suicidal ideation, although the related effect size was not on the high side. However, hopelessness was the most important predictor, while father–adolescent communication and emotional competence were less significant than the other correlates. Because Chinese culture emphasizes emotional inhibition and discouragement of expression of feelings (Shek 2001), emotional competence might be regarded as less important by the Chinese adolescents as it was by their Western counterparts. Besides, father–adolescent communication was less emphasized than mother–adolescent communication. Traditionally, fathers have performed the breadwinner role, while mothers have played the socialization and care-giving roles in Chinese society. Hence adolescents usually turned to their mothers, rather than their fathers, for emotional support and expression of feelings. The satisfaction and quality ratings for father–adolescent communication were lower than those based on mother–adolescent communication (Shek et al. 2006). Although parent–adolescent communication was found to be significantly related to Chinese adolescent psychological well-being (Shek et al. 2006), father–adolescent communication was regarded as a less significant predictor for adolescent suicidal ideation. The direct effects model thus support the hopelessness theory in explaining adolescent suicidal ideation (Rudd 2000).

From the path analyses, hopelessness mediated the relationship between the personal correlates (emotional competence and social problem-solving), family correlates (parent–adolescent communication and family functioning), and adolescent suicidal ideation. This is in line with previous findings suggesting that hopelessness mediated the relationship between problem-solving deficits and suicidal ideation (Dixon et al. 1994; Miros 2000; Rudd et al. 1994). Besides, there was considerable evidence supporting the link between social problem-solving skills (problem orientation and problem-solving skills) and hopelessness (Ciarrochi et al. 2003; D'Zurilla et al. 1998; Kant et al. 1997).

With regard to emotional competence, a study found that effective emotional control and level of emotional awareness had significant incremental value over stressful events in predicting hopelessness (Ciarrochi et al. 2003). Since inhibiting emotions was cognitively demanding and stressful, this hindered the individual's ability to work through difficult life problems. Hence, this might have further led to the sense of hopelessness (Richards and Gross 1999), which, in turn, increased suicidal ideation. Nevertheless, the effect size of the related regression coefficients was not particularly impressive.

Moreover, studies had indicated that parental qualities (including parent–adolescent conflict, frequency of parent–adolescent communication, feelings related to parent–adolescent communication, and parent–adolescent relationship) were associated with adolescent hopelessness (Shek 1999; Tobin 2000). With reference to family functioning, a number of studies had shown that problematic family functioning was significantly related to hopelessness in both clinical and non-clinical adolescents (Adams 1998; Shek 1999). Positive personal and family factors might have enhanced the adolescents' sense of hope, which lessened their suicidal ideation. Although previous studies had found that hopelessness mediated the relationship between other personal factors (e.g., depression, anxiety, and rumination) and suicidal ideation (e.g., MacLeod et al. 2005; Smith et al. 2006; Thompson et al. 2005), this study was pioneering in identifying the mediating role of hopelessness among emotion competence, parent–adolescent communication, family functioning, and adolescent suicidal ideation, which was different from Levy et al.'s (1995) findings.

Decomposition of the direct and indirect effects of the personal and family correlates showed that social problem-solving had the greatest total effect on adolescent suicidal ideation, while emotional competence had the smallest total effect. Previous research also showed that when problem-solving deficits combined with impulsiveness, suicidal behaviors became life-threatening, independent of levels of depression and hopelessness (Arffa 1983; Spirito et al. 1989). Hence, there was empirical evidence that social problem-solving was the most important predictor of adolescent suicidal ideation, when hopelessness was controlled for. Inasmuch as the direct effects model assumed that all personal and family predictors contribute directly to adolescent suicidal ideation, the mediating model was a better description of the relationship among the predictors and suicidal ideation.

Since this study underscores the important roles of hopelessness, social problem-solving, parent–adolescent communication (particularly mother–adolescent communication), family functioning, and emotional competence in adolescent suicidal ideation, these factors should be considered as the key building blocks in theoretical models for adolescent suicidal ideation. The present findings are important because there are few theoretical models on both the personal and family determinants of adolescent quality of life (i.e., suicidal ideation) in the Chinese context (Shek 2006). Nevertheless, it is noteworthy that the effect size of the predictors was not high. As such, more studies should be done to replicate the present findings.

Practically, it can be derived from the results that interventions from both the personal and family levels are needed to reduce adolescent suicidal ideation, thus enhancing their quality of life. Workshops and programs can be conducted to help adolescents build up hope and belief in the future, develop positive attitudes toward exploring possible options in life and recognize their own capabilities in goal achievement. Some adventure-based counseling (i.e., adventure activities to enhance self-understanding, coping with adversity, and interpersonal cooperation) can also be introduced so that they can learn to persevere in the face of hardship. Moreover, reinforcement of positive traditional Chinese beliefs about coping with adversity, for example, 'You zhi zhe shi jing cheng' (when there is a will, there is a way) is important for adolescents.

Cognitive behavioral groups can be held to teach the adolescents rational problem-solving skills, such as problem definition and formulation, generation of alternative solutions, decision making, solution implementation, and verification. These will likewise help to cultivate a positive problem orientation and to introduce active coping strategies. To enhance the adolescents' emotional competence, workshops and programs can also be organized to guide them and help them understand and regulate their own emotions, handle other people's emotions, and make effective use of emotions.

Since parent–adolescent communication and family functioning are significant predictors of adolescent suicidal ideation, it is important to involve the parents and the family in reducing suicidal ideation. Parallel groups and workshops on communication skills training can be run for both the parents and the adolescents. Communication barriers (e.g., threatening, criticizing, and ordering), appropriate communication attitudes (e.g., trust, respect, sincerity, and empathy) and effective communication skills (e.g., reflection of content and feeling, self-disclosure, and I-messages) can be introduced in the groups and workshops. In addition, other family members can be involved in the family workshops and programs to enhance family mutuality, harmony, and concern, as well as minimize family conflict and control.

It should be noted that the present study has several limitations. First, suicidal ideation can be transitional, and may not be closely linked to suicidal attempts or self-destructive behavior. This poses a limitation of using suicidal ideation, but not suicidal behaviors, as an indicator of quality of life. However, similar to other psychological symptoms, suicidal ideation has been used in previous studies as an indicator of quality of life (Felce and Perry 1995; Wallander et al. 2001). Second, schools have been approached through agencies providing school social work service, and the resulting samples thus represent convenience samples. Generalization of the present findings to the secondary school population should proceed with caution. Third, as self-report questionnaires were used, the information collected was from the adolescent informants only. If resource permits, the use of multiple informants would give a clearer picture of the problem area. Fourth, the present research predominately used quantitative methodology. One disadvantage of this methodology is that it cannot explore the subjective experiences of adolescents. Another drawback is that it is less process-oriented and makes it difficult to apply the generalized data to individual cases.

Fifth, besides the personal and family quality of life measures utilized in this study, other indicators should be used in the future. Sixth, the use of a cross-sectional design means that it is not possible to claim a causal relationship between the antecedents and adolescent suicidal ideation. There may in fact be a bi-directional relationship between the variables, or a third variable may be present. Hence, a longitudinal research design can be used in future studies. Seventh, while most of the relationships explored were statistically significant, the practical significance of the findings may not be high. Finally, if resource permits, further analyses using structural equation modeling would provide a better understanding of the problem area. However, it is noteworthy that the use of ordinary least square multiple regression analyses to understand psychosocial predictors of adolescent suicidal ideation is not uncommon in the field (Resch et al. 2008; Wong et al. 2007). Despite these limitations, the present study can be regarded as a stimulating and interesting addition to the literature on the relationships between personal and family quality of life measures and adolescent suicidal ideation.

Acknowledgement The preparation for this paper was financially supported by Wofoo Foundation Limited.

References

Adams, D. M. (1998). Child abuse trauma, family functioning and adolescent depression, hopelessness and suicidal behavior. *Dissertation Abstracts International: Section B: The Sciences and Engineering, 58*, 5635.

Arffa, S. (1983). Cognition and suicide: A methodological review. *Suicide and Life-Threatening Behavior, 13*, 109–122.

Beavers, W. R., Hampson, R. B., & Hulgus, Y. F. (1990). *Manual: Beavers Systems Model of Family Assessment.* Dallas: Southwest Family Institute.

Beck, A. T., Weissman, A., Lester, D., & Trexler, L. (1974). The measurement of pessimism: The Hopelessness Scale. *Journal of Consulting and Clinical Psychology, 42*, 861–865.

Belsky, J., Lerner, R. M., & Spanier, G. B. (1984). *The child in the family.* Reading: Addison-Wesley.

Bronfenbrenner, U. (1979). *The ecology of human development: Experiments by nature and design.* Cambridge, MA: Harvard University Press.

Carris, M. J., Sheeber, L., & Howe, S. (1998). Family rigidity, adolescent problem-solving deficits, and suicidal ideation: a mediational model. *Journal of Adolescence, 21*, 459–472.

Chan, D. W. (2003). Dimensions of emotional intelligence and their relationships with social coping among gifted adolescents in Hong Kong. *Journal of Youth and Adolescence, 32*, 409–418.

Cheung, Y. B., Law, C. K., Chan, B., Liu, K. Y., & Yip, S. F. (2006). Suicidal ideation and suicidal attempts in a population-based study of Chinese people: Risk attributable to hopelessness, depression, and social factors. *Journal of Affective Disorders, 90*, 193–199.

Ciarrochi, J., Deane, P., & Anderson, S. (2002). Emotional intelligence moderates the relationship between stress and mental health. *Personality and Individual Differences, 32*, 197–209.

Ciarrochi, J., Scott, G., Deane, P., & Heaven, C. L. (2003). Relations between social and emotional competence and mental health: a construct validation study. *Personality and Individual Differences, 35*, 1947–1963.

Cukrowicz, K. C., Wingate, L. R., Driscoll, K. A., & Joiner, T. E. (2004). A standard of care for the assessment of suicide risk and associated treatment: The Florida State University psychology clinic as an example. *Journal of Contemporary Psychotherapy, 34*, 87–100.

Dixon, W. A., Heppner, P. P., & Rudd, M. D. (1994). Problem-solving appraisals, hopelessness, and suicide ideation: Evidence for a mediational model. *Journal of Counseling Psychology, 38*, 51–56.

D'Zurilla, T. J., Chang, C., Nottingham, J., & Faccini, L. (1998). Social problem-solving deficits and hopelessness, depression, and suicidal risk in college students and psychiatric inpatients. *Journal of Clinical Psychology, 54*, 1091–1107.

D'Zurilla, T. J., Nezu, A. M., & Maydeu-Olivares, A. (1996). *Manual for the Social Problem–Solving Inventory-Revised (SPSI-R).* North Tonawanda, NY: Multi-Health System, Inc.

Ellis, A., & Bernard, M. E. (2006). *Rational emotive behavioral approaches to childhood disorders: Theory, practice and research.* New York: Springer.

Epstein, N. B., Bishop, D., Ryan, C., Miller, I., & Keitner, G. (1993). The McMaster Model: View of healthy family functioning. In F. Walsh (Ed.), *Normal family processes* (pp. 138–160). New York: Guilford Press.

Esposito, C. L., & Clum, G. A. (2003). The relative contribution of diagnostic and psychosocial factors in the prediction of adolescent suicidal ideation. *Journal of Clinical Child and Adolescent, 32*, 386.

Everall, R. D., Bostik, K. E., & Paulson, B. L. (2006). Being in the safety zone: Emotional experiences of suicidal adolescents and emerging adults. *Journal of Adolescent Research, 21*, 370–392.

Felce, D., & Perry, J. (1995). Quality of life: Its definition and measurement. *Research in Developmental Disabilities, 16*, 51–74.

Fotti, A., Katz, Y., Afifi, O., & Cox, J. (2006). The associations between peer and parental relationships and suicidal behaviors in early adolescents. *Canadian Journal of Psychiatry, 51*, 698–703.

Fremouw, W., Callahan, T., & Kashden, J. (1993). Adolescent suicidal risk: Psychological problem solving and environmental factors. *Suicide and Life-Threatening Behaviors, 23*, 46–54.

Hallfors, D., Brodish, H., Khatapoush, S., Sanchez, V., Cho, H., & Steckler, A. (2006). Feasibility of screening adolescents for suicide risk in "real-world" high school settings. *American Journal of Public Health, 96*, 282–287.

Kalafat, J. (1997). Prevention of youth suicide. In R. P. Weissberg, T. P. Gullotta, R. L. Hampton, B. A. Ryan, & G. R. Adams (Eds.), *Enhancing children's wellness* (pp. 175–213). Thousand Oaks, CA: Sage.

Kant, G. L., D'Zurilla, T. Z., & Maydeau-Olivares, A. (1997). Social problem solving as a mediator of stress-related depression and anxiety in middle-aged and elderly community residents. *Cognitive Therapy & Research, 21*, 73–96.

Kingsbury, S., Hawton, K., Steinhardt, K., & James, A. (1999). Do adolescents who take overdoses have specific psychological characteristics? A comparative study with psychiatric and community controls. *Journal of the American Academy of Child and Adolescents Psychiatry., 38*, 1125–1131.

Landman-Peeters, K. M. C., Hartman, C. A., van de Pompe, G., den Boer, J. A., Minderaa, R. B., & Ormel, J. (2005). Gender differences in the relation between social support, problem in parent-offspring communication, and depression and anxiety. *Social Science Medicine, 60*, 2549–2559.

Lee, T. Y., Wong, P., Chow, W. Y., & McBride-Chang, C. (2006). Predictors of suicide ideation and depression in Hong Kong adolescents: Perceptions of academic and family climates. *Suicide and life-threatening behavior, 36*, 82–97.

Levy, S. R., Jurkovic, G. L., & Spirito, A. (1995). A multisystems analysis of adolescent suicide attempters. *Journal of Abnormal Child Psychology, 23*, 221–234.

Lynch, F., Mills, C., Daly, I., & Fitzpatick, C. (2006). Challenging times: Prevalence of psychiatric disorders and suicidal behavior in Irish adolescents. *Journal of Adolescence, 29*, 555–573.

MacLeod, K., Tata, P., Tyrer, P., Schmidt, U., Davidson, K., & Thompson, S. (2005). Hopelessness and positive and negative future thinking in parasuicide. *The British Journal of Clinical Psychology, 44*, 495–504.

Miner, M. H., & Coleman, E. (2001). Advances in sex offender treatment and challenges for the future. *Journal of Psychology & Human Sexuality, 13*, 5–24.

Miros, N. J. (2000). Depression, anger, and coping skills as predictors of suicidal ideation in young adults: Examination of the diathesis-stress-hopelessness theory. *Dissertation Abstracts International: Section B: The Sciences and Engineering, 61*, 3286.

Mitchell, M. G., & Rosenthal, D. M. (1992). Suicidal adolescents: Family dynamics and the effects of lethality and hopelessness. *Journal of Youth and Adolescence, 21*, 23–33.

Olson, D. H., Russell, C. S., & Sprenkle, D. H. (1989). *Circumplex Model: Systemic assessment and treatment of families*. New York: Haworth Press.

Pinto, A., & Whisman, M. A. (1996). Negative affect and cognitive biases in suicidal and nonsuicidal hospitalized adolescents. *Journal of the American Academy of Child and Adolescent Psychiatry, 35*, 158–165.

Resch, F., Parzer, P., & Brunner, R. (2008). Self-mutilation and suicidal behavior in children and adolescents: Prevalence and psychosocial correlates: Results of the BELLA study. *European Child and Adolescent Psychiatry, 17*, 92–98.

Richards, J. M., & Gross, J. J. (1999). The cognitive consequences of emotion suppression. *Personality and Social Psychology Bulletin, 25*, 1033–1044.

Rucklidge, J. (2006). Psychosocial functioning of adolescents with and without paediatric bipolar disorder. *Journal of Affective Disorders, 91*, 181–188.

Rudd, M. (2000). The suicidal mode: A cognitive-behavioral mode of suicidality. *Suicide and Life Threatening Behavior, 30*, 18–33.

Rudd, M. D., Rajab, M. H., & Dahm, P. F. (1994). Problem-solving appraisal in suicide ideators and attempters. *American Journal of Orthopsychiatry, 64*, 136–149.

Rutter, P. A., & Behrendt, A. E. (2004). Adolescent Suicide Risk: Four Psychosocial Factors. *Adolescence, 39*, 295.

Schutte, S., Malouff, M., Hall, L., Haggerty, D., Cooper, J., Goldern, C., et al. (1998). Development and validation of a measure of emotional intelligence. *Personality and Individual Differences, 25*, 167–177.

Shek, D. T. L. (1993). Measurement of pessimism in Chinese adolescents: The Chinese hopelessness scale. *Social Behavior and Personality, 21*, 107–120.

Shek, D. T. L. (1999). Parenting characteristics and adolescent psychological well-being: A longitudinal study in a Chinese context. *Genetic, Social and General Psychology Monographs, 125*, 27–44.

Shek, D. T. L. (2000). Assessment of family functioning in Chinese adolescents. In N. N. Singh (Ed.), *International perspectives on child and adolescent mental health*. Holland: Elsevier.

Shek, D. T. L. (2001). Chinese adolescents and their parents' views on a happy family: Implications for family therapy. *Family Therapy, 28*, 73–104.

Shek, D. T. L. (2002). Assessment of family functioning in Chinese adolescents: The Chinese version of the Family Assessment Device. *Research on Social Work Practice, 12*, 502–524.

Shek, D. T. L. (2006). Chinese family research: Puzzles, progress, paradigms, and policy implications. *Journal of Family Issues, 27*, 275–284.

Shek, D. T. L. (2008). Economic disadvantage, perceived family life quality, and emotional well-being in Chinese adolescents: A longitudinal study. *Social Indicators Research, 85*, 169–189.

Shek, D. T. L., & Lee, T. Y. (2005). Hopelessness in Chinese adolescents in Hong Kong. In J. Merrick & G. Zalsman (Eds.), *Suicidal behavior in adolescence: An international perspective* (pp. 105–118). Israel: Freund Publishing House Ltd.

Shek, D. T. L., Lee, B. M., & Lee, T. Y. (2006). Frequency, satisfaction and quality dimensions of perceived parent–adolescent communication among Chinese adolescents in Hong Kong. *International Journal of Adolescent Mental Health, 18*, 259–270.

Siu, M. H., & Shek, T. L. (2005a). Psychometric properties of the Chinese Family Assessment Instrument in Chinese adolescent in Hong Kong. *Adolescence, 40*, 817–830.

Siu, M. H., & Shek, T. L. (2005b). The Chinese version of the Social Problem-Solving Inventory: Some initial results on reliability and validity. *Journal of Clinical Psychology, 61*, 347–360.

Smith, M., Alloy, B., & Abramson, Y. (2006). Cognitive vulnerability to depression, rumination, hopelessness, and suicidal ideation: Multiple pathways to self-injurious thinking. *Suicide and Life-threatening behavior, 36*, 443–454.

Spirito, A., Overholser, J., & Stark, L. J. (1989). Common problems and coping strategies. 2: Findings with adolescent suicide attempts. *Journal of Abnormal Child Psychology, 17*, 213–221.

Stewart, S. M., Kennard, B. D., Lee, P. W. H., Mayes, T., Hughes, C., & Emslie, G. (2005). Hopelessness and suicidal ideation among adolescents in two cultures. *Journal of Child Psychology and Psychiatry, 46*, 364.

Thompson, A., Mazza, J., Herting, R., Randell, P., & Eggert, L. (2005). The mediating roles of anxiety, depression, and hopelessness on adolescent suicidal behaviors. *Suicide and Life-threatening Behavior, 35*, 14–34.

Tobin, J. J. (2000). Adolescent suicide attempters in the year following hospitalization: Does the parent–child relationship predict symptom relapse and recurrent suicidality? *Dissertation Abstracts International: Section B: The Sciences and Engineering, 61*, 2225.

Tse, W. L., & Bagley, C. (2002). *Suicidal behavior, bereavement and death education in Chinese adolescents*. London: Ashgate Publishing Company.

Wallander, J. L., Schmitt, M., & Koot, H. M. (2001). Quality of life measurement in children and adolescents: Issues, instruments and applications. *Journal of Clinical Psychology, 57*, 571–585.

Walsh, F. (Ed.). (1993). *Normal family processes* (2nd ed. ed.). New York: Guilford Press.

Weishaar, M. E., & Beck, A. T. (1992). Hopelessness and suicide. *International Review of Psychiatry, 4*, 177–184.

Wong, P. S., Stewart, S. M., Ho, S. Y., & Lam, T. H. (2007). Risk factors associated with suicide attempts and other self-injury among Hong Kong adolescents. *Suicide and Life-threatening Behavior, 37*, 453–466.

Yang, B., & Clum, G. A. (1996). Effects of early negative life experiences on cognitive functioning and risk for suicide. *Clinical Psychology Review, 16*, 177–185.

Yang, B., & Clum, G. A. (2000). Childhood stress leads to later suicidality via its effect on cognitive functioning. *Suicide and Life-Threatening Behavior, 30*, 183–198.

Yip, S. F., Fu, K. W., Yang, C. T., Ip, Y. T., Chan, L. W., Chen, Y. H., Lee, T. S., Law, Y. W., & Hawton, K., et al. (2006). The effects of a celebrity suicide on suicide rates in Hong Kong. *Journal of Affective Disorders, 93*, 245–252.

Zonj, H. J., & Lude, P. (2002). Regulation of emotion and psychological symptoms in people with spinal cord injury. *Swiss Journal of Psychology Schweizerische Zeitschrift fuer Psychologie Revue Suisse de Psychologie, 61*, 203–210.

Soc Indic Res (2010) 95:421–436
DOI 10.1007/s11205-009-9529-3

School Attachment Among Taiwanese Adolescents: The Roles of Individual Characteristics, Peer Relationships, and Teacher Well-Being

Hsi-Sheng Wei · Ji-Kang Chen

Accepted: 5 July 2009 / Published online: 7 October 2009

Abstract This study examines the effects of individual characteristics (school grade and gender), peer relationships (peer support and peer victimization), and the subjective well-being of teachers (depression and job satisfaction) on students' attachment to school. Twenty-four classes in grades 7 through 9 at two middle schools in Taipei were selected as the sample, and survey data were obtained from students and homeroom teachers. Hierarchical linear modeling was used to conduct a two-level analysis on 720 students and 24 teachers with valid data on all research variables. A series of models were constructed and tested stepwise. The results indicated that students' average school attachment scores varied significantly among classes. A higher school grade was associated with reduced attachment while no gender difference was found. Peer support had a positive influence and peer victimization had a negative effect on school attachment. Finally, job satisfaction of the homeroom teachers positively contributed to students' attachment to school, but teachers' depression had no significant effect. Implications for creating a positive classroom environment were discussed.

Keywords School attachment · Peer victimization · Homeroom teacher · Well-being · Job satisfaction

1 Introduction

School is a crucial environment that has a significant influence on student well-being and development (Roeser and Eccles 1998). Children and adolescents now spend a considerable amount of time in school each day, and are likely to have more interactions with classmates and teachers than with their own parents. School shapes youngsters' beliefs and

H.-S. Wei (✉)
Department of Social Work, National Taipei University, 151, University Rd., San Shia, Taipei 237, Taiwan
e-mail: hswei@mail.ntpu.edu.tw

J.-K. Chen
Department of Social Work, Chinese University of Hong Kong, Shatin, Hong Kong

behaviors profoundly, which further affects their lifespan trajectory and career prospects. As a central part of life, school is regarded as a major area of students' life satisfaction, while educational performance often serves as a core indicator of child well-being (Gilman et al. 2000; Ghysels and Van Vlasselaer 2008). Research has shown that negative school experiences impact students' psychosocial adjustment and can result in a variety of consequences including low self-esteem, loneliness, and depression (Brand et al. 2008; Locker and Cropley 2004; McDougall et al. 2001). Such findings apply not only to Western countries but also in Eastern contexts as well. For example, a large-scale survey of 9,586 adolescents in Taiwan suggested that lower satisfaction with peer relations and less connectedness to school were associated with higher risk of depression (Lin et al. 2008).

Schools may play an even more important role for student well-being in certain Asian regions compared to Western countries. One study compared correlations among domains of life satisfaction for Korean and U.S. adolescents and found that satisfaction with school was highly associated with global life satisfaction for Korean, but not American, students (Park and Huebner 2005). As with many other Confucian-based cultures, the education system of Taiwan is highly academically-oriented and students are preoccupied by competitive exams and evaluations. Parents also have high expectations for their children's educational achievement. As a result, Taiwanese adolescents spend a considerable part of every day in school-related activities. In a survey of 2,764 junior and senior high school students in one metropolitan area of Taiwan, 53.7% of the respondents were attending cram schools after regular school hours (Wei et al. 2006). In the same survey, 84.9% of the respondents reported school performance as a personal concern, which made it the major source of stress for local youth.

Positive attitudes and feelings toward school are beneficial for student well-being and learning. It is human nature to seek connections and bonding, and school is one major social institution that provides a sense of belonging for individuals (Baumeister and Leary 1995). Feelings of emotional connectedness, support, and inclusion in the school environment are often referred to as school attachment or school bonding (Jimerson et al. 2003), and have been shown to impact students' psychological and behavioral adjustment. For example, attachment to school was found to contribute to lower delinquency and aggression as well as higher motivation for achievement (Eccles 2007; Frey et al. 2009). School attachment is also positively linked to better academic performance and self-esteem while negatively correlated with a variety of problem behaviors including substance use and gang involvement (Maddox and Prinz 2003; Catalano et al. 2004; Simons-Morton et al. 1999). For example, one study of sixth to eighth graders found differences in school attachment between bullies, victims, bully-victims, and non-involved peers, and such feelings were associated with their risk for bullying and investment in prosocial beliefs and behaviors (Cunningham 2007). So far, little research has been done in Asian regions to investigate the personal and social factors of school attachment despite the common emphasis on education in Confucian-based cultures. Therefore, the present study hopes to fill in this knowledge gap, examining the effects of individual, peer, and teacher contexts on Taiwanese adolescents' attachment to school.

1.1 Individual Characteristics

On an individual level, gender is one variable that has been extensively examined in the school attachment literature. Girls are constantly found to have more positive feelings and attitudes toward school. One large-scale survey on 431,331 public school students in Arizona showed that girls had higher school satisfaction scores than boys (Okun et al.

1990). Another study surveyed 4,263 6th through 8th graders in seven U.S. middle schools and found female students to have higher school bonding and school adjustment while male students had more problem behaviors (Simons-Morton et al. 1999). Verkuyen and Thijs (2002) examined school satisfaction among 1,090 Dutch children aged 10–12 years and found girls were significantly more satisfied with their schools than boys were. Still another study analyzed data from the National Longitudinal Study of Adolescent Health and showed that girls had higher school attachment than boys in the middle school years, although such differences were only statistically significant in grade 8 (Johnson et al. 2006). Girls were also found to have higher grades and school engagement. These findings are interesting because research in general has shown that girls often have lower self-esteem, higher depression, increased loneliness, and more suicidal ideation during adolescence compared to boys (Polce-Lynch et al. 2001; Mahon et al. 2006; Galambos et al. 2004; Liu et al. 2005). It seems that school is one area where girls have higher enjoyment and adjust better than boys.

Age and school grade differences in school attachment are also shown to be salient in the literature. Student satisfaction and bonding with school have been shown to decrease during middle school years, with the lowest levels in 8th or 9th grade (Johnson et al. 2006; Hawkins et al. 2001; Okun et al. 1990). The common decline in school attachment and motivation during early adolescence following the transition to junior high school has been stated to result from a misfit between student psychological needs and the opportunities provided by the school environment (Eccles et al. 1996). One study of 641 American children from 3rd to 6th grade showed that students' self-reported relatedness to teachers increased between 3rd and 5th grade but fell significantly after entering middle school, as did their classroom engagement (Furrer and Skinner 2003). Another large-scale study revealed a similar trend in which delinquency and problem behaviors went up while students' school bonding and perceived climate continually dropped from 6th to 8th grade (Simons-Morton et al. 1999).

Little research has been done to investigate the potential effect of age and school grade on the well-being and school attachment of Taiwanese adolescents. However, the 9th grade is expected to be a difficult and stressful time for local students since the Basic Competence Test for senior high school entrance is usually held two times in May and July while the middle school students graduate in June. In accordance with this schedule, middle schools in Taiwan increasingly focus on academic performance as adolescents move along the school grade levels, which can result in great distress and negative feelings toward school for students in higher grades. Interestingly, some studies on students from other cultures found exams and evaluations not necessarily threatening or harmful. For example, one UK study of 520 secondary school students found no significant difference in depression between school year (year 9 and year 11) and time points (regular term time and the week immediately prior to the examinations; Locker and Cropley 2004). On the other hand, given the cultural value of academic achievement and high educational expectations from parents, performance pressure and test anxiety are common for students in Asian countries such as Japan, Korea, and Singapore (Ang et al. 2007; Juon et al. 1994; Hawkins and Tanaka 1992). One study compared public middle school pupils' perceptions of test anxiety in the United States and China, and Chinese students reported significantly stronger concerns for the possibility of annoying their parents with unsatisfactory academic achievement than American students (Xing et al. 2005). The pressure from family and school is likely to increase as students approach the critical exam in 9th grade and may make students more likely to avoid attending schools. It is thus hypothesized in the present study that school grade is negatively associated with students' school attachment.

1.2 Peer Relationships

As adolescents' major social environment, school is a multilayer context with a variety of subsystems, among which peers constitute a critical one. Peers become increasingly significant during adolescence and have a considerable influence on children's well-being and development. Peer support, friendships, and positive classroom climate have been found to be associated with higher school liking and school satisfaction (Erath et al. 2008; Verkuyten and Thijs 2002). Positive relationships with peers is also associated with healthy and adaptive outcomes including higher self-esteem, better school performance, and stronger achievement motivation (de Bruyn and van den Boom 2005; Harter et al. 1998; Eshel et al. 2003; Nelson and DeBacker 2008). A large-scale study of 18,735 students in Dutch junior high schools indicated that students with peer acceptance had lower risk of being held back from advancing to the next grade or to go downward in the track system (Lubbers et al. 2006). On the other hand, peer rejection can affect students' learning and result in maladjustment and problem behaviors (Wentzel 2003; Ladd 2006; Pedersen et al. 2007), and can also lead to reduced class engagement and detachment from school (Buhs et al. 2006).

Getting along with peers is not always an easy task for adolescents, and many are actually abused or maltreated by classmates and fellow students. Recent research has clearly shown that peer victimization is prevalent in Western and Eastern countries (Chen and Astor 2009a; Due and Holstein 2008; Koo et al. 2008; Wong et al. 2008; Wei and Chen 2009). Wei and others surveyed a sample of Taiwanese 7th graders and showed that approximately 31% of the students reported being bullied at least once by classmates during their first three months in middle school while almost 24% were bullied by students outside their classes (Wei et al. 2007). Such experiences have a considerable impact on the victims' psychosocial well-being (Hawker and Boulton 2000; Karin Natvig et al. 2001). Students' academic achievement, attachment to school, and even life satisfaction are all likely to be affected (You et al. 2008; Beran et al. 2008). Wei and Williams (2004) analyzed data on 1,022 US 6th grade students and found that peer victimization was associated with lower school attachment, which in turn led to inattentive school behaviors and poor academic performance. Another study in the UK showed that victimization and the fear of future victimization predicted disrupted concentration on class work (Boulton et al. 2008).

The influence of peers is probably more salient in Taiwanese schools than in certain Western counterparts. Middle school students in Taiwan stay with a fixed group of peers every day throughout the school years, which makes peer reputation and status in class extremely important for quality of life in school. Under the current school schedule, Taiwanese students attend school approximately two hundred days a year, and their time with classmates can be as long as nine hours a day, which is much longer compared to many other countries. In addition, Taiwan maintains much of its collectivism characteristics, such as group-orientation and emphasis on interpersonal relations, despite the profound transformation toward Westernization (Ali et al. 2005; Chiou 2001). It is therefore hypothesized in the present study that peer relationship factors, including peer support and peer victimization, are associated with Taiwanese adolescents' attachment to school.

1.3 Teacher Factors in School Attachment

Besides peers, teachers are another major factor affecting students' sense of connectedness and attachment to school. Past research has largely focused on the influence of the teacher–

student relationship on school-related feelings. Perceived teacher support has been shown to be associated with positive perceptions of school climate, school satisfaction, and academic motivation (Danielsen et al. 2009; Frey et al. 2009). A study of 805 American students in 4th to 7th grade found that teacher support led to increased emotional engagement and decreased disaffection (Skinner et al. 2008). Having a warm and trustful relationship with a teacher predicted positive school outcomes for at-risk students (Baker et al. 2008). Davis and Lease (2007) employed a peer-rating procedure with middle school students to map their perceived status of teacher likeability in classrooms. The position in this "teacher-liking space" was found to be associated with students' achievement and teacher relationship quality. Furthermore, Hughes and Kwok (2006) suggested that teacher–student relationship quality contributes to classroom engagement, which in turn impacted students' peer acceptance.

Under the current educational system in Taiwan, one homeroom teacher is assigned to each class in middle school, and this teacher interacts with these students in homeroom on a daily basis for as long as 3 years (Chen and Astor 2009b; Taiwan Ministry of Education 2006). The homeroom teachers play a crucial role in the classroom climate and students' learning due to the great power endorsed to them by the institution and cultural traditions (Fwu and Wang 2002). The Confucian heritage culture of Taiwan emphasizes respect for teachers and an obedient role for students. Teachers are regarded as a parent-like figure and pupils are supposed to follow their instructions without questioning (Wu 2002). As a symbol of authority, they are in control of classroom dynamics and their conduct sets an example for students to imitate. However, teaching is a stressful occupation in Eastern as well as Western countries. A study based on a sample of senior high school teachers in China found that their somatization and depression scores were higher than the Chinese norm (Huang et al. 2006). A large-scale telephone survey in Hong Kong also showed that the prevalence rates of generalized anxiety disorder and major depressive episodes among teachers were higher than the general population, and these symptoms were associated with job-specific stressors (Lee et al. 2007).

Teachers' subjective well-being, such as psychological adjustment and job satisfaction, is closely related to performance and teaching quality. Lower well-being was found to be associated with teacher burnout (Milfont et al. 2008). Betoret (2009) suggested that emotional exhaustion was a key element of burnout, which was largely accounted for by teachers' job stressors. Teachers who perceived their job as highly demanding and low in control were at higher risk of emotional exhaustion and burnout (Santavirta et al. 2007), and teachers who were experiencing burnout were shown to have attention difficulties (van der Linden et al. 2005). A study of Spanish secondary school teachers found emotional exhaustion and job dissatisfaction to be associated with psychiatric sick leave (Moriana and Herruzo 2006). The relationship between job satisfaction and job performance has been well documented (see Judge et al. 2001 for a review), and teachers' distress can interfere with their motivation and ability to teach and care for students, but so far there is little research directly investigating the effect of teacher well-being on student attachment to school. The present study addresses this issue and evaluates the hypothesis that homeroom teachers' depression and job satisfaction predict students' general school attachment in that class.

1.4 The Present Study

A school is a complex environment with multiple layers of contexts (Furlong et al. 2003). From an ecological perspective, the present study aims to integrate individual, peer, and teacher factors into a multilevel model and examine their contributions to middle school students' school attachment. One limitation of previous studies is that they often rely on a single source of data, especially students' self-reports, to assess variables on different levels including class and school contexts. Such practices increase the concern of shared-method variance (Donaldson and Grant-Vallone 2002). This study employs data from both teachers and students in order to reduce the risk of self-report bias. It also delivers a more direct analysis for the link between teachers' well-being and students' feelings toward school, which is a core index of well-being among adolescents. Specifically speaking, this study will test the following research hypotheses:

1. On the individual level, girls have higher school attachment than boys and students in higher grades are less attached to school than students in lower grades.
2. School attachment is positively affected by peer support and negatively affected by peer victimization.
3. Homeroom teacher's depression has a negative effect and his/her job satisfaction has a positive effect on students' attachment to school.

Finally, this study focuses on Taiwanese youth and accounts for the specific educational characteristics under a Confucian heritage culture. The results can provide valuable insights regarding potential cultural differences in school dynamics between Western and Eastern countries.

2 Methods

2.1 Participants

Two middle schools in Taipei were invited to participate in the present study, in which 834 students and 24 homeroom teachers from 24 classes in grades 7–9 were recruited as the research respondents. Written consent was obtained and self-report questionnaires were administered. Only those with complete data on all research variables were included in the following analysis, which results in a final sample of 720 students and 24 teachers. About half (49.7%) of the students ($n = 358$) are male and 50.3% ($n = 362$) are female. Their ages range from 10 to 15 years old with a mean of 13.34 and a standard deviation of .97. The majority of teacher respondents are female (83.3%, $n = 20$) and in their forties (79.2%, $n = 19$).

2.2 Procedures

Data collection for the present study was conducted during the fall semester of 2007. Student respondents were asked to fill out the research questionnaire in class. The self-report questionnaire takes approximately 30 min to complete. The students were advised to read the instructions carefully and not to discuss answers with classmates during the survey. It was clearly stated that respondents could withdraw from the survey at any time with no penalty. The teacher version of the questionnaires was distributed to homeroom teachers and returned after completion.

2.3 Measures

2.3.1 Individual Characteristics

Information on student characteristics, including gender and school grade, were collected through corresponding items on the self-report questionnaire. Male and female were dichotomously coded while the three school grades were coded as 7, 8, and 9, respectively.

2.3.2 Peer Victimization

Students' experiences with peer victimization during the last semester were assessed via seven items on a five-point scale (never–five times or more). These seven items in this scale were selected and adapted from the scale of victimization based on the scale of school violence in Taiwan (Chen and Astor 2009a) as well as adaptive version of California School Climate and Safety Survey (CSCSS; e.g., Benbenishty and Astor 2005; Furlong et al. 1998). The original items in adaptive version of California School Climate and Safety Survey were translated from English to Chinese in Standardized Version. A standard back-translation procedure was employed in order to ensure translation accuracy. Example items include "My classmates beat, kick, punch me or use other instruments to hurt me", "My classmates curse or insult me", and "My classmates boycott me and do not want to play or talk with me". The coefficient alpha was calculated as .91. Regarding validity, California School Climate and Safety Survey was shown to have good construct validity (Furlong et al. 2005).

2.3.3 School Attachment

School attachment was measured by six items on the questionnaire adopted from previous studies (Chen and Astor 2010) and CSCSS (Benbenishty and Astor 2005; Furlong et al. 1998, 2005; Murray and Greenberg 2001) with modifications to assess students' general interests and feelings toward school. Example items include "I feel unsafe in school", "I feel that my school doesn't care about students", and "I like school life". A five-point scale was used (strongly disagree–strongly agree). Negative items were reverse scored and an aggregate score was calculated to represent school attachment. The coefficient alpha of the 6 items in the research sample equals .69. CSCSS demonstrated adequate construct validity (Furlong et al. 2005).

2.3.4 Peer Support

Peer support was measured by two items on the questionnaire: "My classmates encourage and support me in my time of difficulty and frustration" and "My classmates would like to share their thoughts with me". A five-point scale was used (strongly disagree–strongly agree). The coefficient alpha equals .78.

2.3.5 Teacher Depression

Teacher depression was assessed using seven items adopted from the Brief Symptom Rating Scale (BSRS), a Chinese questionnaire used to screen for mental health problems (Lee et al. 1990). The whole battery consists of 50 items, which are divided into ten dimensions such as phobia, depression, and obsession. Only the depression subscale of

BSRS was employed for the present study. Respondents are asked to report their status over the past week on a five-point scale (never–very severe). Example items include "I have suicidal thoughts", "I feel lonely", and "I lose interest in daily activities". The coefficient alpha was calculated as .94. BSRS was suggested by the authors to be a valid screening tool and its scores were found highly correlated with the parental form of the Symptom Check List-90-R (SCL-90-R) among medical populations for each symptom dimension (Lee et al. 1990).

2.3.6 Teacher Job Satisfaction

The Job Satisfaction Scale (JSS; Liu 2004) was adopted to assess teachers' feelings about their current job, including administration and leadership, salary and promotions, relationships with colleagues, psychological rewards, and job content. Example items include "opportunities of job promotion", "campus climate for faculty", and "efficiency of school administration". JSS has a total of 35 items measured on a five-point Likert scale (very unsatisfied–very satisfied). The coefficient alpha was found to be .96. The five factors of JSS accounted for approximately 60% of the variance and good construct validity was suggested by the author (Liu 2004).

2.4 Data Analysis

This study employed hierarchical linear modeling (HLM) as the major analytical approach. HLM is suitable for analyzing data that has nested structures (Raudenbush and Bryk 2002). In this study, the students were nested in classes, and each class had only one homeroom teacher. The student and teacher variables thus constitute two levels of data. The fact that students belonged to classes violates the statistical assumption that all observations are independent of one another. Unlike many traditional regression approaches, HLM takes this non-independence into account and is able to analyze the variance in the outcome variable at multiple levels. In the present study, a stepwise strategy was used in which student-level models were first computed to assess the effects of individual characteristics and peer relationships on school attachment. One regression equation was calculated for each class with intercepts and slopes, which were then used in a class-level analysis to further examine the influence of teacher well-being on students' attachment to school.

3 Results

The descriptive statistics of the research variables are shown in Table 1. As a first step of HLM, a basic two-level model of school attachment without any predictors was specified and tested. The results show a significant difference in average school attachment scores between classes (tau = .98, Chi-square = 65.14, $p < .01$), which provides a rationale to conduct further multi-level analysis. In this unconditional model, the within-group (student-level) variance was found to be 16.02 while between-group variance (teacher-level) was .98. The Intraclass Correlation Coefficient (ICC) was calculated as .06, suggesting that class-level factors account for approximately 6% of the variance in students' school attachment.

Secondly, a model with student-level predictors only was specified, in which gender, school grade, peer support, and peer victimization were included. The results of the model testing are summarized in Table 2. School grade and peer victimization were found to be negatively associated with school attachment while peer support positively contributed to

Table 1 Descriptive statistics of research variables

	Mean	SD	Minimum	Maximum
Outcome variable				
School attachment	20.31	4.12	6.00	30.00
Student-level variables				
Gender[a]	N/A			
School grade	8.18	0.80	7.00	9.00
Peer support	7.07	1.97	2.00	10.00
Peer victimization	10.97	3.99	7.00	28.00
Teacher-level variables				
Depression	31.71	4.30	16.00	35.00
Job satisfaction	122.13	18.77	79.00	165.00

[a] Gender is a variable with only two categories (1 = male and 2 = female)

Table 2 HLM results of the model with student-level predictors only

Student-level variables	Coefficient	Standard error	*T*-ratio	*p* value
Gender	−0.371	0.369	−1.005	0.316
School grade	−0.592	0.267	−2.216	0.027
Peer support	0.704	0.081	8.610	0.00
Peer victimization	−0.095	0.0417	−2.275	0.023

school attachment. An inspection of the mean attachment scores of the three school grades revealed a downward tendency with 7th grade being the highest and 9th grade the lowest. No significant gender difference was found. A supplementary ANOVA was conducted, in which girls were found to have slightly higher school attachment scores than boys although the difference was non-significant [$F(1,718) = .05$, $p = .83$]. Gender was therefore dropped from the consequent analysis.

Finally, teacher depression and job satisfaction were added as teacher-level predictors, and the complete model with variables from the two levels was specified as follows:

Student-level model

$$\text{School attachment} = \text{B0} + \text{B1} * (\text{school grade}) + \text{B2} * (\text{peer support}) + \text{B3} * (\text{peer victimization}) + \text{R}$$

Teacher-level model

$$\text{B0} = \text{G00} + \text{G01} * (\text{teacher depression}) + \text{G02} * (\text{teacher job satisfaction}) + \text{U0}$$

$$\text{B1} = \text{G10} + \text{U1}$$

$$\text{B2} = \text{G20} + \text{U2}$$

$$\text{B3} = \text{G30} + \text{U3}$$

B0 represents the intercept of the student-level equation while B1, B2 and B3 refer to the slopes of school grade, peer support and peer victimization, respectively. The model specifies that teacher-level variables affect the intercept of the student-level equation. In other words, teacher's depression and job satisfaction were used to predict after controlling for individual-level factors including school grade, peer support and peer victimization. All the predictors were centered on the grand mean to obtain more interpretable estimates.

Table 3 HLM results of the final model

	Coefficient	Standard error	*T*-ratio	*p* value
Student-level variables				
School grade	−0.541	0.227	−2.378	0.018
Peer support	0.686	0.079	8.64	0.000
Peer victimization	−0.088	0.039	−2.219	0.027
Teacher-level variables				
Depression	−0.0185	0.037	−0.498	0.62
Job satisfaction	0.028	0.009	2.93	0.008

Table 3 summarizes the results of hierarchical linear modeling. The three student-level variables all significantly contributed to school attachment. It was expected that students in lower grades were more attached to school, and the results supported this hypothesis. Another hypothesis was also supported, in which higher peer support and less peer victimization were associated with higher attachment to school. However, as mentioned earlier, gender was found having no significant effect on student's school attachment, which was inconsistent with one of the student-level hypotheses. At the same time, teacher-level hypotheses were partly supported by the results, in which job satisfaction of the homeroom teacher was found significantly associated with school attachment while no significant relationship was found between depression of the teacher and students' school attachment.

4 Discussion

School is a major institution that plays a critical role in youngsters' education and socialization, and students' feelings toward school are closely related to their learning and well-being. The present study utilizes a multi-level approach and examines the effect of individual characteristics, peer experiences, and teacher well-being on students' school attachment. These factors have not only been studied extensively in past research but also have cultural relevance in the context of Taiwan. Predictors are categorized into two levels and hierarchical linear modeling is the major analytic strategy. The results largely support the research hypotheses. First, higher school grade was found to be significantly associated with lower school attachment, which confirmed one of our student-level hypotheses. As mentioned earlier, middle school students in Taiwan are required to take the Basic Competence Test in 9th grade, and this major exam determines their future in high school and thus becomes a major source of stress for many students. School classes are more and more exam-oriented as the exam approaches, and teachers also put stronger emphasis on students' academic performance and test scores. Based on the results of this study, it seems that such pressures actually reduced students' positive attitudes toward school, which may be damaging for their learning and well-being. The study also highlights the need for mental health services among students in higher school grades. However, this study did not assess students' academic stress nor examine the class contents and schedules between different school grades, which constitutes a limitation and makes it difficult to draw any definitive conclusion. In order to better understand the decrease in school attachment with increasing grades, future investigation is needed to reveal the underlying mechanisms through which the school grade impacts those youngsters' bonding with school.

Another student-level hypothesis concerning gender difference was rejected by the results. Although girls had slightly higher scores on school attachment, no significant gender difference was found in this study, which is inconsistent with past research in Western countries. Interestingly, a recent cross-national survey on adolescents showed that American and Irish male respondents reported significantly lower school satisfaction scores than their female peers while no such differences were found for Chinese and South Korean adolescents (Gilman et al. 2008). A closer examination of the present data revealed that girls in 7th grade had higher school attachment than boys (although the difference was not significant), but the situation was reversed for 8th graders, in which girls had lower scores than boys. Both genders reached an identical lowest level in 9th grade. The middle school transition and school environment seem to be somewhat gender-unfriendly for female students in Taiwan. One contributing factor may be the patriarchic culture and gender-insensitive practice in many Taiwanese schools. Lee (2007) examined the organization of a Taiwanese high school and suggested the existence of gendered discourses in which a men-strong/women-weak differentiation was reinforced and a sexist school culture was reproduced. Further investigation is called for to identify the exact factors causing girls' rapid decline in school attachment during this period, and more efforts are needed in gender education and gender mainstreaming in order to promote a friendly environment for both boys and girls.

Results of this study supported our hypothesis that school attachment is positively affected by peer support and negatively affected by peer victimization. The findings are consistent with the previous studies and confirmed the impact of peer relationships on students' attitude toward school. Given the nature of class structure in Taiwanese schools, where students spend all of their time with the same group of peers, these classmates are expected to play an important role in adolescents' learning and well-being. At the same time, the collectivist cultural tradition of Taiwan puts great emphasis on maintaining relational harmony and interdependence (Lu 2008), which may make peer maltreatment more problematic for victims. Akiba (2004) suggested that acceptance by the group was crucial in a collective society like Japan, and ijime (the Japanese word for bullying) was mostly a collective behavior in which a group of perpetrators abuse one single student. Sometimes the whole class may join in as bullies against the victim. More in-depth studies should be conducted to analyze group dynamics in the classroom and the cultural implications of peer relationships for Taiwanese adolescents.

In a Confucian heritage tradition, teachers are regarded as a symbol of authority while the students assume a passive and obedient role to be hard-working, humble, and silent (Ho et al. 2001). Teachers' conduct and manners serve as a model example for youngsters to look up to. Given their central role in education, the well-being of teachers is expected to be tied to students' feelings toward school. This study tested such hypotheses through a direct assessment of teachers' subjective well being, which provides some advantages over previous research. In partial support of our hypothesis, homeroom teachers' job satisfaction, but not their depression, was associated with students' school attachment. The considerable correlation between depression and job satisfaction ($r = .50$) implies their close relationship, but the latter appears to be a stronger predictor of students' connectedness to school. In a sense, students' attitudes correspond to teacher's attitudes since those with unsatisfied homeroom teachers are less attached to school. However, the small ICC mentioned earlier suggests that only a small portion of the variance in students' school attachment was accounted for by teacher-level variables. This is possibly due to the small sample size (720 students and 24 teachers) of the present study, which constitutes a limitation and calls for further investigation to better evaluate the magnitude of teacher influence in students' bonding to school.

The findings of this study point to a number of implications for research and practice. First, the specific mechanisms and processes connecting teachers' and students' well-being need to be identified. Teachers experiencing job stress are likely to have negative perceptions toward school, which may impact their teaching competence and reduce their ability to care about the students. This underscores the necessity of mental health screening and care for school teachers. One study in Hong Kong showed that only 8.5% of local teachers with mental disorders sought professional help due to concerns of stigmatization (Lee et al. 2007). Schools should provide adequate and confidential mental health services not only for students but also for teachers in order to ensure their psychosocial adjustment and well-being. Since much of the teachers' dissatisfaction and emotional exhaustion is associated with job stress, the above discussion highlights another important issue, which is the improvement of the school organization and culture. Lu (2007) found that middle school teachers' perceptions of organizational politics affected their burnout through job satisfaction. School support is another important factor for teachers' emotional well-being and professional disengagement (Galand et al. 2007).

Students need a warm and friendly environment in order to fulfill their potential, as do teachers. Therefore, effective strategies to promote school attachment must be inclusive, and a whole school approach is recommended in order to build a caring community for all individuals involved (Rowe et al. 2007; Battistich et al. 2004). Adolescents' developmental demands and life changes during this stage should also be taken into consideration. Social support for the needs of both autonomy and relatedness is likely to enhance students' quality of life over their transition to secondary school (Gillison et al. 2008). Teachers can be active participants in creating a positive school environment. Increased teacher support and respect for student perspectives have been found to be associated with less drug use and depression as well as perception of a respectful climate among students (LaRusso et al. 2008). Children and adolescents are valuable assets in our society and efforts have been made to enhance their positive development beyond mere survival. This study provides a comprehensive framework to explore adolescents' school attachment in an Asian context, which can help in the development of effective and culture-sensitive programs to promote the well-being and growth of youth in Taiwan.

References

Akiba, M. (2004). Nature and correlates of ijime: Bullying in Japanese middle schools. *International Journal of Educational Research, 41*, 216–236.

Ali, A., Lee, M., Hsieh, Y., & Krishnan, K. (2005). Individualism and collectivism in Taiwan. *Cross Cultural Management, 12*(4), 3–15.

Ang, R., Huan, V., & Braman, O. (2007). Factorial structure and invariance of the academic expectations stress inventory across Hispanic and Chinese adolescent samples. *Child Psychiatry & Human Development, 38*(1), 73–87.

Baker, J., Grant, S., & Morlock, L. (2008). The teacher–student relationship as a developmental context for children with internalizing or externalizing behavior problems. *School Psychology Quarterly, 23*(1), 3–15.

Battistich, V., Schaps, E., & Wilson, N. (2004). Effects of an elementary school intervention on students' 'connectedness' to school and social adjustment during middle school. *Journal of Primary Prevention, 24*(3), 243–262.

Baumeister, R. F., & Leary, M. R. (1995). The need to belong: Desire for interpersonal attachments as a fundamental human motivation. *Psychological Bulletin, 117*, 497–529.

Benbenishty, R., & Astor, R. A. (2005). *School violence in context: Culture, neighborhood, family, school, and gender*. New York, NY: Oxford University Press.
Beran, T., Hughes, G., & Lupart, J. (2008). A model of achievement and bullying: Analyses of the Canadian national longitudinal survey of children and youth data. *Educational Research, 50*(1), 25–39.
Betoret, F. (2009). Self-efficacy, school resources, job stressors and burnout among Spanish primary *and* secondary school teachers: A structural equation approach. *Educational Psychology, 29*(1), 45–68.
Boulton, M., Trueman, M., & Murray, L. (2008). Associations between peer victimization fear of future victimization and disrupted concentration on class work among junior school pupils. *British Journal of Educational Psychology, 78*(3), 473–489.
Brand, S., Felner, R., Seitsinger, A., Burns, A., & Bolton, N. (2008). A large scale study of the assessment of the social environment of middle and secondary schools: The validity and utility of teachers' ratings of school climate, cultural pluralism, and safety problems for understanding school effects and school improvement. *Journal of School Psychology, 46*(5), 507–535.
Buhs, E. S., Ladd, G. W., & Herald, S. L. (2006). Peer exclusion and victimization: Processes that mediate the relation between peer group rejection and children's classroom engagement and achievement? *Journal of Educational Psychology, 98*(1), 1–13.
Catalano, R. F., Haggerty, K. P., Oesterle, S., Fleming, C. B., & Hawkins, J. D. (2004). The importance of bonding to school for healthy development: Findings from the social development research group. *Journal of School Health, 74*(7), 252–261.
Chen, J. K., & Astor, R.A. (2009a). The perpetration of school violence in Taiwan: An analysis of gender, grade level, school type. *School Psychology International* (in press). doi:10.1177/01430343090.
Chen, J. K., & Astor, R. A. (2009b). Students' reports of violence against teachers in Taiwanese schools. *Journal of School Violence, 8*(1), 2–17.
Chen, J. K., & Astor R. A. (2010). School violence perpetration in Taiwan: Examining how western risk factors predict school violence in an Asian culture. *Journal of Interpersonal Violence* (in press).
Chiou, J. (2001). Horizontal and vertical individualism and collectivism among college students in the United States, Taiwan, and Argentina. *Journal of Social Psychology, 141*(5), 667–678.
Cunningham, N. (2007). Level of bonding to school and perception of the school environment by bullies, victims, and bully victims. *The Journal of Early Adolescence, 27*(4), 457–478.
Danielsen, A., Samdal, O., Hetland, J., & Wold, B. (2009). School-related social support and students' perceived life satisfaction. *Journal of Educational Research, 102*(4), 303–318.
Davis, H., & Lease, A. (2007). Perceived organizational structure for teacher liking: The role of peers' perceptions of teacher liking in teacher–student relationship quality, motivation, and achievement. *Social Psychology of Education, 10*(4), 403–427.
de Bruyn, E., & van den Boom, D. (2005). Interpersonal behavior, peer popularity and self-esteem in early adolescence. *Social Development, 14*(4), 555–573.
Donaldson, S., & Grant-Vallone, E. (2002). Understanding self-report bias in organizational behavior research. *Journal of Business and Psychology, 17*(2), 245–260.
Due, P., & Holstein, B. (2008). Bullying victimization among 13 to 15 year old school children: Results from two comparative studies in 66 countries and regions. *International Journal of Adolescent Medicine and Health, 20*(2), 209–221.
Eccles, J. (2007). Families, schools, and developing achievement-related motivations and engagement. In J. E. Grusec & P. D. Hastings (Eds.), *Handbook of socialization: Theory and research* (pp. 665–691). New York, NY: Guilford.
Eccles, J., Lord, S., & Buchanan, C. (1996). School transitions in early adolescence: What are we doing to our young people? In J. A. Graber, J. Brooks-Gunn, & A. C. Petersen (Eds.), *Transitions through adolescence: Interpersonal domains and context* (pp. 251–284). Hillsdale, NJ: Lawrence Erlbaum Associates.
Erath, S., Flanagan, K., & Bierman, K. (2008). Early adolescent school adjustment: Associations with *friendship* and peer victimization. *Social Development, 17*(4), 853–870.
Eshel, Y., Sharabany, R., & Bar-Sade, E. (2003). Reciprocated and unreciprocated dyadic peer *preferences* and academic achievement of Israeli and immigrant students: A longitudinal study. *Journal of Social Psychology, 143*(6), 746–762.
Frey, A., Ruchkin, V., Martin, A., & Schwab-Stone, M. (2009). Adolescents in transition: School and family characteristics in the development of violent behaviors entering high school. *Child Psychiatry & Human Development, 40*(1), 1–13.
Furlong, M. J., Greif, J.L., Bates, M. P., Whipple, A. D., Jimenez, T. C., & Morrison, R. (2005). Development of California school climate and safety survey-short form. *Psychology in the Schools, 42*(2), 137–149.

Furlong, M. J., Morrison, R., Bates, M., & Chung, A. (1998). School violence victimization among secondary students in California: Grade, gender, and racial-ethnic incidence patterns. *The California School Psychologist, 3*, 71–87.

Furlong, M., Whipple, A., Jean, G., Simental, J., Soliz, A., & Punthuna, S. (2003). Multiple contexts of school engagement: Moving toward a unifying framework for educational research and practice. *California School Psychologist, 8*, 99–113.

Furrer, C., & Skinner, E. (2003). Sense of relatedness as a factor in children's academic engagement and performance. *Journal of Educational Psychology, 95*(1), 148–162.

Fwu, B. J., & Wang, H. H. (2002). The social status of teachers in Taiwan. *Comparative Education, 38*(2), 211–224.

Galambos, N., Leadbeater, B., & Barker, E. (2004). Gender differences in and risk factors for depression in adolescence: A 4-year longitudinal study. *International Journal of Behavioral Development, 28*(1), 16–25.

Galand, B., Lecocq, C., & Philippot, P. (2007). School violence and teacher professional disengagement. *British Journal of Educational Psychology, 77*(2), 465–477.

Ghysels, J., & Van Vlasselaer, E. (2008). Child well-being in Flanders: A multidimensional account. *Social Indicators Research, 89*(2), 283–304.

Gillison, F., Standage, M., & Skevington, S. (2008). Changes in quality of life and psychological need satisfaction following the transition to secondary school. *British Journal of Educational Psychology, 78*(1), 149–162.

Gilman, R., Huebner, E. S., & Laughlin, J.-E. (2000). A first study of the multidimensional students' life satisfaction scale with adolescents. *Social Indicators Research, 52*(2), 135–160.

Gilman, R., Huebner, E., Tian, L., Park, N., O'Byrne, J., Schiff, M., et al. (2008). Cross-national adolescent multidimensional life satisfaction reports: Analyses of mean scores and response style differences. *Journal of Youth and Adolescence, 37*(2), 142–154.

Harter, S., Waters, P., & Whitesell, N. (1998). Relational self-worth: Differences in perceived worth as a person across interpersonal contexts among adolescents. *Child Development, 69*(3), 756–766.

Hawker, D. S. J., & Boulton, M. J. (2000). Twenty years' research on peer victimization and psychosocial maladjustment: A meta-analytic review of cross-sectional studies. *Journal of Child Psychology and Psychiatry, 41*, 441–455.

Hawkins, J., Guo, J., Hill, K., Battin-Pearson, S., & Abbott, R. (2001). Long-term effects of the Seattle social development intervention on school bonding trajectories. *Applied Developmental Science, 5*(4), 225–236.

Hawkins, J., & Tanaka, Y. (1992). Japanese education: A context for test anxiety. *Anxiety, Stress & Coping: An International Journal, 5*(3), 195–203.

Ho, Y. F., Peng, S. Q., & Chan, S. F. (2001). Authority and learning in Confucian-heritage education: A relational methodological analysis. In C. Y. Chiu, F. Salili, & Y. Y. Hong (Eds.), *Multiple competencies and self-regulated learning: Implications for multicultural education* (pp. 29–47). Greenwich, CT: Information Age.

Huang, L., Yan, H., Chen, Q., Zhang, X., & Li, H. (2006). Correlative analysis of psychological health status and personality characteristics of grade three teachers of senior high school. *Chinese Journal of Clinical Psychology, 14*(5), 518–519.

Hughes, J., & Kwok, O. (2006). Classroom engagement mediates the effect of teacher–student support on elementary students' peer acceptance: A prospective analysis. *Journal of School Psychology, 43*(6), 465–480.

Jimerson, S., Campos, E., & Greif, J. (2003). Toward an understanding of definitions and measures of school engagement and related terms. *California School Psychologist, 8*, 7–27.

Johnson, M., Crosnoe, R., & Thaden, L. (2006). Gendered patterns in adolescents' school attachment. *Social Psychology Quarterly, 69*(3), 284–295.

Judge, T., Thoresen, C., Bono, J., & Patton, G. (2001). The job satisfaction-job performance relationship: A qualitative and quantitative review. *Psychological Bulletin, 127*(3), 376–407.

Juon, H., Nam, J., & Ensminger, M. (1994). Epidemiology of suicidal behavior among Korean adolescents. *Journal of Child Psychology and Psychiatry, 35*(4), 663–676.

Karin Natvig, G., Albrektsen, G., & Qvarnstrom, U. (2001). Psychosomatic symptoms among victims of school bullying. *Journal of Health Psychology, 6*(4), 365–377.

Koo, H., Kwak, K., & Smith, P. (2008). Victimization in Korean schools: The nature, incidence, and distinctive features of Korean bullying or wang-ta. *Journal of School Violence, 7*(4), 119–139.

Ladd, G. (2006). Peer rejection, aggressive or withdrawn behavior, and psychological maladjustment from ages 5 to 12: An examination of four predictive models. *Child Development, 77*(4), 822–846.

LaRusso, M., Romer, D., & Selman, R. (2008). Teachers as builders of respectful school climates: Implications for adolescent drug use norms and depressive symptoms in high school. *Journal of Youth and Adolescence, 37*(4), 386–398.

Lee, M., Lee, Y., Yen, L., Lin, M., & Lue, B. (1990). Reliability and validity of using a brief psychiatric symptom rating scale in clinical practice. *Journal of the Formosan Medical Association, 89*, 1081–1087.

Lee, S. (2007). The shaping of a gendered school: A case study. *Formosan Education and Society, 13*, 121–152.

Lee, S., Tsang, A., & Kwok, K. (2007). Stress and mental disorders in a representative sample of teachers during education reform in Hong Kong. *Journal of Psychology in Chinese Societies, 8*(2), 159–178.

Lin, H., Tang, T., Yen, J., Ko, C., Huang, C., Liu, S., et al. (2008). Depression and its association with self-esteem, family, peer and school factors in a population of 9586 adolescents in southern Taiwan. *Psychiatry and Clinical Neurosciences, 62*(4), 412–420.

Liu, C. H. (2004). *A study on the relationships among the personality traits and job satisfaction for the professional subject teachers of public industrial vocational senior high school in Taiwan.* Unpublished Master's thesis, National Changhua University of Education, Taiwan.

Liu, X., Tein, J., Zhao, Z., & Sandler, I. (2005). Suicidality and correlates among rural adolescents of China. *Journal of Adolescent Health, 37*(6), 443–451.

Locker, J., & Cropley, M. (2004). Anxiety, depression and self-esteem in secondary school children: An investigation into the impact of standard assessment tests (SATs) and other important school examinations. *School Psychology International, 25*(3), 333–345.

Lu, L. (2008). The individual-oriented and social-oriented Chinese bicultural self: Testing the theory. *Journal of Social Psychology, 148*(3), 347–373.

Lu, Y. (2007). Perceptions of organizational politics' influences on teachers' job satisfaction and burnout. *Chinese Journal of Clinical Psychology, 15*(4), 376–377.

Lubbers, M., Van Der Werf, M., Snijders, T., Creemers, B., & Kuyper, H. (2006). The impact of peer relations on academic progress in junior high. *Journal of School Psychology, 44*(6), 491–512.

Maddox, S., & Prinz, R. (2003). School bonding in children and adolescents: Conceptualization, assessment, and associated variables. *Clinical Child and Family Psychology Review, 6*(1), 31–49.

Mahon, N., Yarcheski, A., Yarcheski, T., Cannella, B., & Hanks, M. (2006). A meta-analytic study of predictors for loneliness during adolescence. *Nursing Research, 55*(5), 308–315.

McDougall, P., Hymel, S., Vaillancourt, T., & Mercer, L. (2001). The consequences of childhood peer rejection. In M. R. Leary (Ed.), *Interpersonal rejection* (pp. 213–247). New York, NY: Oxford University Press.

Milfont, T., Denny, S., Ameratunga, S., Robinson, E., & Merry, S. (2008). Burnout and wellbeing: Testing the Copenhagen burnout inventory in New Zealand teachers. *Social Indicators Research, 89*(1), 169–177.

Moriana, J., & Herruzo, J. (2006). Variables related to psychiatric sick leave taken by Spanish secondary school teachers. *Work & Stress, 20*(3), 259–271.

Murray, C., & Greenberg, M. (2001). Relationships with teachers and bonds with school: Social emotional adjustment correlates for children with and without disabilities. *Psychology in the Schools, 38*(1), 25–41.

Nelson, R., & DeBacker, T. (2008). Achievement motivation in adolescents: The role of peer climate and best friends. *Journal of Experimental Education, 76*(2), 170–189.

Okun, M. A., Braver, M. W., & Weir, R. M. (1990). Grade level differences in school satisfaction. *Social Indicators Research, 22*, 419–427.

Park, N., & Huebner, E. S. (2005). A cross-cultural study of the levels and correlates of life satisfaction among adolescents. *Journal of Cross-Cultural Psychology, 36*(4), 444–456.

Pedersen, S., Vitaro, F., Barker, E., & Borge, A. (2007). The timing of middle-childhood peer rejection and friendship: Linking early behavior to early-adolescent adjustment. *Child Development, 78*(4), 1037–1051.

Polce-Lynch, M., Myers, B., Kliewer, W., & Kilmartin, C. (2001). Adolescent self-esteem and gender: Exploring relations to sexual harassment, body image, media influence, and motional expression. *Journal of Youth and Adolescence, 30*(2), 225–244.

Raudenbush, S. W., & Bryk, A. S. (2002). *Hierarchical linear models: Applications and data analysis methods*. Thousand Oaks: Sage.

Roeser, R., & Eccles, J. (1998). Adolescents' perceptions of middle school: Relation to longitudinal changes in academic and psychological adjustment. *Journal of Research on Adolescence, 8*(1), 123–158.

Rowe, F., Stewart, D., & Patterson, C. (2007). Promoting school connectedness through whole school approaches. *Health Education, 107*(6), 524–542.

Santavirta, N., Solovieva, S., & Theorell, T. (2007). The association between job strain and emotional exhaustion in a cohort of 1,028 Finnish teachers. *British Journal of Educational Psychology, 77*(1), 213–228.

Simons-Morton, B., Crump, A., Haynie, D., & Saylor, K. (1999). Student-school bonding and adolescent problem behavior. *Health Education Research, 14*(1), 99–107.

Skinner, E., Furrer, C., Marchand, G., & Kindermann, T. (2008). Engagement and disaffection in the classroom: Part of a larger motivational dynamic? *Journal of Educational Psychology, 100*(4), 765–781.

Taiwan Ministry of Education. (2006). *Education in Taiwan, 2006*. Taipei: Author.

van der Linden, D., Keijsers, G., Eling, P., & van Schaijk, R. (2005). Work stress and attentional difficulties: An initial study on burnout and cognitive failures. *Work & Stress, 19*(1), 23–36.

Verkuyen, M., & Thijs, J. (2002). School satisfaction of elementary school children: The role of performance, peer relations, ethnicity and gender. *Social Indicators Research, 59*(2), 203–228.

Wei, H. S., Chang, H. Y., & Chen, J. K. (2006). *Taichung city youth life conditions survey*. Taichung: Children's Bureau.

Wei, H. S., & Chen, J. K. (2009). Social withdrawal, peer rejection and victimization: An examination of path models. *Journal of School Violence, 8*(1), 18–28.

Wei, H., Jonson-Reid, M., & Tsao, H. (2007). Bullying and victimization among Taiwanese 7th graders: A multi-method assessment. *School Psychology International, 28*(4), 479–500.

Wei, H., & Williams, J. (2004). Relationship between peer victimization and school adjustment in sixth-grade students: Investigating mediation effects. *Violence and Victims, 19*(5), 557–571.

Wentzel, K. (2003). Sociometric status and adjustment in middle school: A longitudinal study. *The Journal of Early Adolescence, 23*(1), 5–28.

Wong, D., Lok, D., Lo, T., & Ma, S. (2008). School bullying among Hong Kong Chinese primary schoolchildren. *Youth & Society, 40*(1), 35–54.

Wu, S. (2002). Filling the pot or lighting the fire? Cultural variations in conceptions of pedagogy. *Teaching in Higher Education, 7*(4), 387–395.

Xing, L., Huang, X., Huang, H., Sanchez, K., & Ye, R. (2005). Middle school students' parent-related test anxiety: Comparisons between United States and China. *Chinese Mental Health Journal, 19*(8), 509–512.

You, S., Furlong, M., Felix, E., Sharkey, J., Tanigawa, D., & Green, J. (2008). Relations among school connectedness, hope, life satisfaction, and bully victimization. *Psychology in the Schools, 45*(5), 446–460.

Soc Indic Res (2010) 95:437–453
DOI 10.1007/s11205-009-9530-x

Children's Resilience-Related Beliefs as a Predictor of Positive Child Development in the Face of Adversities: Implications for Interventions to Enhance Children's Quality of Life

Tak-yan Lee · Wai-man Kwong · Chau-kiu Cheung · Michael Ungar · Maria Y. L. Cheung

Accepted: 23 July 2009 / Published online: 13 October 2009

Abstract This paper reports the findings of a longitudinal childhood resilience study which investigated the relationship between resilience-related beliefs and positive child development. Three waves of data collection (T1, T2, and T3) were completed in January 2005, July 2005, and January 2006 with a sample of 843 grade 4 pupils, drawn from six primary schools in Hong Kong, and their parents or guardians. At T1, parents/guardians responded to a 24-item inventory of life adversities affecting their children since birth; at T1 and T3, they completed a 25-item *Parental Assessment of Child's Habit*, which provided parental evaluation of children's performance at home and in school. At T1, T2, and T3, children responded to a 58-item *Child and Youth Resilience Measure*, a 9-item scale on *Chinese cultural beliefs about adversity*, and an 11-item *Chinese Resilience Measure for Children and Adolescents in Hong Kong*. Regression analyses, based on linear mixed models, controlling for gender, T1 and T2 scores, personal variables, and random effects of schools, were conducted to test and validate the hypothesis that children's resilience beliefs are predictive of positive child development, and that this predictive relationship is stronger with increasing adversity in children's lives. Implications of these findings for the development of resilience-based interventions to enhance the quality of life of children facing adversities are examined.

An earlier version of this paper was presented at the International Conference on Human Development and the Environment: Advances in Quality of Life Studies. December 12–13, 2008, The Chinese University of Hong Kong, Hong Kong S.A.R., China.

T. Lee (✉) · W. Kwong · C. Cheung
Department of Applied Social Studies, City University of Hong Kong, 83 Tat Chee Avenue, Kowloon, Hong Kong S.A.R., China
e-mail: sstakyan@cityu.edu.hk

M. Ungar
Maritime School of Social Work, Dalhousie University, Halifax, NS B3H 3J5, Canada

M. Y. L. Cheung
Faculty of Social Work, University of Manitoba, Winnipeg, MB R3T 2N2, Canada

Keywords Adversity · Resilience · Positive child development · Behavioral quality of life · Chinese children

1 Introduction

Worrisome social phenomena, such as mental health problems, family violence, school bullying, teenage suicide, and broken families undermine positive child development in Hong Kong (Wong and Lee 2005). To helping professionals, a critical question is how to mitigate potentially harmful effects of these social trends on child development. The concept of resilience was introduced into the mental health field in the 1980s. It gave rise to a new paradigm for mental health practice (Cicchetti 1989; Rutter 1987). Since then, there has been a growing body of research to discern the processes whereby some young people are able to achieve positive development despite exposure to acute and chronic adversities (Howard et al. 1999; Kim-Cohen et al. 2004; Luthar et al. 2000; Myers and Taylor 1998). However, definitional ambiguity remains unresolved (Luthar et al. 2000; Ungar 2008). The term was given multiple uses (Kirby and Fraser 1997). Masten et al. (1990) defined resilience as a "process of, or capacity for, or the outcome of successful adaptation despite challenging and threatening circumstances" (p. 426). Werner and Smith (1982) considered resilience as the capacity to moderate internal (physiological) vulnerabilities (e.g., stress) as well as external stressors (e.g., family discord). Sagor (1996) likened resilience to an antibody that enabled children to ward off formidable attackers that might stop healthy development even among the most seemingly resourceful youth. It appears that resilience is not a single construct but a constellation of complex processes associated with discrete aspects of health (Gordon and Song 1994).

2 Resilience as a Culturally Embedded and Contextually Sensitive Phenomenon

The resilience construct has gone through several conceptual revisions, beginning with a focus on the individual—traits, characteristics, capacities, abilities, and internal resources—and later evolving into an ecological framework, seeing resilience as a product of the interactions between and among external risk factors, protective factors, and a person's internal resources, with protective processes mitigating harmful effects on children to differing extents depending on the nature of risks (Luthar et al. 2000). However, adopting the ecological perspective necessarily presupposes certain entities as adversities, risk factors, and protective factors, and embraces certain normative judgment of what constitutes outcomes that are indicative of resilience. Given unresolved definitional ambiguities, a large and inconsistent set of variables have been used to study young people growing up under adversity, resulting in inconclusive research findings. Lately, there has been a growing critique of the ecological view of resilience and an emerging awareness of the need to incorporate culture and diversity into the study of risk and resilience (Arrington and Wilson 2000; Ungar 2004, 2008).

To account for cultural and contextual specificity regarding how resilience is expressed, Ungar (2004) advances a constructionist interpretation of resilience as:

> the outcome of negotiation between individuals and their environments to maintain self-definition as healthy … [and] resilience is successful negotiation by individuals for health resources, with success depending for its definition on the reciprocity

individuals experience between themselves and the social constructions of well-being that shape their interpretations of their health status (p. 352).

Central to such an interpretation of resilience is a person's construction of the meaning of adversity and what s/he perceives to be behavioral options. Thus, even the most vulnerable youth may access inner resources such as self-esteem, attachment, and sense of belonging despite performing what may generally be perceived as delinquent and maladjusted behaviors (Ungar and Teram 2000).

Qualitative findings of an international study of childhood resilience, conducted at 14 research sites in eleven countries/regions (Ungar et al. 2007), point to a culturally embedded and contextually sensitive understanding of the phenomenon of resilience, in that childhood resilience is about how young people navigate "unique and culturally embedded pathways to health in the face of adversity" (p. 307). This led to a definition of resilience as "both the capacity of individuals to navigate their way [through these tensions] to health-sustaining resources...and a condition of the individual's family, community and culture to provide these health resources and experiences in culturally meaningful way" (Ungar 2008, p. 225). Seen in this light, the interactions between risk factors and protective factors in the ecological model of resilience can be conceptualized as a dynamic convergence of tensions. Outcomes associated with resilience and the processes which mitigate risk and contribute to well-being are dependent upon how people resolve these tensions to attain healthy functioning, acknowledging that the latter is a culturally embedded and context specific normative judgment and may not align with the person's subjective point of view (Ungar 2004).

3 Cultural Beliefs and Resilience

In a scenario where a young person grows up in a home environment impacted by poverty, social discrimination, domestic violence, troubled parents, and/or a distressed parental marriage, the ecological view regards resilience as the resulting interaction between the individual's personal qualities that are predictive of positive development and the burden imposed on him/her by complex ecological systems, not the least of which is the child's immediate family (Lerner 2006). Resilience is the outcome, but the interaction leading to it is a 'black box'.

Ungar's (2004) constructionist conceptualization of resilience refocuses on the individual, not in terms of personal attributes or internal resources, but in terms of agency as well as the significance of culture and context. As a young person navigates his/her way in the face of adversity to find health resources and culturally (and sub-culturally) meaningful experiences, the meaning s/he makes of the adversity and the behavioral options being perceived and considered will influence, if not determine, what action the person will take. We hypothesize that cultural beliefs will significantly influence how people perceive, experience, and approach adversities in life. For instance, a child's individual belief system that has been transgenerationally transmitted will influence which aspects of the child's environment are experienced as most protective. As such, parental expectation for a child to succeed in school may be experienced by the child as a useful psychosocial resource if the family and the society value education and if the child also perceives a successful future as contingent upon his or her school performance (Cross 1998).

In a cross-sectional study, Shek (2004) explores the mitigating effect of positive Chinese cultural beliefs about adversity on adjustment problems and psychological well-being of adolescents in Hong Kong. It was found that stronger endorsement of positive cultural beliefs about adversity was associated with a higher level of positive mental health, better school adjustment, and less problem behaviors, even more so for adolescents facing adversity (such as economic disadvantage). The author suggests that "identification with traditional positive Chinese beliefs on adversity is an important factor for adolescents with economic disadvantage in Hong Kong" (p. 76). A follow-up longitudinal study confirmed this (Shek 2005). The author reasons that "culture plays an important role in defining the problem and behavioral options" (p. 404). For instance, cultural beliefs may shape the degree of optimism and coping patterns of a person experiencing hardship. Further research findings indicate that optimism contributes to successful adjustment in the midst of adversity (Affleck et al. 2001; Floyd 1996, cited in Shek 2004, p. 76). A positive outlook, even if it is no more than "positive illusions", sustains hope in the face of crisis (Walsh 2006).

The significance of belief systems is given even greater prominence in the family resilience literature. Walsh (2006) identifies several key factors that facilitate effective family functioning in the face of adversity. She singles out positive beliefs and values, particularly beliefs about the meaning of adversity and a positive outlook on life, as the core of family resilience: "When we can construct some valuable meanings out of our life struggles, they can become the most powerful options of all" (Walsh 1998, p. 75). In the same vein, McCubbin and McCubbin (1993) note that adjusting to stress is a function of, among other things, the meaning that is ascribed to the stress. Faith, family love, and mutual support help stressed families cope and maintain meaning in spite of lack of control over life circumstances resulting from economic poverty (Vandsburger et al. 2008). A review of family research and conceptual literature has identified positive outlook—an optimistic confidence in overcoming odds—as a prominent characteristic of resilient families (Black and Lobo 2008). A Korean study which sought to clarify and delineate the concept of family resilience concludes that resilient families are those characterized by, among other things, positive outlook and a collective orientation (Lee et al. 2004). Likewise, a cross-sectional study (Coyle et al. 2009) of the nature of family resilience in families affected by parental alcohol abuse lends support to the importance of family beliefs or schemas in influencing a family's ability to problem-solve and cope with stressful events. Family resilience is culturally specific. As Walsh (2006) states:

> How a problem is viewed and how distress is handled vary with different families and cultural norms. How families make sense of a crisis situation and how they endow it with meaning are most crucial for resilience...when hardship or tragedy can be viewed as instructive and can serve as an impetus for growth...[and] the definition and meaning of struggle and adversity is culturally varied" (pp. 66–67).

4 The Study

The foregoing review of the research and theoretical literature on individual and family resilience identifies the presence of a prominent cultural dimension in the most current discourse on resilience, suggesting that cultural beliefs and folk notions supply a person with cognitive resources to cope with adversity. The place of culture in the resilience discourse should be even more significant in Hong Kong because the traditional Chinese culture embraces resilience as a virtue, as evident in the Confucian teaching documented in the Analects (Lun Yü). Researching resilience in the local context should factor in the cultural dimension as a major contextual variable. Indeed, Choi (2003) proposes a model of cultural heritage for understanding adolescent resilience, positing that the development of resilience is a result of cultural heritage that embraces the Chinese value orientation and an ethical orientation.

In this study, we sought to establish the presence of a predictive relationship between resilience beliefs in Chinese culture and childhood resilience. We hypothesized that endorsement of Chinese cultural beliefs that cherish and prize a positive outlook in facing adversities are predictive of positive child development (resilient outcomes). Furthermore, as resilience grows from adversity, such a predictive relationship will be stronger with greater adversities in a child's life.

For this study the focus was on Chinese Primary 4 pupils. There are three reasons for this sample selection. Firstly, pupils who have faced a number of different adversities since infancy would have a higher chance of being identified as being a student at risk during their Primary 4 year (pupils are expected to do their work more independently and face increasing academic demands). Secondly, research shows that behavioral problems among Chinese students typically emerge as early as Primary 4 (Lau et al. 1998). Thirdly, Primary 4 pupils are able to respond to a questionnaire themselves, answering questions about their thoughts, feelings, beliefs, and behaviors, thus making this age group ideal for a study that includes both self-report and parental reports of behavior and attitudes related to resilience.

5 Method

5.1 Participants and Procedures

The data for the present analysis come from a longitudinal study on resilience and behavior of children in Hong Kong. Data are from 843 fourth graders (mean age 9.48 years) and their parents or guardians, collected while the pupils attended one of six primary schools. These six schools are located in five different districts and receive guidance counselor and social work service from a large social service agency. Consent from the school principals was obtained to conduct the study. Pupils responded to the survey three times (T1, T2, and T3) over the course of a year, with 6 month intervals between each survey response. At each wave of data collection, the purpose of the study was mentioned, and the confidentiality of the data collected was repeatedly emphasized to all of the pupils in attendance on the day of testing. The pupils were asked to indicate their wish if they did not want to participate in the study (i.e., "passive" informed consent was obtained from the pupils). All participants responded as a group to all the scales included in the questionnaire, but in a self-administration format. Special arrangements were made to read the questionnaire to pupils who had some learning difficulties. Adequate time was provided for the participants to complete the questionnaire. The questionnaire took roughly 20 35 min to complete. Parents or guardians were invited to respond to the survey twice (T1 and T3) with 12 months between administrations of measures. To encourage the completion and return of questionnaires, an invitation letter and stamped return envelopes were provided. Pupils were requested to bring the questionnaires home for their parents.

Analysis proceeded according to a panel design that matched data from pupils and parents or guardians. Female students constituted 53.3% of the initial T1 sample. At T2, 768 pupils from the original sample, who could be identified as having participated at T1, responded to the survey (response rate: 91.1%). At T3, 731 parents or guardians, who could be identified as having completed the questionnaire at T1 and whose children followed through with the T3 survey, participated in the survey again. The attrition rate was 13.3%.

These 731 matched pairs constituted the final sample for the study. The two attrition rates compare favorably with previous studies (e.g., DuBois et al. 1994; Shek and Lee 2007).

5.2 Instruments

5.2.1 The Parental Assessment of Child's Habit Scale

The *Parental Assessment of Child's Habit Scale* was specifically developed for the study. Items were gathered from social workers who work with children and their families. The scale includes two dimensions: (1) a comprehensive coverage of bio-psycho-social aspects of habits in general; and (2) habits displaying unfavorable behaviors found in the local context. Items of physical habits were related to diet, physical exercise, sleep, and personal hygiene. Psychological habits were related to self-review and problem solving. Habits within the social-emotional domain were related to schoolwork, leisure activity, getting along well with the family, getting along well with friends, and studying. Fourteen items were included in the behavioral habit sub-scale as follows: indulgence in videos, indulgence in computer activity, eating junk food, eating or drinking excessively, staying in bed too long, loss of temper, drinking alcohol, smoking, abusing substances, indulgence in gambling, lying, being late, procrastination, and shirking responsibility.

The anchors for the 1–10 score were set at two extremes from 'very bad' to 'very good', 'never' or 'seldom' to 'frequent' and/or 'consistent'. For the sub-scale on general habits, the minimum score is 11 and the maximum is 110. The results at T3 show parental assessment tends to be on the positive side (mean = 77.26; SD = 17.032). For the sub-scale on behavioral habits, the minimum score is 14 and the maximum is 140. The result of parental assessment is on the low end (mean = 44.02; SD = 15.682). The composite habit scale (25 items in two dimensions) represents the parental evaluation of the child's positive development, covering general bio-psycho-social habits and habits of engaging in specific unfavorable behaviors. The *Parental Assessment of Child's Habit Scale* attained reliability (α) coefficients of .859 and .890 for T1 and T3 (second administration), respectively.

5.2.2 Assessment of Adversity

The parents or guardians were invited to respond to three adversity measures at T1 on a 0–2 frequency scale (never, occasionally, often): (1) adversity when the child was 0–2 years old (7 items); (2) adversity since the child's second birth day (13 items); and (3) overall adversity since the child's birth (4 items). The assessment of adversity was the average of standard scores of 24 items. To assess adversity from birth to 2 years of age, seven items were assessed: (1) the child's habit making the mother feel distressed; (2) the child not living with the mother; (3) the child's birth causing distress in the family; (4) the father's absence from the home due to work; (5) parental conflict; (6) the child's premature birth; and (7) the child having younger siblings. To assess adversity since the child's second birthday, thirteen items were developed: (1) father away for long periods of time; (2) mother away for long periods of time; (3) father chronically ill; (4) mother chronically ill; (5) mother working long hours; (6) family members experiencing conflict; (7) child experiencing conflict with family members; (8) elder siblings running away; (9) sibling's death; (10) parental separation; (11) having a step father or mother; (12) father's death; and (13) mother's death. To assess overall patterns of adversity since birth, four items were included in the questionnaire: (1) child having a chronic illness; (2) child living in a children's home; (3) family member abusing substances; and (4) a parent suffering from serious illness.

5.2.3 Assessment of Resilience Beliefs

In contrast to the parent's or guardian's report of the child's adversity and habits, the child indicated his or her resilience-related beliefs on two locally developed five-point scales. Firstly, respondents were given the *Chinese Resilience Measure for Children and Adolescents in Hong Kong*, constructed by Lee et al. (2006). There are eleven items in this scale: (1) I believe that as a person, one should live with human feelings; (2) I believe that as a person, one should be reasonable; (3) If one wants to succeed, he/she needs the support from family; (4) Even though life may become worse tomorrow, I would still live on; (5) I am proud to be Hong Kong people; (6) We should be responsible for family members, however difficult, even it would mean going beyond our limit; (7) Although poverty, misfortune, and illness may be my destiny, I am still not afraid; (8) Despite difficulties, people should live with integrity, relying on self rather than others; (9) When life isn't good, take a break and cast it out of one's mind; (10) I believe that as a person, one needs to abide by law; and (11) People should find a way to forgive and let go. It was subsequently found in the data analysis that four items (items 4, 6, 7 and 10), measuring across four domains, were predictive of positive child development (see Table 1). Secondly, respondents responded to the scale on *Chinese cultural beliefs about adversity*. This scale was developed by a group of psychologists and social workers in Hong Kong (Shek 2004, 2005; Shek et al. 2003). There are nine items in this scale as follows: (1) Hardship increases stature; (2) Whether a life is good or bad depends on fate; (3) When there is a will, there is a way; (4) If you work hard enough, you can turn an iron rod into a needle; (5) Poverty stifles ambition; (6) Diligence is an important factor to overcome poverty; (7) Man is the master of his own fate; (8) Happy is he who is contented; and (9) Man is not born to greatness, he achieves it by his own effort. While items 2 and 5 were concerned with negative cultural beliefs, the rest of the items can be regarded as items assessing positive cultural beliefs. Since children might have difficulty in understanding the meanings embedded in the original classical Chinese expressions, all items were listed with the equivalent meaning in plain Chinese language. No item was found to be predictive of positive child development.

5.2.4 Child and Youth Resilience Measure (CYRM)

This scale consists of resilience belief statements adapted from a measure constructed during a multi-national study of childhood resilience in eleven countries (Ungar 2008; Ungar et al. 2008). Results show that the CYRM is a reliable measure of concepts related to resilience in all sites, with items relating to one another as hypothesized in an ecological model. Specifically the subscales of individual (23 items), relational (7 items), community (15 items) and cultural (12 items) factors all showed good reliability (Cronbach alphas .84, .66, .79, .71, respectively). However, no item was found to be predictive of positive child development.

5.2.5 Measure of Acquiescence

Respondents may give a high rating to measures regardless of the contents of the measures used in the study. For control purposes in predictive analysis, a measure of acquiescence, meaning the tendency of high rating, was the average of all items. This calculation was done for both the child and the parent/guardian at all waves.

Table 1 Means and standard deviations

Variable	Scoring	Wave 1 *M*	Wave 3 *M*	Wave 1 SD	Wave 3 SD
Habit	1–10	7.17	7.20	1.10	1.06
Diet	1–10	6.63	6.64	2.31	2.11
Schoolwork	1–10	6.02	6.28	2.19	2.06
Physical exercise	1–10	5.64	5.68	2.50	2.38
Leisure activity	1–10	6.17	6.20	2.27	2.21
Getting along well with the family	1–10	7.81	7.88	3.13	1.86
Getting along well with friends	1–10	7.36	7.52	1.98	1.88
Sleep	1–10	7.67	7.40	2.16	2.02
Personal hygiene	1–10	7.42	7.50	1.95	1.87
Studying	1–10	6.21	6.24	2.21	2.07
Self-review	1–10	5.49	5.67	2.27	2.15
Problem solving	1–10	6.11	6.12	2.25	2.03
Indulgence in videos	1–10	5.26	5.26	2.75	2.66
Indulgence in computer activity	1–10	4.51	5.03	2.74	2.73
Eating junk food	1–10	5.96	5.71	2.28	2.19
Eating or drinking excessively	1–10	4.10	4.14	2.37	2.24
Staying in bed too long	1–10	4.47	4.42	2.78	2.66
Loss of temper	1–10	5.39	5.27	2.55	2.41
Drinking alcohol	1–10	1.13	1.15	0.77	0.73
Smoking	1–10	1.07	1.08	0.69	0.68
Abusing substances	1–10	1.08	1.05	0.66	0.49
Indulgence in gambling	1–10	1.10	1.11	0.72	0.71
Lying	1–10	3.27	3.29	2.15	2.03
Being late	1–10	1.75	1.82	1.51	1.54
Procrastination	1–10	4.45	4.31	2.69	2.57
Shirking responsibility	1–10	3.59	3.44	2.40	2.30
Adversity during age 0–2	Sum	2.70		1.92	
Child's habit making the mother feel distressed	0–2	0.76		0.66	
Child not living with the mother	0–2	0.29		0.61	
Child's birth causing distress in the family	0–2	0.29		0.53	
Father's absence from the home due to work	0–2	0.80		0.80	
Parental conflict	0–2	0.35		0.56	
Child's premature birth	0–2	0.10		0.30	
Child's having younger siblings	0–2	0.21		0.41	
Adversity since age 2	Sum	1.91		1.93	
Father away for long periods of time	0–2	0.52		0.73	
Mother away for long periods of time	0–2	0.19		0.49	
Father chronically ill	0–2	0.08		0.33	
Mother chronically ill	0–2	0.10		0.37	
Mother working long hours	0–2	0.43		0.67	

Table 1 continued

Variable	Scoring	Wave 1 *M*	Wave 3 *M*	Wave 1 SD	Wave 3 SD
Family members experiencing conflict	0–2	0.27		0.50	
Child experiencing conflict with family members	0–2	0.15		0.38	
Elder siblings running away	0–2	0.04		0.19	
Sibling's death	0–2	0.01		0.08	
Parental separation	0–2	0.09		0.29	
Having a step father or mother	0–2	0.02		0.15	
Father's death	0–2	0.02		0.14	
Mother's death	0–2	0.01		0.08	
Adversity since birth	Sum	0.25		0.58	
Child having a chronic illness	0–2	0.16		0.40	
Child living in a children's home	0–2	0.03		0.19	
Family member abusing substances	0–2	0.03		0.19	
A parent suffering from serious illness	0–2	0.05		0.25	
Resilient belief	1–5	4.25	4.17	0.72	0.72
Even though life may become worse tomorrow, I would still live on	1–5	4.32	4.21	0.97	1.00
We should be responsible for family members, however difficult, even it would mean going beyond our limit	1–5	4.29	4.17	1.07	0.99
Although poverty, misfortune, and illness may be my destiny, I am still not afraid	1–5	4.18	4.06	1.01	1.00
I believe that as a person, one needs to abide by law	1–5	4.22	4.25	1.01	0.99

6 Results

The distribution of status of 731 adult respondents at T3 was as follows: fathers 20.8%; mothers 70.1%; relatives 3.1%; male guardians 0.8%; female guardians 3.1%; and missing 1.9%. Among the 731 matched pupils, the mean age was 10.63 years. The age composition was as follows: pupils aged 10 years (51.7%); 11 years (31.6%); 12 years (8.8%); 13 years (2.4%); 14 years (0.8%); 16 years (0.1%); and 4.6% of pupils did not report their age.

Linear regression analysis was conducted on the panel data using three different measures, i.e., *Child and Youth Resilience Measure* (54-item), *Chinese cultural beliefs about adversity* (9-item), and *Chinese Resilience Measure for Children and Adolescents in Hong Kong* (11-items); no significant results were obtained. However, four items of the *Chinese Resilience Measure for Children and Adolescents in Hong Kong* (items 4, 6, 7 and 10), measuring across four domains, were predictive of a child's favorable habits. These items are: Even though life may become worse tomorrow, I would still live on; We should be responsible for family members, however difficult, even it would mean going beyond our limit; Although poverty, misfortune, and illness may be my destiny, I am still not afraid; and I believe that as a person, one needs to abide by law. The four-item composite measure of the child's resilience beliefs, with reliability coefficients of .670 and .678 for T1 and T2, respectively, was used for subsequent analysis.

Linear regression analysis was performed on the panel data to determine a mixed-effect model; the latter was required to estimate and thereby adjust for random variations among the six schools (Hedeker et al. 1994). The analysis employed a mixed procedure using SPSS, taking standard scores of the variables involved to display standardized effects (Peugh and Enders 2005). The *main effect* of resilience-related beliefs on positive child development addresses Hypothesis 1, and is measured by the *Parental Assessment of Child's Habit Scale*. The *interaction effect*, due to the interplay between adversity and resilience-related beliefs, addresses Hypotheses 2, that is, whether the positive effect of resilience-related beliefs on child development is stronger with greater adversities in children's lives.

In addition, a sensitivity analysis (Atkins 2005) estimated variations in the *main effects* and *interaction effects* due to gender, prior habits and behavioral problems of the child, and the school of the child. This analysis sought to predict a child's favorable habits based upon his/her earlier resilience-related beliefs within the context of each of four versions of, or ways of framing, adversity, i.e., adversity during age 0–2; adversity since age 2; adversity since birth; and the total of all these three adversity measures. Conducting four separate analyses minimized the problems of multicollinearity among the child's resilience-related beliefs in the two waves and the four versions of adversity.

The parental assessment on the child's development yielded an overall score for the 25 items on the child's general habits and behavioral habits. On the average, the overall score was on the positive side for the two waves of data at T1 & T3 ($M = 7.17$ & 7.20, see Table 1). Among these 25 items, "getting along well with the family" received the most positive rating ($M = 7.81$ & 7.88), whilst "smoking" and "substance abuse" were very rare, with the overall scores close to the lowest point on the scale (see Table 1). Adversity tended to be rare in every aspect (see Table 1). For the period between birth and 2 years of age, the adversity score was highest for the following items: "distress caused by the child's habits" ($M = 0.76$) and "father's absence from the home due to work" ($M = 0.80$). The child's resilience belief was, on average, rather high in both waves ($M = 4.25$ & 4.17).

Analysis of the child's habits in Wave 3, as reported by parent or guardian, generated findings to support both Hypotheses 1 and 2 (see Tables 2, 3). First, the child's resilience reflected in either Wave 1 or Wave 2 data showed a significant positive effect on the child's Wave 3 habits ($\beta = .107$ to $.119$). Second, the interaction between adversity and

Table 2 Standardized effects of wave 1 resilience belief and others on wave 3 habit

Measure	Adversity at age 0–2	Adversity since age 2	Adversity since birth	Adversity: overall
Female	.071*	.068*	.070*	.070*
Adversity	−.088**	−.102**	−.093**	−.117**
Habit, wave 1	.570***	.560***	.564***	.562***
Child's acquiescence, wave 1	.005	.013	.010	.009
Mother's acquiescence, wave 1	−.023	−.021	−.017	−.022
Resilience belief at wave 1	.111**	.107*	.114**	.111**
Resilience belief at wave 1 × adversity	.057#	.059#	.036	.086*
R^2	.415	.417	.415	.419
R^2 due to school	.000	.000	.000	.000

# $p < .10$. * $p < .01$. ** $p < .001$. *** $p < .0001$

Table 3 Standardized effects of wave 2 resilience belief and others on wave 3 habit

Measure	Adversity at age 0–2	Adversity since age 2	Adversity since birth	Adversity: overall
Female	.059	.061	.060	.062*
Adversity	−.077*	−.087**	−.044	−.091*
Habit, wave 1	.583***	.577***	.596***	.580***
Child's acquiescence, wave 1	.030	.036	.035	.037
Mother's acquiescence, wave 1	−.081*	−.077	−.078*	−.079*
Child's acquiescence, wave 2	−.010	−.008	−.014	−.010
Mother's acquiescence, wave 2	.082*	.080*	.082*	.083**
Resilience belief at wave 2	.111*	.109*	.119*	.107*
Resilience belief at wave 2 × adversity	.092**	.061*	.035	.081*
R^2	.438	.438	.430	.439
R^2 due to school	.001	.002	.002	.002

* $p < .01$. ** $p < .001$. *** $p < .0001$

Table 4 Variation in the main and interaction effects of resilience on wave 3 habit

Source of variation	Adversity at age 0–2	Adversity since age 2	Adversity since birth	Adversity: overall
Wave 1 main effect				
Female	.005	.011	−.002	.018
Habit, wave 1	−.098**	−.062	−.106**	−.083*
School	.000	.000	.000	.000
Wave 1 interaction effect				
Female	.021	−.052	.024	−.003
Habit, wave 1	−.038	−.036	−.046	−.091*
School	.000	.050	.000	.096
Wave 2 main effect				
Female	.032	.042	.026	.021
Habit, wave 1	.017	−.005	−.038	−.009
School	.000	.100	.000	.036
Wave 2 interaction effect				
Female	.057	−.050	.013	−.036
Habit, wave 1	−.078*	−.018	−.015	−.041
School	.000	.000	.000	.122

* $p < .01$. ** $p < .001$. *** $p < .0001$

the child's resilience in either Wave 1 or Wave 2 contributed to a significant positive effect on the child's Wave 3 habits (see Table 3). Such findings were consistent across the eight analyses using resilience belief in different waves and four different versions of adversity. The only exception was that the interaction between the version of adversity "Since the Child's Birth" and the child's resilience in either Wave 1 or Wave 2 did not show a significant effect on the child's Wave 3 habits. Nevertheless, the effect of such an interaction was still positive (0.035, see Table 3). Moreover, a significant positive interaction effect emerged from the analysis that employed the overall adversity, combining various instances of adversity in different periods ($\beta = .086$ & .081). All these effects were net of those of the child's Wave 1 habits, acquiescence, and other background characteristics. Therefore, the main and interaction effects involving the child's resilience belief tended to make a significant change toward favorable habits, by holding prior habits as a constant. Obviously, controlling for prior habits was necessary because of the strong effect of Wave 1 habits on Wave 3 habits ($\beta = .560$ to .596). In addition, adversity displayed a significant negative effect on the child's Wave 3 habits in all analyses, except when using the version of adversity since birth and the child's Wave 2 resilience belief as predictors.

Sensitivity analysis indicated that only 5 significant variations occurred out of the 48 variations examined in the main and interaction effects of the child's resilience beliefs on Wave 3 habits (Table 4). Hence, the main and interaction effects generally held across genders, schools, and levels of prior habits. The exception was that the effects were less positive when prior habits were more favorable. This reduction in effects reflected the ceiling effect, which constrained further improvement in habits when the habits were highly favorable.

7 Discussion

This paper reports data on the predictive relationship between resilience beliefs in Chinese culture—as a protective factor in the resilience discourse—and the positive development of children in Hong Kong. It was expected that children with stronger endorsement of these resilience beliefs would experience more positive life development, and that the predictive relationship would be stronger for children having been exposed to greater adversities.

Results show that those who had a stronger endorsement of Chinese resilience beliefs displayed more favorable habits and less behavioral problems as reported by their parents or guardians. Furthermore, data reveals that children growing up with adversities had similar results, i.e., identification with the resilience beliefs was predictive of a larger number of favorable habits and fewer behavioral problems. As Shek (2002) notes, there are few studies in the resilience literature investigating adversity and resilience in childhood and adolescence in Hong Kong. Our findings are consistent with Shek's (2004) findings on the relationship between Chinese beliefs about adversity and adolescent adjustment.

Results consistently support hypotheses regarding the contribution of the child's resilience to behavioral quality of life. With reference to the first hypothesis, the present study shows that the child's resilience belief fosters the child's positive child development. Furthermore, the present findings suggest that the children with personal or family adversity will have a poorer quality of life and demonstrate less favorable habits and more behavioral problems as perceived by the parent. Regarding the second hypothesis, the present study again shows that the child's resilience belief fosters the child's favorable habits, as reported by the parent, particularly in the presence of adversity.

Results of this study are significant in that they demonstrate the predictive, facilitating, and healing effects of the child's resilience belief, comprising only four items, on the parent's evaluation of behavior quality of life. This study demonstrates the value of resilience beliefs embedded in Chinese culture that children acquire through cultural transmission, four of which were identified as significant in mitigating harmful effects of adversity on child development. Endorsement of these resilience beliefs was predictive of positive development, as indicated by more favorable habits and less problem behaviors reported by their parents or guardians 6 months later. This effect holds even after controlling for reported favorable habits and problem behaviors of the child at T1. Hence, the contribution of resilience belief is likely to be causal, and is useful for the early detection and prevention of unfavorable habits and problem behaviors. It is unlikely that the effect reflects a co-occurrence of belief and behavior at the same time. Such co-occurrence will be too momentary as to be useful for designing preventive intervention. As the present findings suggest that the contribution of resilience belief to positive development is likely to be causal, it is useful for preventive interventions to foster these resilience beliefs among vulnerable groups of children.

In addition to having a main effect on positive development, these resilience beliefs also exert a moderating effect that is contingent on the degree of adversity that the child has been exposed to. This moderating effect is reminiscent of the buffering or stress-attenuating effect to counter stress. This confirms the value of resilience beliefs with regard to living well despite adversity; in other words, resilience beliefs are a cognitive resource contributing to the maintenance of quality of life in the face of adversity. Moreover, only a small set of resilience beliefs, as identified in this study, will predispose children to the kind of positive outlook that enables them to navigate their way to the attainment of positive development despite adversities. Arguably, the construction of resilience beliefs need not be a highly complicated matter. A limited set of beliefs appears to be sufficient for these children to achieve resilience. Such a parsimonious concept of resilience belief clearly affirms and refines the focus on research and practice to foster the child's behavioral quality of life.

However, it is also noteworthy that the mitigating effect of resilience beliefs appeared to be weaker for adversities that a child was exposed to since birth. Despite the notable contribution of resilience belief, the effect on the version of adversity since the child's birth was less beneficial than the effects on other versions of adversity. Adversity experienced since the child's birth is obviously more chronic and resistant to change than that which begins at a later age and is experienced for shorter duration. Hence, the findings simply indicate that resilience belief is less effective for healing more chronic or severe adversity. Furthermore, the cross-informant relationship of parent and child effectively minimizes bias and increases the validity of our findings.

Few studies have been conducted to examine the possible mediating factors involved in the relationship between endorsement of resilience beliefs and childhood adjustment. Research efforts along this line will facilitate a better understanding of what helps children navigate their lives towards positive development in the face of adversities. One such research area is the relationship between resilience beliefs and the degree of optimism, and how an optimistic outlook shapes a child's coping pattern in the face of personal and family hardship, as optimism is a crucial factor contributing to successful adjustment in the midst of adversity (Affleck et al. 2001; Reivich and Shatté 2002; Shatté et al. 2003).

We acknowledge that a single study is unable to offer conclusive findings with certainty. The present study is notably limited by the fact that it only studied primary school students in Hong Kong, and that it adopted a correlational design. These two limitations restrict the generalizability of the present findings. Possibly, the four resilience ideas that constituted children's resilience belief may be pertinent only to primary school children in Hong Kong. Hence, the urban, industrialized, and somewhat westernized and affluent setting of Hong Kong may be responsible for the significance of the four resilience ideas. Replication in other contexts is necessary.

Despite these limitations, given the present findings, it is clear that there are factors to be found among Hong Kong primary school children that mitigate adversity. Cultivating a child's resilience belief over a prolonged period of time is likely to produce better quality of life. A child's resilience belief is not, however, a panacea, especially in tackling chronic adversity. His/her personal resources are likely to be limited in the effective promotion of behavioral quality of life. Structural changes that affect the manifestation of the child's inner resources remain critical to conceptualizations of resilience (Ungar 2008). In this regard, our research suggests only one aspect of resilience: the contextually specific beliefs of a child. Nonetheless, it is clear that there are cognitive resources that help primary school children in Hong Kong to navigate their lives toward positive development in the face of adversities. Cultivating resilience beliefs in children furnishes them with the cognitive resources for resisting hardships in life.

8 Implications

In Hong Kong, preventive interventions have moved toward the direction of early identification of at-risk young people and developing resilience-based primary and secondary prevention, mostly in school-settings, that increase their capacity for resisting adversities and enhance their competencies to acquire resources for positive development. Weinreb's (1997) findings show that resilience can shore up protective mechanisms in young children. Research on risk and resilience in childhood (Clark 1995; Connell et al. 1994; Grossman et al. 1992; Guetzloe 1994; Rak and Patterson 1996; Sagor 1996; Weinreb 1997) holds the promise of informing preventive measures to mitigate harmful effects of adversities on young people. However, as definitions of success and healthy functioning are social constructions that are culturally and contextually embedded, and reflect the values of a population, Ungar (2004) cautions that the factors predicting positive growth under adversity need to be meaningful to young people who are the target population of resilience-based intervention programs. The Understanding Adolescents Project (UAP) is an exemplar of large scale, school-based, preventive programs that are premised on early risk identification and resilience-based intervention (Lee et al. 2007; Wong and Lee 2005). The project seeks to foster in children three key elements that contribute to childhood resilience: (a) personal competence; (b) a sense of belonging; and (c) a sense of optimism. The present study furnishes empirical support to inject resilience beliefs already embedded in Chinese culture into intervention designs, thus providing cognitive resources for young people—and also their families—that reframe or give positive meanings to hardship and difficulties in life. That said, even large-scale programmatic effort will not be sufficient to raise a generation of young people who are optimistic about their future. "Quality of Life" is a far more embracing concept than a conceptualization of resilience that promises grand outcomes for young people in terms of being hardy, optimistic, and able to navigate their lives toward positive development.

The resilience discourse on what constitutes the outcome of resilience has evolved from a focus on a reduction of negative outcome to a focus on positive development, such as psychological well-being and a positive outlook—and this overlaps with the concept of quality of life (QOL). The latter covers the domains of emotional, material, physical, social, and productive well-being (Felce and Perry 1995; Wallander et al. 2001). It is important to note that the quality of family environment and experience makes significant contributions to children's quality of life. Indeed, family is considered the most important source of social capital (Putnam 1995). In a review of the studies on quality of life, Shek et al. (2005) note that QOL research with reference to the family system ("family quality of life") is not substantial. Two dimensions of the concept of "family quality of life" are identified: (a) systemic family functioning (e.g., family climate and communication among family members); and (b) dyadic relationships within the family (Siu and Shek 2005). These two dimensions of "family quality of life" influence the resilience of family members when facing adversity—and this overlaps with the concept of family resilience. The more children experience better family quality of life, the more resilient they will be in the face of adversity.

Acknowledgments The work described in this paper was fully supported by a grant from the Research Grants Council of the Hong Kong Special Administrative Region, China [Project No. (RGC Ref. No.), CityU 1318/04H]. The authors wish to thank Wong Ying for her assistance in collecting the data.

References

Affleck, G., Tennen, H., & Apter, A. (2001). Optimism, pessimism, and daily life with chronic illness. In E. C. Chang (Ed.), *Optimism and pessimism: Implications for theory, research, and practice* (pp. 172–200). Washington, DC: American Psychological Association.

Arrington, E. G., & Wilson, M. N. (2000). A re-examination of risk and resilience during adolescence: Incorporating culture and diversity. *Journal of Child and Family Studies, 9*, 221–230.

Atkins, D. C. (2005). Using multilevel models to analyze couple and family treatment data: Basic and advanced issues. *Journal of Family Psychology, 19*, 98–110.

Black, K., & Lobo, M. (2008). A conceptual review of family resilience factors. *Journal of Family Nursing, 14*, 33–55.

Choi, P. Y. W. (2003). Resilience: Beyond skills. In *Proceedings of the conference on resilience: Fostering children's resilience*. Hong Kong: Save Children Fund.

Cicchetti, D. (Ed.). (1989). *The emergence of a discipline: Rochester symposium on developmental pathology* (Vol. 1). Hillsdale, NJ: Lawrence Erlbaum.

Clark, P. (1995). *Risk and resiliency in adolescence: The current status of research on gender differences*. Columbus: Ohio State University.

Connell, J. P., Spencer, M. B., & Aber, J. L. (1994). Educational risk and resilience in African-American youth: Context, self, action, and outcomes in school. *Child Development, 65*, 493–506.

Coyle, J. P., Nochajski, T., Maguin, E., Safyer, A., DeWit, D., & Macdonald, S. (2009). An exploratory study of the nature of family resilience in families affected by parental alcohol abuse. *Journal of Family Issues*. doi:10.1177/0192513x09339478.

Cross, T. L. (1998). Understanding family resiliency from a relational world view. In H. I. McCubbin, E. A. Thompson, A. I. Thompson, & J. E. Fromer (Eds.), *Resiliency in native American and immigrant families* (pp. 143–157). Thousand Oaks, CA: Sage.

DuBois, D. L., Eitel, S. K., & Felner, R. D. (1994). Effects of family environment and parent–child relationships on school adjustment during the transition to early adolescence. *Journal of Marriage and the Family, 56*, 405–414.

Felce, D., & Perry, J. (1995). Quality of life: Its definition and measurement. *Research in Developmental Disabilities, 16*, 51–74.

Gordon, E. W., & Song, L. D. (1994). Variations in the experience of resilience. In M. C. Wang & E. W. Gordon (Eds.), *Educational resilience in inner-city America* (pp. 27–43). Hillsdale: Erlbaum.

Grossman, F. K., Beinashowitz, J., & Anderson, L. (1992). Risk and resilience in young adolescents. *Journal of Youth and Adolescence, 21*, 529–550.

Guetzloe, E. (1994). Risk, resilience, and protection. *Journal of Emotional and Behavioral Problems, 3*, 2–5.

Hedeker, R., Gibbons, R. O., & Flay, B. R. (1994). Random-effect regression models for clustered data with an example from smoking prevention research. *Journal of Consulting and Clinical Psychology, 60*, 757–765.

Howard, S., Dryden, J., & Johnson, B. (1999). Childhood resilience: Review and critique of the literature. *Oxford Review of Education, 25*, 307–323.

Kim-Cohen, J., Moffitt, T. E., Caspi, A., & Taylor, A. (2004). Genetic and environmental processes in young children's resilience and vulnerability to socioeconomic deprivation. *Child Development, 75*, 651–668.

Kirby, L. D., & Fraser, M. W. (1997). Risk and resilience in childhood. In M. W. Fraser (Ed.), *Risk and resilience in childhood: An ecological perspective* (pp. 10–33). Washington, DC: NASW Press.

Lau, S., Siu, C. K. K., & Chik, M. P. Y. (1998). The self-concept development of Chinese primary schoolchildren: A longitudinal study. *Childhood, 5*, 69–97.

Lee, I., Lee, E. O., Kim, H. S., Park, Y. S., Song, M., & Park, Y. H. (2004). Concept development of family resilience: A study of Korean families with a chronically ill child. *Journal of Clinical Nursing, 13*, 636–645.

Lee, T. Y., Kwong, W. M., Ungar, M., & Cheung, M. (2006). *Psychometric properties of the Chinese resilience measures for children and adolescents in Hong Kong*. Paper presented at the 5th international conference on social work in health and mental health, HKSAR, China.

Lee, T. Y., Shek, D. T. L., & Kwong, W. M. (2007). Chinese approaches to understanding and building resilience in at-risk populations. *Child and Adolescent Psychiatric Clinics of North America, 16*, 377–392.

Lerner, R. M. (2006). Resilience as an attribute of the developmental system: Comments on the papers of Professors Masten & Wachs. In B. M. Lester, A. S. Masten, & B. McEwen (Eds.), *Resilience in children* (pp. 40–51). Boston, MA: Blackwell.

Luthar, S. S., Cicchetti, D., & Becker, B. (2000). The construct of resilience: A critical evaluation and guidelines for future work. *Child Development, 71*, 543–562.

Masten, A., Best, K., & Garmezy, N. (1990). Resilience and development: Contributions from the study of children who overcome adversity. *Development and Psychopathology, 2*, 425–444.

McCubbin, M. A., & McCubbin, H. I. (1993). Families coping with illness: The resiliency model of family stress, adjustment, and adaptation. In C. Danielson, B. P. H. Bissell, & P. Winstead-Fry (Eds.), *Families, health, and illness: Perspectives on coping and intervention* (pp. 21–63). St. Louis, MO: Mosby.

Myers, H. F., & Taylor, S. (1998). Family contributions to risk and resilience in African American children. *Journal of Comparative Family Studies, 29*, 215–230.

Peugh, J. L., & Enders, C. K. (2005). Using the SPSS mixed procedure to fit cross-sectional and longitudinal multilevel models. *Educational and Psychological Measurement, 65*, 811–835.

Putnam, R. D. (1995). Bowling alone: America's declining social capital. *Journal of Democracy, 6*, 65–77.

Rak, C. L., & Patterson, L. E. (1996). Promoting resilience in at-risk children. *Journal of Counseling and Development, 74*, 368–373.

Reivich, K., & Shatté, A. (2002). *The resilience factor: 7 Essential skills for overcoming life's inevitable obstacles*. New York: Broadway Books.

Rutter, M. (1987). Psychosocial resilience and protective mechanisms. *American Journal of Orthopsychiatry, 57*, 316–331.

Sagor, R. (1996). Building resiliency in students. *Educational Leadership, 54*, 38–43.

Shatté, A. J., Seligman, M. E. P., Gillham, J. E., & Reivich, K. (2003). The role of positive psychology in child, adolescent, and family development. In R. E. Lerner, D. Wertlieb, & F. Jacobs (Eds.), *Handbook of applied developmental science: Adding value to youth and family development* (pp. 207–226). Thousand Oaks, CA: Sage Publications.

Shek, D. T. L. (2002). The relation of parental qualities to psychological well-being, school adjustment, and problem behavior in Chinese adolescents with economic disadvantage. *American Journal of Family Therapy, 30*, 215–230.

Shek, D. T. L. (2004). Chinese cultural beliefs about adversity: Its relationship to psychological well-being, school adjustment and problem behavior in Hong Kong adolescents with and without economic disadvantage. *Childhood, 11*, 63–80.

Shek, D. T. L. (2005). A longitudinal study of Chinese cultural beliefs about adversity, psychological well-being, delinquency and substance abuse. *Social Indicators Research, 71*, 385–409.

Shek, D. T. L., Chan, Y. K., & Lee, P. S. N. (2005). Quality of life in the global context: A Chinese response. *Social Indicators Research, 71*, 1–10.

Shek, D. T. L., & Lee, T. Y. (2007). Family life quality and emotional quality of life in Chinese adolescents with and without economic disadvantage. *Social Indicators Research, 80*, 393–410.

Shek, D. T. L., Tang, V., Lam, M. C., Lam, C. M., Tsoi, K. W., & Tsang, K. M. (2003). The relationship between Chinese cultural beliefs about adversity and psychological adjustment in Chinese families with economic disadvantage. *American Journal of Family Therapy, 31*, 427–443.

Siu, M. H., & Shek, D. T. L. (2005). Relations between social problem solving and indicators of interpersonal and family well-being among Chinese adolescents in Hong Kong. *Social Indicators Research, 71*, 517–539.

Ungar, M. (2004). A constructionist discourse on resilience: Multiple contexts, multiple realities among at-risk children and youth. *Youth and Society, 35*, 341–365.

Ungar, M. (2008). Resilience across cultures. *British Journal of Social Work, 38*, 218–235.

Ungar, M., Brown, M., Liebenberg, L., Othman, R., Kwong, W. M., Armstrong, M., et al. (2007). Unique pathways to resilience across cultures. *Adolescence, 42*, 287–310.

Ungar, M., Liebenberg, L., Boothroyd, R., Kwong, W. M., Lee, T. Y., Leblanc, J., et al. (2008). The study of youth resilience across cultures: Lessons from a pilot study of measurement development. *Research in Human Development, 5*, 166–180.

Ungar, M., & Teram, E. (2000). Drifting towards mental health: High-risk adolescents and the process of empowerment. *Youth & Society, 32*, 228–252.

Vandsburger, E., Harrigan, M., & Biggerstaff, M. (2008). In spite of all, we make it: Themes of stress and resiliency as told by women in families living in poverty. *Journal of Family Social Work, 11*, 17–35.

Wallander, J. L., Schmitt, M., & Koot, M. H. (2001). Quality of life measurement in children and adolescents: Issues, instruments and applications. *Journal of Clinical Psychology, 57*, 571–585.

Walsh, F. (1998). Beliefs, spirituality, and transcendence: Keys to family resilience. In M. McGoldrick (Ed.), *Re-visioning family therapy: Race, culture, and gender in clinical practice* (pp. 62–77). New York: Guilford Press.

Walsh, F. (2006). *Strengthening family resilience* (2nd ed.). New York: Guilford.

Weinreb, M. L. (1997). Be a resiliency mentor: You may be a lifesaver for a high-risk child. *Young Children, 52*, 14–20.

Werner, E., & Smith, R. (1982). *Vulnerable but invincible*. New York: McGraw Hill.

Wong, K. Y., & Lee, T. Y. (2005). Professional discourse among social workers working with at-risk adolescents in Hong Kong: Risk or resilience? In M. Ungar (Ed.), *Handbook for working with children and youth: Pathways to resilience across cultures and contexts* (pp. 313–327). Thousand Oaks: Sage Publications.

Soc Indic Res (2010) 95:455–474
DOI 10.1007/s11205-009-9531-9

Life Satisfaction, Positive Youth Development, and Problem Behaviour Among Chinese Adolescents in Hong Kong

Rachel C. F. Sun · Daniel T. L. Shek

Accepted: 13 May 2009 / Published online: 10 October 2009

Abstract This paper examines the relationships among life satisfaction, positive youth development, and problem behaviour. A total of 7,975 Secondary One students (4,169 boys and 3,387 girls; with most aged 12) of Chinese ethnicity recruited from 48 schools responded to validated measures of life satisfaction, positive youth development and problem behaviour. While life satisfaction was positively correlated with different measures of positive youth development, these measures were negatively correlated with measures of substance abuse, delinquency and intention to engage in problem behaviour. Based on a series of structural equation models, a non-recursive model was found to best fit the data, which suggests that adolescents having higher levels of positive youth development are more satisfied with life and have fewer problem behaviour, with life satisfaction and problem behaviour negatively reinforcing each other.

Keywords Adolescents · Positive youth development · Life satisfaction · Problem behaviour

1 Introduction

In the past two decades, increasing attention has been paid to positive youth development and adolescent subjective well-being (SWB). Park (2004) pointed out that "SWB serves not only as a key indicator of positive development but also as a broad enabling factor that promotes and maintains optimal mental health" (p. 27). Similarly, based on their work in primary prevention, Meyers and Meyers (2003) proposed that positive youth development could be enhanced by strengthening one's subjective well-being, competence and social

R. C. F. Sun
Department of Social Work, The Chinese University of Hong Kong, Shatin, New Territories, Hong Kong

D. T. L. Shek (✉)
Department of Applied Social Sciences, The Hong Kong Polytechnic University, Hung Hom, Kowloon, Hong Kong
e-mail: Daniel.shek@polyu.edu.hk

support, and at the same time mitigating poor individual predisposition, stress and exploitation. In short, researchers have argued that subjective well-being and its cognitive components (such as life satisfaction, Diener et al. 1999) are factors enabling positive development (Child Trends 2003; Damon 2004). However, before assuming that life satisfaction is an indicator of positive youth development, the operational definition of positive youth development must first be outlined.

In their review of positive youth development programs in North America, Catalano et al. (2004) pointed out that positive youth development comprises fifteen inter-related constructs—bonding, social competence, emotional competence, cognitive competence, behavioural competence, moral competence, self-efficacy, prosocial norms, resilience, self-determination, spirituality, clear and positive identity, beliefs in the future, prosocial involvement, and recognition of positive behaviour (for definitions of these constructs, see Table 1). Among these positive youth development constructs, many were found to associate with life satisfaction: Paxton et al. (2006) showed that bonding to adults and owning meaningful social roles were closely related to adolescent life satisfaction; Stein and Newcomb (1999) reported that intimate relationships formed in early adulthood contributed to life satisfaction in later adulthood; Ciarrochi et al. (2003) found that social and emotional competencies were significant predictors of life satisfaction. Academic and social self-efficacy (Vecchio et al. 2007), prosocial motivation and behaviour (Caprara and Steca 2005; Gebauer et al. 2008), spirituality and religiosity (Laudet and White 2008; Zullig et al. 2006), as well as mastery and ethnic identity (Sam 1998) were also found to be significant predictors of life satisfaction. In sum, using Catalano et al.'s (2004) definition of positive youth development, the above studies demonstrate that positive youth development predicts life satisfaction. Unfortunately, the possible influence of life satisfaction on positive youth development was not examined in these studies.

In addition, positive youth development was found to associate with positive behaviour but negatively relate to problem behaviour, such as substance abuse and delinquency. According to Catalano et al.'s review (2004) on 25 well-evaluated positive youth development programs, about 76% increased adolescents' positive behaviour and about 96% reduced problem behaviour. Since the fifteen positive youth development constructs proposed by Catalano et al. (2004) refer to how individuals' internal and external resources help them deal with challenges, they can be regarded as protective factors alleviating the development of problem behaviour, as proposed in the resilience literature on risk and protective factors (e.g., Jessor et al. 2003). This concept and related theories of protective factors suggest a predictive relationship of positive youth development to problem behaviour.

Empirically speaking, the findings on the predictive effects of positive youth development on life satisfaction and problem behaviour were quite piecemeal because not all the fifteen constructs were examined simultaneously in a single study. Moreover, although integrative models were tested by using structural-equation modelling or hierarchical regressions to demonstrate the predictive effect of positive youth development on problem behaviour (Jessor et al. 2003; Lent et al. 2005), these cross-sectional studies did not examine the *reverse* predictive effect of problem behaviour on positive youth development. This research gap can be filled by testing the predictive relationship of positive youth development to life satisfaction and problem behaviour, as well as possible reverse or even bidirectional relationships.

Studies have shown that life satisfaction is negatively associated with adolescent problem behaviour: sexual risk-taking behaviours (Valois et al. 2002); substance abuse, such as cigarette smoking, chewing tobacco, marijuana, cocaine, regular alcohol use, binge drinking (Desousa et al. 2008; Piko et al. 2005; Zullig et al. 2001); and violence and aggression, such as carrying a gun or weapon, physical fighting, stealing or damaging

Table 1 Definitions of the theoretical constructs, reliability statistics (mean inter-item correlation coefficients and coefficient alphas), and mean and standard deviations

Theoretical construct	Definition	Mean inter-item correlation	Alpha	Mean (SD)
Life satisfaction (LS): 5 items	Global judgment of one's quality of life.	.49	.81	4.12 (1.04)
Bonding (BO): 6 items	Development of positive relationship with healthy adults and positive peers.	.45	.83	4.82 (.79)
Resilience (RE): 6 items	Capacity for adapting to changes and stressful events in healthy and adaptive ways.	.44	.82	4.70 (.81)
Social competence (SC): 7 items	Interpersonal skills such as communication and conflict resolution skills.	.42	.83	4.63 (.77)
Recognition for positive behaviour (RB): 4 items	Systems for rewarding, recognizing or reinforcing positive behaviour.	.44	.76	4.50 (.88)
Emotional competence (EC): 6 items	Skills to recognize feelings in oneself and others and emotional self-management strategies.	.44	.83	4.25 (.90)
Cognitive competence (CC): 6 items	Cognitive skills such as problem solving and goal setting.	.47	.84	4.46 (.84)
Behavioural competence (BC): modified 5 items	Behavioural skills such as taking action skills and provision of reinforcement for effective behaviour choices and action pattern.	.38	.76	4.72 (.77)
Moral competence (MC): 6 items	Ability to differentiate right and wrong and respect for rules and standards as well as social justice.	.37	.78	4.47 (.81)
Self-determination (SD): 5 items	Sense of autonomy, independent thinking, or self-advocacy.	.40	.76	4.74 (.77)
Self-efficacy (SE): modified 2 items	Skills for coping and mastery.	.34	.50	4.33 (1.03)
Clear and positive identity (ID): 7 items	Development of healthy identity formation and achievement.	.43	.84	4.19 (.89)
Beliefs in the future (BF): modified 3 items	Ability to develop future potential goals, choices, or options.	.61	.82	4.45 (1.09)
Prosocial involvement (PI): 5 items	Activities and events to make positive contribution to groups.	.49	.83	4.54 (.91)
Prosocial norms (PN): 5 items	Development of clear and explicit standards for prosocial engagement.	.40	.77	4.68 (.86)
Spirituality (SP): 7 items	Sense of purpose and meaning in life, hope, or beliefs in a higher power.	.51	.88	5.24 (1.21)
Positive youth development (PYD): 80 items	Positive adolescent development defined in terms of healthy, holistic, and valuable developmental attributes, assets, and potentials.	.54	.94	4.58 (.67)
Substance abuse (SA): 8 items	Consumption of alcohol and drugs.	.51	.88	NA
Delinquency (DE): 12 items	Engagement in antisocial behaviour.	.56	.76	NA
Intention to engage in problem behaviour (BI): 5 items	Purpose of involving in high-risk behaviour.	.47	.76	NA

Table 1 continued

Theoretical construct	Definition	Mean inter-item correlation	Alpha	Mean (SD)
Problem behaviour (PB): 25 items	Problem behaviour defined in terms of substance abuse, delinquency and intention to engage in problem behaviour.	.53	.75	NA

property at school, and drinking and driving (MacDonald et al. 2005; Valois et al. 2001). In addition, life satisfaction was found to act as a predictor of suicide ideation (Heisel and Flett 2004). Theoretically, adolescents who were dissatisfied with life might have had poor strategies to cope with life stress and thus engaged in sexual behaviours, substance abuse and even delinquency and suicide attempts (Kim and Kim 2008). On the other hand, longitudinal research also pointed out that heavy substance or tobacco use in adolescence was a precursor of lower levels of life satisfaction, relationship satisfaction, and physical and mental health in adulthood (Fergusson and Boden 2008; Georgiades and Boyle 2007). Since research findings on the relationships between life satisfaction and problem behaviour are equivocal, investigation of the predictive contribution of life satisfaction to problem behaviour, as well as that of problem behaviour to life satisfaction, and even their bidirectional relationship, is needed.

The picture of the relationships among positive youth development, life satisfaction and adolescent problem behaviour becomes more complicated when researchers treat life satisfaction as a mediator. While most of the existing studies treated life satisfaction either as an outcome variable (e.g., Gebauer et al. 2008; Laudet and White 2008; Vecchio et al. 2007) or as a predictor (e.g., Heisel and Flett 2004; Swami et al. 2007), several studies examined the mediating influence of life satisfaction on problem behaviour. For instance, McKnight et al. (2002) found that life satisfaction partially mediated the relationship between stressful life events and adolescent problem behaviour. Suldo and Huebner (2004) also demonstrated that life satisfaction had not only a partial mediating effect between authoritative parenting and adolescent problem behaviour, but also a full mediating effect between parental involvement and adolescent problem behaviour. Based on these findings, further examination of the mediating role of life satisfaction to problem behaviour is needed.

In the Hong Kong context, studies on life satisfaction among adolescents have commonly used the correlational method (e.g., Shek 1998a, 1998b; Shek et al. 2006a). A few used multivariate statistical analyses, like multiple regression (Chan 2007; Chang et al. 2003) and structural equation modelling (Leung and Zhang 2000), but predictors were limited to family factors (such as parent-adolescent relationship, parental warmth and emotional detachment) and intrapersonal factors (such as self-concept and perfectionism). No study has been conducted in Hong Kong to examine positive youth development involving the fifteen constructs developed by Catalano et al. (2004) as predictors of life satisfaction, though there is an emerging body of positive youth development literature.

From a Hong Kong perspective, there are four reasons to examine the relationships among life satisfaction, positive youth development and adolescent problem behaviour. First, since harmonious relationships, moral values, prosocial norms and behaviours are highly valued in Chinese culture, it is interesting to study how these factors are related to adolescent life satisfaction and problem behaviour. Second, despite problem behaviour being less common among Chinese adolescents than among their Western counterparts

(Jessor et al. 2003), there is a rising trend of adolescent developmental problems, such as abuse of psychotropic substances (Shek 2007), adolescent suicide (Sun and Hui 2007) and school violence (Wong 2004). Third, because of the addictive nature of problem behaviour, it is valuable to examine adolescents' intention of engaging in problem behaviour such as substance abuse and delinquency. Finally, while Western studies show that positive youth development predicts life satisfaction and problem behaviour (e.g., Catalano et al. 2004), relevant studies are almost non-existent in the Chinese contexts and it remains unknown whether isolated Western findings can be generalized to the Chinese culture.

Against this background, the main goal is to test the structural models of the predictive relationships among positive youth development, life satisfaction and problem behaviour. Theoretically, with structural equation modelling, a model could clearly delineate predictive relationships between the predictor and criterion variables. From the literature review, it is hypothesized that positive youth development is positively related with life satisfaction, and that both of them are negatively related with problem behaviour.

To answer the research question of whether there would be direct, indirect, mediating, reverse or bidirectional paths among the three variables, six hypothetical models were proposed with reference to the positive youth development theoretical framework (Catalano et al. 2004), empirical research findings, and logical deductions. First, with structural equation modelling, the possible partial or full mediation role of life satisfaction (Model 1 and Model 2) was tested. Second, due to the cross-sectional nature of the present data, a possible reverse predictive relationship (Model 3) was examined to further demonstrate the predictive directionality of the variables. Third, alternative bidirectional relationships among the variables based on logical reasoning were also tested (Models 4 and 5), though the bidirectional relationship between life satisfaction and problem behaviour (Model 6) was rather clearly shown by the previous studies. After model testing and comparison, the model with the most optimal fit indices would be considered.

- Model 1: It was hypothesized that positive youth development would have a positive effect on life satisfaction but a negative effect on problem behaviour, with life satisfaction partially mediating the impact of positive youth development on problem behaviour relationship. (i.e., partial mediation model)
- Model 2: It was hypothesized that positive youth development would have a positive effect on life satisfaction, and that life satisfaction would have a negative effect on problem behaviour. (i.e., full mediation model)
- Model 3: It was hypothesized that adolescent problem behaviour would have negative effects on positive youth development as well as life satisfaction, and that life satisfaction would have a positive effect on positive youth development. (i.e., reverse effect model)
- Model 4: It was hypothesized that positive youth development and life satisfaction would have a bidirectional relationship. Both positive youth development and life satisfaction would have negative effects on problem behaviour. (i.e., non-recursive model with a bidirectional path between exogenous and one endogenous variables)
- Model 5: It was hypothesized that positive youth development would have a bidirectional relationship on life satisfaction and a negative effect on problem behaviour. Also, life satisfaction and problem behaviour would have a bidirectional relationship. (i.e., non-recursive model with two bidirectional paths)
- Model 6: It was hypothesized that positive youth development would have a positive effect on life satisfaction and a negative effect on problem behaviour, with life satisfaction and problem behaviour having a bidirectional relationship. (i.e., non-recursive model with a bidirectional path between two endogenous variables)

2 Method

2.1 Participants and Procedure

Project Positive Adolescent Training through Holistic Social Programmes (P.A.T.H.S.) is a pioneering positive youth development program designed for junior secondary-school students in Hong Kong, with the aim of promoting holistic development among adolescents. In the first year of the Full Implementation Phase (the 2006–2007 school year), a total of 24 experimental schools ($n = 4{,}121$ students) and 24 control schools ($n = 3{,}854$ students) were randomly selected to join a longitudinal study. In Wave 1 of the data collection, all the Secondary One students ($N = 7{,}975$) completed the objective outcome questionnaire prior to program implementation. Of these, 4,169 (52.3%) were boys and 3,387 (42.5%) were girls, with the remaining 5.2% not reporting their gender. A majority of the students reported their age as 12 (60.5%), 13 (14.9%) or 11 (12.5%). Further details of the project can be seen in studies by Shek and Ma (2006) and Shek and Sun (2009).

Data were collected at the schools by trained research staff and/or school teachers with adequate advance briefings. Parental and school consent were obtained prior data collection. At the time of data collection, student consent was sought, the purpose of the study was mentioned, and the confidentiality of the data collected was repeatedly emphasized to all students. After giving instructions, adequate time was provided for all participants to respond to all scales in the questionnaires in a self-administration format. No students refused to complete the questionnaires.

2.2 Instruments

The study used an objective outcome evaluation questionnaire (Shek et al. 2006b) in Chinese, containing measures of positive youth development, life satisfaction, adolescent problem behaviour and demographic characteristics.

2.2.1 Assessment of Positive Youth Development

Positive youth development was measured by the modified Chinese Positive Youth Development Scale (Shek et al. 2008). A detailed description of the scale, as well as its items and psychometric properties, can be found in Shek et al.'s study (2007). The scale includes 15 subscales: bonding, social competence, emotional competence, cognitive competence, behavioural competence, moral competence, self-efficacy, prosocial norms, resilience, self-determination, spirituality, clear and positive identity, beliefs in the future, prosocial involvement, and recognition of positive behaviour (see Table 1). Except spirituality, which was measured by a seven-point rating scale, all categories had a six-point rating scale. Positive youth development was represented by these 15 indicators—a final score was obtained by averaging the items in each subscale.

2.2.2 Assessment of Life Satisfaction

Life satisfaction was measured by the five-item Life Satisfaction Scale on a 6-point rating scale (Diener et al. 1985), which assesses one's own global judgment of one's quality of life. The Chinese translation was found to have acceptable psychometric properties (Shek 2004).

2.2.3 *Assessment of Problem Behaviour*

Problem behaviour was measured by three subscales. The first was an eight-item measure of substance abuse, examining via a seven-point rating scale the respondent's frequency of using alcohol, tobacco, ketamine, cannabis, cough mixture, organic solvent, pills, and narcotics. The second subscale is a 12-item measure of delinquency, examining via a seven-point rating scale the respondent's frequency of engaging in antisocial behaviour such as stealing, cheating, truancy, running away from home, damaging property, assault, having sexual relationship with others, gang fighting, speaking foul language, staying away from home without parental consent, strong-arming others, and breaking into residences. The third subscale uses a four-point rating scale and is a five-item measure of intention to engage in problem behaviour, including consuming alcohol, smoking, consuming illicit drugs, engaging in sexual behaviour, and gambling. These subscales were found to have acceptable construct validity (Shek 2004). Problem behaviour was represented by these three indicators, which were obtained by averaging the items in each subscale.

2.3 Data Analyses

The hypothetical models were tested by structural equation modelling (LISREL 8, linear structural relations; Jöreskog and Sörbom 1999). Since the present study was based on a community adolescent sample, it was predicted that the problem behaviour data would be positively skewed and kurtosic (i.e., not normally distributed). To tackle the issue of data non-normality, maximum likelihood (ML) in the latest version of LISREL 8.80 and PRELIS 2.54 was used to estimate the free parameters in the models. PRELIS 2.80 gives the estimations of polychoric covariance and asymptotic covariance matrices, which allow ML to provide the Satorra–Bentler scaled chi-squares in the LISREL 8.80 solutions for estimating the non-normal data. Evaluation of model fit was based on multiple criteria, including the theoretical meaningfulness of the model, absolute-fit indices (how well a model fits the data, without comparing to a baseline model), incremental fit measures (how much better the model fits than a baseline model) and model cross-validation (how the model can be replicated with an independent sample). Absolute fit indices include Satorra–Bentler scaled chi-square (χ^2), root mean square error of approximation (RMSEA), goodness-of-fit index (GFI), and standardized root mean residual (SRMR). Incremental fit measures include the non-normed fit index (NNFI) and the comparative fit index (CFI). For model cross-validation, the total sample was split randomly into two sub-samples for model exploration and validation, respectively, and a cross-validation index (CVI) was computed to indicate discrepancies among the sub-samples.

3 Results

Reliability analyses showed that all the scales and subscales except the self-efficacy subscale were highly reliable, i.e., they had alpha coefficients above .75 (Table 1). Results in Table 2 showed that the prevalence of problem behaviour was very low among Chinese early adolescents. More than 90% of the respondents reported that they had never smoked or abused drugs (other than drinking alcohol) in the previous 6 months. While about half of the respondents reported that they had cheated somebody and/or spoken foul language, a majority had never been involved in other kinds of delinquent behaviours, such as a sexual relationship in the previous 6 months. However, some respondents did intend to drink

Table 2 Summary table of the reported frequency and percentage of problem behaviour

	Never	1–2 times	3–5 times	>5 times	Several times per month	Several times per week	Every day	Missing	Total
Substance abuse in past 6 months									
Tobacco	7,356 (92.2%)	283 (3.5%)	79 (1.0%)	77 (1.0%)	25 (.3%)	30 (.4%)	56 (.7%)	69 (.9%)	7,975 (100%)
Alcohol	5,921 (74.2%)	1,090 (13.7%)	356 (4.5%)	330 (4.1%)	128 (1.6%)	41 (.5%)	21 (.3%)	88 (1.1%)	7,975 (100%)
Ketamine	7,867 (98.6%)	20 (.3%)	10 (.1%)	4 (.1%)	2 (.0%)	1 (.0%)	8 (.1%)	63 (.8%)	7,975 (100%)
Cannabis	7,869 (98.7%)	8 (.1%)	2 (.0%)	11 (.1%)	2 (.0%)	1 (.0%)	10 (.1%)	72 (.9%)	7,975 (100%)
Cough mixture	7,708 (96.7%)	40 (.5%)	15 (.2%)	20 (.3%)	4 (.1%)	3 (.0%)	10 (.1%)	175 (2.2%)	7,975 (100%)
Organic solvent	7,626 (95.6%)	104 (1.3%)	22 (.3%)	18 (.2%)	6 (.1%)	3 (.0%)	11 (.1%)	185 (2.3%)	7,975 (100%)
Pills	7,772 (97.5%)	13 (.2%)	3 (.0%)	5 (.1%)	3 (.0%)	3 (.0%)	11 (.1%)	165 (2.1%)	7,975 (100%)
Narcotics	7,777 (97.5%)	6 (.1%)	1 (.0%)	4 (.1%)	0 (0%)	3 (.0%)	10 (.1%)	174 (2.2%)	7,975 (100%)
Delinquency in past 6 months									
Stealing	7,270 (91.2%)	403 (5.1%)	70 (.9%)	17 (.2%)	18 (.2%)	3 (.0%)	22 (.3%)	172 (2.2%)	7,975 (100%)
Cheating	4,405 (55.2%)	2,025 (25.4%)	619 (7.8%)	250 (3.1%)	79 (1.0%)	26 (.3%)	368 (4.6%)	203 (2.5%)	7,975 (100%)
Truancy	7,479 (93.8%)	163 (2.0%)	47 (.6%)	35 (.4%)	10 (.1%)	4 (.1%)	47 (.6%)	190 (2.4%)	7,975 (100%)
Running away from home	7,438 (93.3%)	232 (2.9%)	43 (.5%)	21 (.3%)	12 (.2%)	6 (.1%)	21 (.3%)	202 (2.5%)	7,975 (100%)
Damaging others' properties	7,066 (88.6%)	517 (6.5%)	86 (1.1%)	39 (.5%)	16 (.2%)	13 (.2%)	39 (.5%)	199 (2.5%)	7,975 (100%)
Assault	7,176 (90.0%)	388 (4.9%)	93 (1.2%)	35 (.4%)	19 (.2%)	10 (.1%)	60 (.8%)	194 (2.4%)	7,975 (100%)
Having sexual relationship with others	7,720 (96.8%)	58 (.7%)	15 (.2%)	5 (.1%)	1 (.0%)	1 (.0%)	14 (.2%)	161 (2.0%)	7,975 (100%)
Gang fighting	7,509 (94.2%)	178 (2.2%)	42 (.5%)	21 (.3%)	8 (.1%)	2 (.0%)	31 (.4%)	184 (2.3%)	7,975 (100%)
Speaking foul language	3,666 (46.0%)	2,093 (26.2%)	608 (7.6%)	295 (3.7%)	123 (1.5%)	62 (.8%)	929 (11.6%)	199 (2.5%)	7,975 (100%)
Staying away from home without parental consent	7,462 (93.6%)	167 (2.1%)	59 (.7%)	29 (.4%)	10 (.1%)	11 (.1%)	50 (.6%)	187 (2.3%)	7,975 (100%)
Strong-arming others	7,010 (87.9%)	483 (6.1%)	121 (1.5%)	63 (.8%)	21 (.3%)	17 (.2%)	89 (1.1%)	171 (2.1%)	7,975 (100%)
Breaking into others' places	7,579 (95.0%)	137 (1.7%)	29 (.4%)	9 (.1%)	10 (.1%)	3 (.0%)	28 (.4%)	180 (2.3%)	7,975 (100%)

Table 2 continued

	Absolutely not	Probably not	Probably yes	Absolutely yes	Missing	Total
Intention to engage in problem behaviour in coming 2 years						
Consuming alcohol	5,027 (63.0%)	1,019 (12.8%)	1,327 (16.6%)	336 (4.2%)	266 (3.3%)	7,975 (100%)
Smoking	6,925 (86.8%)	424 (5.3%)	241 (3.0%)	112 (1.4%)	273 (3.4%)	7,975 (100%)
Consuming illicit drugs	7,461 (93.6%)	133 (1.7%)	43 (.5%)	69 (.9%)	269 (3.4%)	7,975 (100%)
Engaging in sexual behaviour	7,113 (89.2%)	345 (4.3%)	159 (2.0%)	91 (1.1%)	267 (3.3%)	7,975 (100%)
Gambling	6,616 (83.0%)	579 (7.3%)	361 (4.5%)	142 (1.8%)	277 (3.5%)	7,975 (100%)

alcohol (20.8%), gamble (6.3%), smoke (4.4%), have sex (3.1%), and consume illicit drugs (1.4%) in the subsequent 2 years.

As shown in Table 3, analyses based on Pearson correlation showed that all variables were correlated in the expected directions (with a two-tailed multistage Bonferroni correction). Life satisfaction was positively correlated with different measures of positive youth development and global positive youth development, while negatively correlated with substance abuse, delinquency, intention to engage in problem behaviour, and global problem behaviour.

As expected, variables were normally distributed, except the values of drug and delinquency of problem behaviour variables which showed positive skewness and kurtosis. In two-step modelling (Anderson and Gerbing 1988), the measurement models of the positive youth development, life satisfaction, and problem behaviour were tested first. Results showed that the fifteen-indicator positive youth development fit the data [Satorra–Bentler scaled χ^2 (90, $n = 3{,}987$) = 1,580.48; RMSEA = 0.06; GFI = 0.89; SRMR = 0.041; NNFI = 0.99; CFI = 0.99; CVI = 0.95] and that the three-indicator problem behaviour had excellent fit indices [Satorra–Bentler scaled χ^2 (0, $n = 3{,}987$) = 0; CVI = 0.02]. The construct validity of both scales was supported. For the five-indicator life satisfaction, the goodness-of-fit indices indicated that the model did not fit well. Since item 5 had a relatively lower loading and measures a hypothetical situation which is different from the other items, item 5 was dropped. The modified four-indicator life satisfaction had a significant χ^2-difference ($\Delta\chi^2 = 199.7$, $\Delta df = 3$, $p < 0.01$), and good fit [Satorra–Bentler scaled χ^2 (2, $n = 3{,}987$) = 9.14; RMSEA = 0.03; GFI = 1.00; SRMR = 0.010; NNFI = 1.00; CFI = 1.00; CVI = 0.95], which indicated that the scale would be better represented by four items which measure life satisfaction in similar contexts.

To examine the structural model of quality of life, the proposed models were tested and compared. The one showing optimal fit was selected to represent the final model.

3.1 Step (1): Testing Model 1

As shown in Table 4, the fit indices of Model 1 were adequate [Satorra–Bentler scaled χ^2 (206, $n = 3{,}987$) = 2,230.55; RMSEA = 0.05; GFI = 0.90; SRMR = 0.041; NNFI = 0.99; CFI = 0.99; CVI = 21.75] (see Fig. 1).

3.2 Step (2): Testing Model 2 with Model 1

The fit indices of Model 2 were adequate [Satorra–Bentler scaled χ^2 (207, $n = 3{,}987$) = 2,264.01; RMSEA = 0.05; GFI = 0.90; SRMR = 0.049; NNFI = 0.99; CFI = 0.99; CVI = 21.43] (Table 4; see Fig. 2). When compared with Model 1, although Model 2's CVI was a bit lower, its fit indices were not better than those of Model 1. Therefore, Model 1 was preferred. The findings suggested that life satisfaction partially mediated the relationship of positive youth development to problem behaviour. This was used as a baseline model for further model comparison.

3.3 Step (3): Testing Model 3 with Model 1

The fit indices of Model 3 were also adequate [Satorra–Bentler scaled χ^2 (206, $n = 3{,}987$) = 2,230.55; RMSEA = 0.05; GFI = 0.90; SRMR = 0.041; NNFI = 0.99; CFI = 0.99; CVI = 34.47] (Table 4; see Fig. 3), but it had a higher CVI, when compared

Table 3 Intercorrelation matrix for variables of positive youth development, life satisfaction, and problem behaviour

Variables	LS	BO	RE	SC	RB	EC	CC	BC	MC	SD	SE
Life satisfaction (LS)	1										
Bonding (BO)	.47**	1									
Resilience (RE)	.47**	.60**	1								
Social competence (SC)	.43**	.60**	.62**	1							
Recognition for positive behaviour (RB)	.45**	.63**	.56**	.59**	1						
Emotional competence (EC)	.52**	.57**	.61**	.65**	.56**	1					
Cognitive competence (CC)	.52**	.54**	.68**	.66**	.57**	.72**	1				
Behavioural competence (BC)	.45**	.54**	.59**	.64**	.53**	.64**	.70**	1			
Moral competence (MC)	.49**	.56**	.58**	.61**	.56**	.63**	.66**	.65**	1		
Self-determination (SD)	.44**	.51**	.57**	.59**	.48**	.60**	.65**	.64**	.60**	1	
Self-efficacy (SE)	.36**	.33**	.40**	.39**	.35**	.39**	.46**	.41**	.40**	.48**	1
Clear and positive identity (ID)	.59**	.52**	.55**	.58**	.51**	.62**	.64**	.57**	.58**	.61**	.48**
Beliefs in the future (BF)	.51**	.47**	.57**	.54**	.45**	.54**	.61**	.54**	.53**	.58**	.46**
Prosocial involvement (PI)	.51**	.59**	.55**	.57**	.59**	.56**	.60**	.57**	.60**	.54**	.39**
Prosocial norms (PN)	.43**	.50**	.52**	.51**	.51**	.50**	.54**	.54**	.59**	.51**	.36**
Spirituality (SP)	.57**	.53**	.54**	.46**	.45**	.53**	.52**	.46**	.48**	.45**	.33**
Positive youth development (PYD)	.64**	.74**	.78**	.78**	.73**	.80**	.84**	.78**	.79**	.77**	.59**
Substance abuse (SA)	−.10**	−.18**	−.16**	−.14**	−.17**	−.13**	−.14**	−.13**	−.14**	−.10**	−.07**
Delinquency (DE)	−.20**	−.28**	−.24**	−.20**	−.25**	−.24**	−.23**	−.21**	−.26**	−.16**	−.11**
Intention to engage in problem behaviour (BI)	−.18**	−.24**	−.21**	−.15**	−.21**	−.19**	−.19**	−.19**	−.23**	−.15**	−.09**
Problem behaviour (PB)	−.21**	−.29**	−.25**	−.20**	−.26**	−.23**	−.24**	−.22**	−.27**	−.17**	−.11**

Table 3 continued

Variables	ID	BF	PI	PN	SP	PYD	SA	DE	BI	PB
Life satisfaction (LS)										
Bonding (BO)										
Resilience (RE)										
Social competence (SC)										
Recognition for positive behaviour (RB)										
Emotional competence (EC)										
Cognitive competence (CC)										
Behavioural competence (BC)										
Moral competence (MC)										
Self-determination (SD)										
Self-efficacy (SE)										
Clear and positive identity (ID)	1									
Beliefs in the future (BF)	.72**	1								
Prosocial involvement (PI)	.59**	.56**	1							
Prosocial norms (PN)	.48**	.51**	.65**	1						
Spirituality (SP)	.54**	.52**	.50**	.42**	1					
Positive youth development (PYD)	.80**	.77**	.78**	.71**	.70**	1				
Substance abuse (SA)	−.10**	−.12**	−.14**	−.18**	−.17**	−.18**	1			
Delinquency (DE)	−.19**	−.22**	−.23**	−.28**	−.28**	−.30**	.63**	1		
Intention to engage in problem behaviour (BI)	−.16**	−.19**	−.21**	−.26**	−.27**	−.26**	.47**	.49**	1	
Problem behaviour (PB)	−.19**	−.22**	−.24**	−.30**	−.30**	−.31**	.80**	.87**	.81**	1

Note: ** Significant when a two-tailed multistage Bonferroni procedure was used (210 pairs)

Table 4 Goodness-of-fit indices of structural models

Structural Model	$\chi^2(df)$	$\Delta\chi^2(\Delta df)$	RMSEA	GFI	SRMR	NNFI	CFI	CVI
(1) Model 1	2,230.55 (206)		0.05	0.90	0.041	0.99	0.99	21.75
(2) Model 2	2,264.01 (207)		0.05	0.90	0.049	0.99	0.99	21.43
Model 2 vs. Model 1		33.51 (1)**						
(3) Model 3	2,230.55 (206)		0.05	0.90	0.041	0.99	0.99	34.47
Model 3 vs. Model 1		0 (0)						
(4) Model 4	2,275.99 (206)		0.05	0.89	0.20	0.99	0.99	1.40
Model 4 vs. Model 1		45.44 (0)**						
(5) Model 5	2,263.09 (206)		0.05	0.89	0.19	0.99	0.99	1.40
Model 5 vs. Model 1		32.54 (0)**						
(6) Model 6	2,214.19 (206)		0.05	0.90	0.044	0.99	0.99	21.88
Model 6 vs. Model 1		16.36 (0)**						

Note: A better fitting model was judged by Satorra–Bentler scaled χ^2, RMSEA < 0.08, GFI, NNFI and CFI > 0.90, SRMR < 0.05, a low CVI value, and a significant χ^2-difference (** $p < 0.01$)

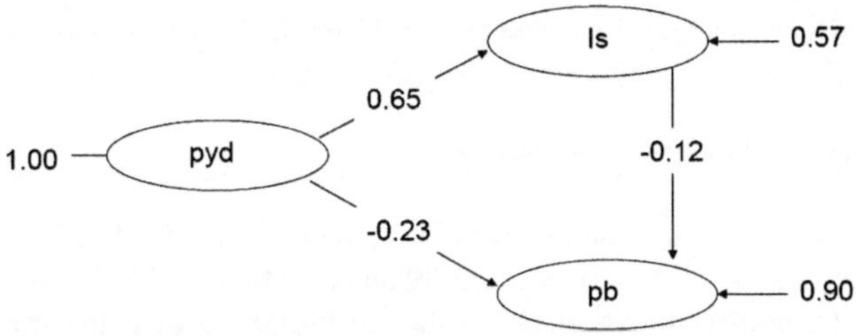

Fig. 1 Tested model 1: partial mediation model

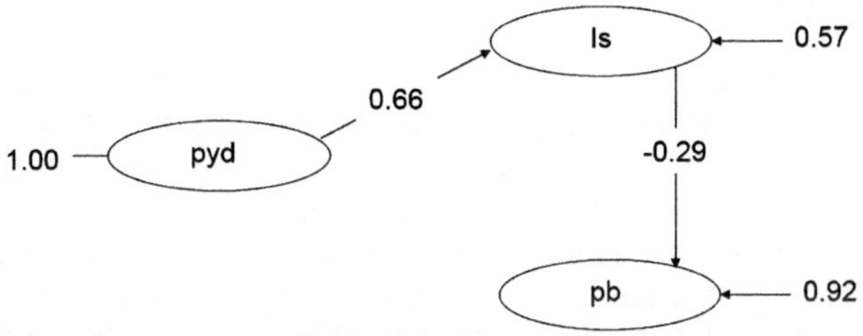

Fig. 2 Tested model 2: full mediation model

with Model 1. The model suggested that the directionality from problem behaviour to life satisfaction and positive youth development could not be easily replicated across subsamples. Therefore, Model 3 was rejected.

3.4 Step (4): Testing Model 4 with Model 1

When compared with Model 1, although Model 4 had a lower CVI, it had higher Satorra–Bentler scaled χ^2 (206, n = 3,987) = 2,275.99 and SRMR = 0.20 (Table 4; see Fig. 4). It suggested that the bidirectional relationship between positive youth development and life satisfaction was not preferred. Therefore, Model 4 was rejected.

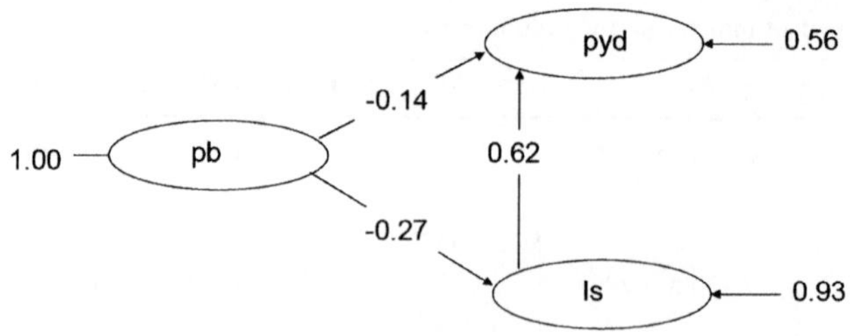

Fig. 3 Tested model 3: reverse effect model

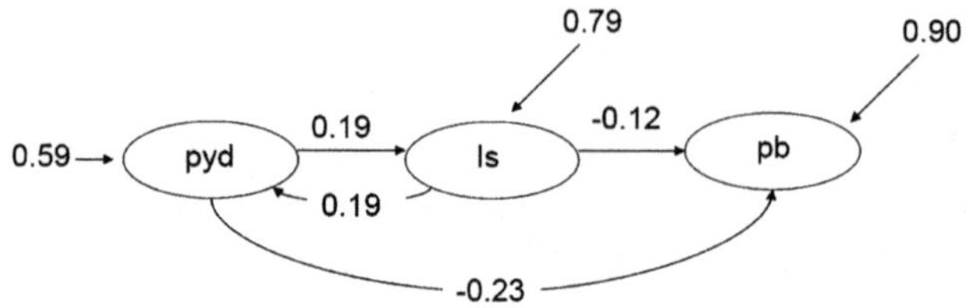

Fig. 4 Tested model 4: non-recursive model with a bidirectional path between exogenous and one endogenous variables

3.5 Step (5): Testing Model 5 with Model 1

When compared with Model 1, although Model 5 had a lower CVI, it had higher Satorra–Bentler scaled χ^2 (206, n = 3,987) = 2,263.09 and SRMR = 0.19 (Table 4; see Fig. 5). It suggested that the non-recursive model with two bidirectional paths was not preferred. Therefore, Model 5 was rejected.

3.6 Step (6): Testing Model 6 with Model 1

The fit indices of Model 6 were adequate [Satorra–Bentler scaled χ^2 (206, n = 3,987) = 2,214.19; RMSEA = 0.05; GFI = 0.90; SRMR = 0.044; NNFI = 0.99; CFI = 0.99; CVI = 21.88] (Table 4; see Fig. 6). When compared with Model 1, although Model 6's CVI was a bit higher, its fit indices were better than those of Model 1, and it had a significant χ^2 difference. Model 6 was preferred and accepted as the model of quality of life in the present study because it had the most optimal fit indices, although it is noteworthy that it is only slightly better than Model 1. Moreover, the direct effects of positive youth development on both life satisfaction and problem behaviour, and the reciprocal relationship between life satisfaction and problem behaviour, have been supported by different studies (e.g., Catalano et al. 2004; Desousa et al. 2008; Fergusson and Boden

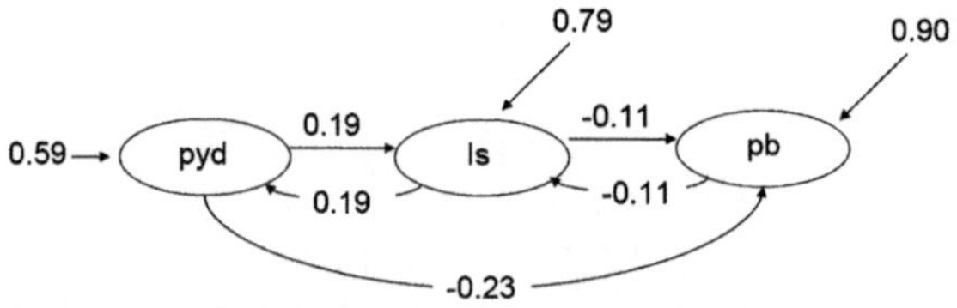

Note.

pyd: positive youth development

ls: life satisfaction

pb: problem behaviour

Fig. 5 Tested model 5: non-recursive model with two bidirectional paths

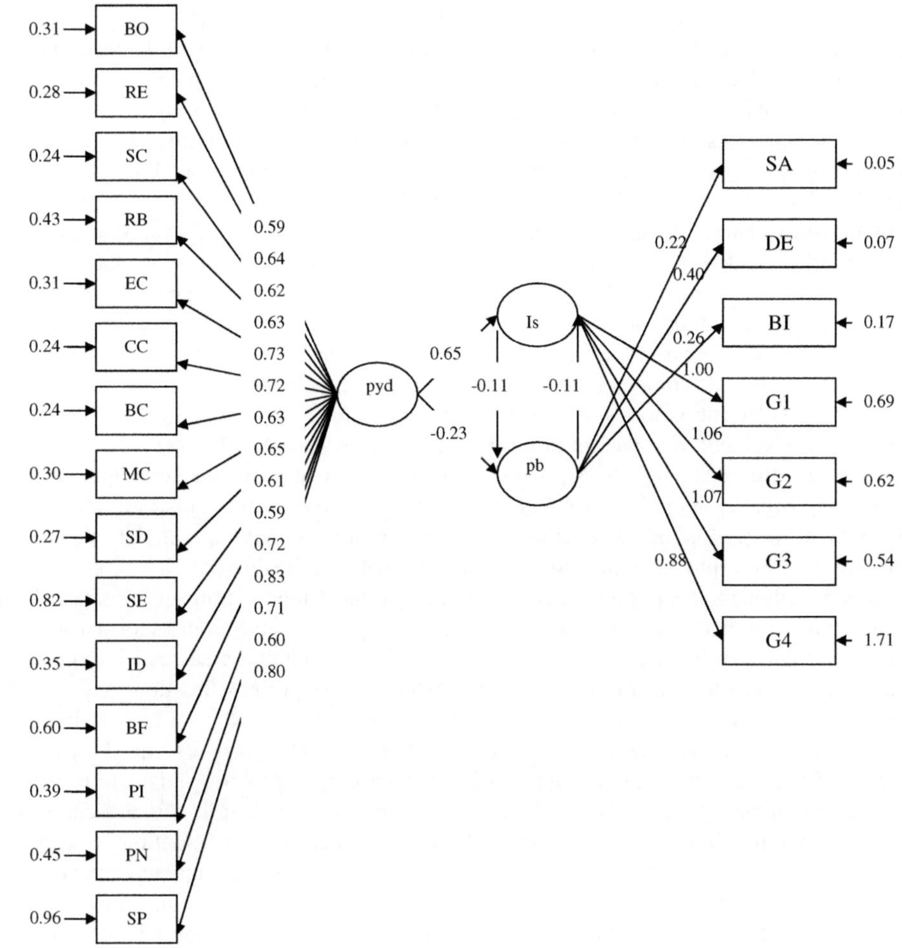

Note.
pyd: positive youth development
ls: life satisfaction
pb: problem behaviour
BO: bonding
RE resilience
SC: social competence
RB: recognition for positive behaviour
EC: emotional competence
CC: cognitive competence
BC: behavioural competence
MC: moral competence
SD: self-determination
SE: self-efficacy
ID: positive identity
BF: beliefs in the future
PI: prosocial involvement
PN: prosocial norms
SP: spirituality
SA: substance abuse
DE: delinquency
BI: intention to engage in problem behaviour
G1-G4: 4 indicators of Life Satisfaction Scale

Fig. 6 Tested model 6: non-recursive model with a bidirectional path between two endogenous variables

2008). Such a non-recursive model explained 46% of the variance in life satisfaction and 12% of the variance in problem behaviour.

4 Discussion

The main goal of the present study was to test the different models pertinent to the relationships among positive youth development, life satisfaction, and problem behaviour in Chinese early adolescents. There were several unique features of this study. First, the present study is a positive response to the observation that there are few related studies in this area, particularly in the Chinese context. Second, because of the paucity of studies on adolescent quality of life (Shek et al. 2005; Shek and Lee 2007), Chinese adolescents were recruited in the present study. Third, a large sample was used in this study. Fourth, validated assessment tools were employed. Finally, latent variables analyses were performed which permit comparison of different models.

Apart from generating findings on the internal consistency of the scales of positive youth development, life satisfaction, and problem behaviour, the present study further demonstrated the validity of these constructs via confirmatory factor analyses. First, the present study affirmed that positive youth development is comprised of fifteen inter-related constructs, namely, bonding, social competence, emotional competence, cognitive competence, behavioural competence, moral competence, self-efficacy, prosocial norms, resilience, self-determination, spirituality, clear and positive identity, beliefs in the future, prosocial involvement, and recognition for positive behaviour (Catalano et al. 2004), with beliefs in the future having the strongest influence on positive youth development, followed by spirituality (Fig. 6). Therefore, future studies can compute global positive youth development, instead of using separate sub-scales, in order to have a complete picture of how positive development relates to adolescent growth and health.

Second, although the psychometric properties of the Chinese translation of the Life Satisfaction Scale had been proved (Shek 2004), the present study indicated that a scale item, "If I could live my life over, I would change almost nothing" assesses a hypothetical situation that is different from the other items, which assess present situations, e.g., "I am satisfied with my life". It is possible that a person who is dissatisfied with life does not want to change things if s/he is also helpless and hopeless. The present study showed that removal of this item could contribute to a better measurement of life satisfaction, with a better alpha value (0.83, mean inter-item correlation = .56). Third, the present study showed that three indicators—substance abuse, delinquency, and intention to commit problem behaviour—could represent problem behaviour, with delinquency having the strongest loading (Fig. 6). Besides examining substance abuse and delinquency as indicators of problem behaviour, this study added to the literature by examining "intention to engage in problem behaviour" as another indicator. It suggests that a better measurement of problem behaviour could be obtained by assessing both past behaviour and intention for future behaviour.

Consistent with previous studies, positive youth development was positively related to life satisfaction, and both were negatively associated with problem behaviour as hypothesized. Since most existing studies have focused on bonding, social competence, emotional competence, behavioural competence, prosocial behaviour, and spirituality (e.g., Ciarrochi et al. 2003; Laudet and White 2008; Paxton et al. 2006), this study demonstrated that other positive youth development constructs, including resilience and beliefs in the future, also have significant correlations with life satisfaction. In particular, adolescents having more positive identity were more likely to have higher life satisfaction. Furthermore, problem behaviour was found to have weak, yet significant, correlation with positive youth development and life satisfaction. Interestingly, we found that adolescents are less likely to be involved in problem behaviour when they are more satisfied with life, have strong relationship with healthy adults and peers (i.e., bonding), have a sense of purpose and meaning in life (i.e., spirituality), and have clear standards for prosocial engagement (i.e., prosocial norms).

Most importantly, the present study contributed to existing knowledge by proposing a predictive model (Model 6), which demonstrates that positive youth development predicts life satisfaction and problem behaviour, with life satisfaction and problem behaviour having a bidirectional relationship. It showed that early adolescents having poor positive development have lower life satisfaction and higher levels of substance abuse, delinquency, and intention to engage in problem behaviour. These unidirectional paths from positive youth development to life satisfaction and problem behaviour were in line with Western literature on resilience and positive youth development (e.g., Catalano et al. 2004). Since existing local studies have mainly looked at family factors (bonding) and self-concept (identity) as determinants of life satisfaction (e.g., Chan 2007; Leung and Zhang 2000), the present study contributed by underscoring the contribution of positive youth development to adolescent life satisfaction. As positive youth development directly affects adolescents' behaviour and appraisal of life, the present findings suggest that promoting positive youth development is of paramount importance in enabling satisfaction with life and mitigating risk-taking behaviour among early adolescents. Furthermore, consistent with previous literature (Fergusson and Boden 2008; Georgiades and Boyle 2007), this study highlights the relationship of life dissatisfaction and problem behaviour, with lower levels of life satisfaction encouraging adolescents to engage in problem behaviour, and vice versa. As life satisfaction is a cognitive appraisal of the quality of one's life, it is understandable that adolescents having negative appraisal of life would engage in various kinds of problem behaviour as an outlet. Nevertheless, continuous involvement in problem behaviour would also strengthen the negative evaluation of one's life, resulting in a vicious cycle between life dissatisfaction and problem behaviour. In short, the contribution of the present findings is twofold: (i) unidirectional path models may not be adequate in delineating the relationships among positive youth development, life satisfaction, and adolescent problem behaviour; and (ii) the non-recursive model demonstrates a reciprocal causation between problem behaviour and life satisfaction.

Although the full and partial mediating role of life satisfaction (Model 1 and Model 2) was not supported by the present findings, this is not to say that the mediating role of life satisfaction should be denied—these models still showed adequate fit indices, but both models were slightly poorer when compared with Model 6. Also, the mediating effects of life satisfaction on problem behaviour are supported by Western studies in which stressful life events and parenting were treated as exogenous variables (McKnight et al. 2002; Suldo and Huebner 2004). As the present study used positive youth development as an antecedent variable, the mediating effect of life satisfaction on problem behaviour might not be prominent. In addition, this cross-sectional study did not support the reverse impact of problem behaviour on life satisfaction and positive youth development (Model 3) or that of life satisfaction on positive youth development proposed by the researchers (e.g., Meyers and Meyers 2003), and thus further demonstrated the directionality from positive youth development to life satisfaction and problem behaviour. Furthermore, this study did not support bidirectional relationships between positive youth development and life satisfaction or between positive youth development and problem behaviour (Model 4 and Model 5), which were logically deduced from the literature. In sum, the structural equation modelling analyses and model comparisons indicated that positive youth development was a strong exogenous variable having predictive contributions to life satisfaction and problem behaviour, with the latter two endogenous variables reciprocally related. Selection of this non-recursive model as the final model was not arbitrary. Adoption of the model was based on both the theoretical meaningfulness of the model and fit indices. However, as other competing models were only slightly inferior, it is necessary to replicate the present findings in the future.

There are several limitations of the present study. First, although the present model was based on a large sample collected in the Hong Kong Chinese context, the generalizability and replicability of the preferred model should be further examined. Second, causal inferences based on this cross-sectional study should proceed with caution. As the present study was based on Wave 1 data of a longitudinal study, future studies utilizing the data from several waves is necessary to validate the directionality of the variables in the model. Third, as there are certain percentages of unexplained variance in the model, it indicates that other potential variables should be included in the model to give a better prediction. Nevertheless, the amount of variance explained could not be regarded as low. Fourth, as the data were collected by students' self-reporting, the effects of social desirability and self-serving biases should be taken into consideration. Despite these limitations, the present study demonstrates that positive youth development plays an important role in the quality of life of Chinese adolescents. The present findings represent an important advance in the literature on positive youth development, particularly in the Chinese context.

Acknowledgment The preparation for this paper and the Project P.A.T.H.S. were financially supported by The Hong Kong Jockey Club Charities Trust.

References

Anderson, J. C., & Gerbing, D. W. (1988). Structural equation modeling in practice: A review and recommended two-step approach. *Psychological Bulletin, 103*, 411–423.

Caprara, G. V., & Steca, P. (2005). Self-efficacy beliefs as determinants of prosocial behavior conducive to life satisfaction across ages. *Journal of Social and Clinical Psychology, 24*(2), 191–217.

Catalano, R. F., Berglund, M. L., Ryan, J. A. M., Lonczak, H. S., & Hawkins, J. D. (2004). Positive youth development in the United States: Research findings on evaluations of positive youth development programs. *The Annals of the American Academy of Political and Social Science, 591*, 98–124.

Chan, D. W. (2007). Positive and negative perfectionism among Chinese gifted students in Hong Kong: Their relationships to general self-efficacy and subjective well-being. *Journal for the Education of the Gifted, 31*(1), 77–102.

Chang, L., McBride-Chang, C., Stewart, S. M., & Au, E. (2003). Life satisfaction, self-concept, and family relations in Chinese adolescents and children. *International Journal of Behavioral Development, 27*(2), 182–189.

Child Trends (2003) *Indicators of positive development conference summary*. Retrieved March 1, 2005 from http://www.childtrends.org.

Ciarrochi, J., Scott, G., Deane, F. P., & Heaven, P. C. L. (2003). Relations between social and emotional competence and mental health: A construct validation study. *Personality and Individual Differences, 35*, 1947–1963.

Damon, W. (2004). What is positive youth development? *Annals of the American Academy of Political and Social Science, 591*, 13–24.

Desousa, C., Murphy, S., Roberts, C., & Anderson, L. (2008). School policies and binge drinking behaviours of school-aged children in Wales—A multilevel analysis. *Health Education Research, 23*(2), 259–271.

Diener, E., Emmons, R. A., Larsen, R. J., & Griffin, S. (1985). The satisfaction with life scale. *Journal of Personality Assessment, 49*, 71–75.

Diener, E., Suh, E. M., Lucas, R. E., & Smith, H. L. (1999). Subjective well-being: Three decades of progress. *Psychological Bulletin, 125*, 276–302.

Fergusson, D. M., & Boden, J. M. (2008). Cannabis use and later life outcomes. *Addiction, 103*, 969–976.

Gebauer, J. E., Riketta, M., Broemer, P., & Maio, G. R. (2008). Pleasure and pressure based prosocial motivation: Divergent relations to subjective well-being. *Journal of Research in Personality, 42*, 399–420.

Georgiades, K., & Boyle, M. H. (2007). Adolescent tobacco and cannabis use: Young adult outcomes from the Ontario child health study. *Journal of Child Psychology and Psychiatry, 48*(7), 724–731.

Heisel, M. J., & Flett, G. L. (2004). Purpose in life, satisfaction with life, and suicide ideation in a clinical sample. *Journal of Psychopathology and Behavioral Assessment, 26*(2), 127–135.

Jessor, R., Turbin, M. S., Costa, F. M., Dong, Q., Zhang, H., & Wang, C. (2003). Adolescent problem behavior in China and the United States: A cross-national study of psychosocial protective factors. *Journal of Research on Adolescence, 13*(3), 329–360.

Jöreskog, K. G., & Sörbom, D. (1999). *LISREL 8: Structural equation modeling with the SIMPLIS command language*. Hillsdale, NJ: Lawrence Erlbaum Associates.

Kim, H. S., & Kim, H. S. (2008). Risks factors for suicide attempts among Korean adolescents. *Child Psychiatry and Human Development, 39*, 221–235.

Laudet, A. B., & White, W. L. (2008). Recovery capital as prospective predictor of sustained recovery, life satisfaction, and stress among former poly-substance users. *Substance Use and Misuse, 43*, 27–54.

Lent, R. W., Singley, D., Sheu, H. B., Gainor, K. A., Brenner, B. R., Treistman, D., et al. (2005). Social cognitive predictors of domain and life satisfaction: Exploring the theoretical precursors of subjective well-being. *Journal of Consulting Psychology, 52*(3), 429–442.

Leung, J. P., & Zhang, L. W. (2000). Modelling life satisfaction of Chinese adolescents in Hong Kong. *International Journal of Behavioral Development, 24*, 99–104.

MacDonald, J. M., Piquero, A. R., Valois, R. F., & Zullig, K. J. (2005). The relationship between life satisfaction, risk-taking behaviors, and youth violence. *Journal of Interpersonal Violence, 20*(11), 1495–1518.

McKnight, C. G., Huebner, E. S., & Suldo, S. (2002). Relationships among stressful life events, temperament, problem behavior, and global life satisfaction in adolescents. *Psychology in the Schools, 39*(6), 677–687.

Meyers, J., & Meyers, B. (2003). Bi-directional influences between positive psychology and primary prevention. *School Psychology Quarterly, 18*(2), 222–229.

Park, N. (2004). The role of subjective well-being in positive youth development. *The Annals of the American Academy of Political and Social Science, 591*, 25–39.

Paxton, R. J., Valois, R. F., Huebner, E. S., & Drane, J. W. (2006). Opportunity for adult bonding/meaningful neighbourhood roles and life-satisfaction among USA middle school students. *Social Indicators Research, 79*, 291–312.

Piko, B. F., Luszczynska, A., Gibbons, F. X., & Teközel, M. (2005). A culture-based study of personal and social influences of adolescent smoking. *European Journal of Public Health, 15*(4), 393–398.

Sam, D. L. (1998). Predicting life satisfaction among adolescents from immigrant families in Norway. *Ethnicity & Health, 3*(1/2), 5–18.

Shek, D. T. L. (1998a). A longitudinal study of the relations between parent-adolescent conflict and adolescent psychological well-being. *Journal of Genetic Psychology, 159*(1), 53–67.

Shek, D. T. L. (1998b). A longitudinal study of the relationship between family functioning and adolescent psychological well-being. *Journal of Youth Studies, 1*(2), 195–209.

Shek, D. T. L. (2004). Chinese cultural beliefs about adversity: Its relationship to psychological well-being, school adjustment and problem behavior in Chinese adolescents with and without economic disadvantages. *Childhood, 11*, 63–80.

Shek, D. T. L. (2007). Tackling adolescent substance abuse in Hong Kong: Where we should go and should not go. *TheScientificWorldJournal, 19*, 2021–2030.

Shek, D. T. L., Chan, Y. K., & Lee, P. S. N. (2005). Quality of life in the global context: A Chinese response. *Social Indicators Research, 71*(1), 1–10.

Shek, D. T. L., & Lee, B. M. (2007). A comprehensive review of quality of life (QOL) research in Hong Kong. *TheScientificWorldJournal, 7*, 1222–1229.

Shek, D. T. L., Lee, B. M., Lee, T. Y., & Lam, C. M. (2006a). Frequency, satisfaction and quality dimensions of perceived parent-adolescent communication among Chinese adolescents in Hong Kong. *International Journal of Adolescent Medicine and Health, 18*(2), 259–270.

Shek, D. T. L., & Ma, H. K. (2006). Design of a positive youth development program in Hong Kong. *International Journal of Adolescent Medicine and Health, 18*(3), 315–327.

Shek, D. T. L., Siu, A. M. H., & Lee, T. Y. (2007). The Chinese positive youth development scale: A validation study. *Research on Social Work Practice, 17*, 380–391.

Shek, D. T. L., Siu, A. M. H., Lee, T. Y., Cheng, H., Tsang, S., Chui, Y. H., et al. (2006b). Development and validation of a positive youth development scale in Hong Kong. *International Journal of Adolescent Medicine and Health, 18*(3), 547–558.

Shek, D. T. L., Siu, A. M. H., Lee, T. Y., Cheung, C. K., & Chung, R. (2008). Effectiveness of the tier 1 program of project P.A.T.H.S.: Objective outcome evaluation based on a randomized group trial. *TheScientificWorldJournal, 8*, 4–12.

Shek, D. T. L., & Sun, R. C. F. (2009). Development, implementation and evaluation of a holistic positive youth development program: Project P.A.T.H.S. in Hong Kong. *International Journal on Disability and Human Development 8*(2), 107–117.

Stein, J. A., & Newcomb, M. D. (1999). Adult outcomes of adolescent conventional and agentic orientations: A 20-year longitudinal study. *The Journal of Early Adolescence, 19*, 39–65.

Suldo, S. M., & Huebner, E. S. (2004). The role of life satisfaction in the relationship between authoritative parenting dimensions and adolescent problem behavior. *Social Indicators Research, 66*, 165–195.

Sun, R. C. F., & Hui, E. K. P. (2007). Psychosocial factors contributing to adolescent suicidal ideation. *Journal of Youth and Adolescence, 36*(6), 775–786.

Swami, V., Chamorro-Premuzic, T., Sinniah, D., Maniam, T., Kannan, K., Stanistreet, D., et al. (2007). General health mediates the relationship between loneliness, life satisfaction and depression. *Social Psychiatry and Psychiatric Epidemiology, 42*, 161–166.

Valois, R. F., Zullig, K. J., Huebner, E. S., & Drane, J. W. (2001). Relationship between life satisfaction and violent behaviors among adolescents. *American Journal of Health Behavior, 25*(4), 353–366.

Valois, R. F., Zullig, K. J., Huebner, E. S., Kammermann, S. K., & Drane, J. W. (2002). Association between life satisfaction and sexual risk-taking behaviors among adolescents. *Journal of Child and Family Studies, 11*(4), 427–440.

Vecchio, G. M., Gerbino, M., Pastorelli, C., Del Bove, G., & Caprara, G. V. (2007). Multi-faceted self-efficacy beliefs as predictors of life satisfaction in late adolescence. *Personality and Individual Differences, 43*, 1807–1818.

Wong, D. S. W. (2004). School bullying and tackling strategies in Hong Kong. *International Journal of Offender Therapy and Comparative Criminology, 48*, 537–553.

Zullig, K. J., Vaolis, R. F., Huebner, E. S., Oeltmann, J. E., & Drane, J. W. (2001). Relationship between perceived life satisfaction and adolescents' substance abuse. *Journal of Adolescent Health, 29*, 279–288.

Zullig, K. J., Ward, R. M., & Horn, T. (2006). The association between perceived spirituality, religiosity, and life satisfaction: The mediating role of self-rated health. *Social Indicators Research, 79*, 255–274.

Soc Indic Res (2010) 95:475–487
DOI 10.1007/s11205-009-9532-8

Using Students' Weekly Diaries to Evaluate Positive Youth Development Programs: Are Findings Based on Multiple Studies Consistent?

Daniel T. L. Shek

Accepted: 9 April 2009 / Published online: 8 October 2009

Abstract Asking clients to document their perceived quality of life during and after intervention is a popular approach employed by helping professionals to evaluate intervention programs. In the Project *P*ositive *A*dolescent *T*raining through *H*olistic *S*ocial Programmes (P.A.T.H.S.), students participating in the Experimental Implementation Phase and Full Implementation Phase were invited to write reflective journals in the form of weekly diaries to reveal their perceptions and feelings regarding the program and the perceived benefits of the program. Based on multiple studies, results showed that the respondents generally (a) had positive views on the program, (b) had positive views on the instructors, and (c) perceived that they had acquired competencies at the societal, familial, interpersonal and personal levels and their quality of life was promoted after joining the program. Acknowledging the limitations of diaries, the present qualitative findings provide support for the effectiveness of the Tier 1 Program of the Project P.A.T.H.S. in Hong Kong.

Keywords Weekly diaries · Positive youth development · Chinese adolescents · Qualitative evaluation

1 Introduction

The main purpose of this paper is to report evaluation findings of the Project P.A.T.H.S. which is a positive youth development program in Hong Kong. To promote holistic development among adolescents in Hong Kong, The Hong Kong Jockey Club Charities Trust has approved HK$400 million to launch a project entitled "P.A.T.H.S. to Adulthood: A Jockey Club Youth Enhancement Scheme". The word "P.A.T.H.S." denotes *P*ositive *A*dolescent *T*raining through *H*olistic *S*ocial Programmes. There are two tiers of programs (Tier 1 and Tier 2 Programs) in this project. The Tier 1 Program is a universal positive youth development program in which students in Secondary 1 to Secondary 3 will

D. T. L. Shek (✉)
Department of Applied Social Sciences, The Hong Kong Polytechnic University,
Hunghom, Hong Kong, People's Republic of China
e-mail: daniel.shek@polyu.edu.hk

participate, normally with 20 h of training in the school year at each grade. Because research findings suggest that roughly one-fifth of adolescents would need help of a deeper nature, Tier 2 Program will generally be provided for at least one-fifth of the students who have greater psychosocial needs at each grade (i.e., selective program). In this paper, three qualitative studies based on student diaries collected from the students were reported to understand the perceived attributes of the Tier 1 Program and perceived benefits of the Tier 1 Program on the quality of life (such as psychosocial competencies) of the program participants.

Several characteristics are intrinsic to the curriculum design of the Tier 1 Program. First, although the number of hours for each grade of the junior secondary school is 20, schools with special needs may choose to use the core units only (i.e., 10 h for the Tier 1 Program), so that they can allocate manpower and resource to serve more needy students, at a deeper level, in the Tier 2 Program. Second, there are 40 units per grade (each lasting for 30 min), with a total of 120 units for the whole Tier 1 Program. Third, the program was developed by the Research Team by integrating existing research findings, programs, local adolescent needs, cultural characteristics and experiences (such as trial teaching) gained from the Experimental Implementation Phase of the Project. Fourth, relevant adolescent developmental concerns (e.g., drug issues, sexuality, financial management, sense of responsibility, and life meaning) and adolescent developmental strengths (e.g., high level of concern for society and high proficiency in information technology) were incorporated in the program. Fifth, to cater for the needs of the students, the program is implemented by teachers and/or social workers.

The final attribute of the curriculum design is that the Project P.A.T.H.S. covers 15 positive youth developmental constructs which were identified from the existing successful positive youth development programs (Catalano et al. 2002). These constructs include: promotion of bonding, cultivation of resilience, promotion of social competence, promotion of emotional competence, promotion of cognitive competence, promotion of behavioral competence, promotion of moral competence, cultivation of self-determination, promotion of spirituality, development of self-efficacy, development of a clear and positive identity, promotion of beliefs in the future, provision of recognition for positive behavior, provision of opportunities for prosocial involvement, and fostering prosocial norms.

There are two implementation phases in this project—Experimental Implementation Phase and Full Implementation Phase. For the Experimental Implementation Phase (2005/2006 to 2007/2008 academic year), 52 secondary schools participated in the project with the objectives of accumulating experience in program implementation and familiarizing frontline workers with the program design and philosophy. In 2006/2007 school year, the programs were implemented on a full scale at Secondary 1 level. In 2007/2008 school year, the programs were implemented at Secondary 1 and Secondary 2 levels. In 2008/2009 school year, the programs were implemented at Secondary 1, Secondary 2 and Secondary 3 levels. In the present study, student diaries written by students participating in the Secondary 1 Program (Experimental and Full Implementation Phases) and Secondary 2 Program (Experimental Implementation Phase) were collected to evaluate the Tier 1 Program.

The Project P.A.T.H.S. is a positive youth development program. In contrast to mainstream approaches that focus on youth developmental problems, the field of positive youth development (PYD) focuses on the talents, strengths, interests, and future potentials in children and adolescents (Damon 2004). According to Catalano et al. (2002), there are several attributes of the positive youth development approach, including emphasis on integrated youth development (i.e., focusing on a range of youth developmental possibilities and problems) rather than dealing with a single youth problem, upholding the belief that "problem-free is not fully prepared", emphasis of person-in-environment perspective, and focus on developmental models on how young people grow, learn and change.

Although there are different views on the strengths that should be developed in adolescents, many researchers suggested that building cognitive, academic, social and emotional competence is a fundamental task in adolescence (Graczyk et al. 2000). For example, Weissberg and O'Brien (2004) suggested that there are 5 core social-emotional competencies to be targeted in positive youth development programs: self-awareness, social awareness, self-management, relationship skills and responsible actions. Guerra and Williams (2003) similarly highlighted five core competencies for healthy youth development, including positive identity (positive self-concept, hopefulness, future goals), personal agency (self-efficacy, effective coping, locus of control, attributional style), self-regulation (affective, behavioral, and cognitive self-regulation, impulse control), social relationship skills (social problem solving skills, empathy, conflict resolution, capacity for intimacy), and prosocial system of beliefs (attitudes, norms, values, moral engagement).

The concept of positive youth development is closely linked to the construct of quality of life. Although there are different views on the definitions of quality of life, there is general agreement amongst researchers (e.g., Felce and Perry 1995; Wallander et al. 2001) that the concept is a multi-dimensional one, including material well-being (finance, income, housing quality, transport), physical well-being (health, fitness, mobility, personal safety), social well-being (personal relationships, community involvement), emotional well-being (positive affect, mental health, fulfillment, satisfaction, faith/belief, self-esteem), and productive well-being (competence, productivity). Obviously, positive youth development can be regarded as a cause, concomitant, component or consequence of quality of life, particularly with reference to social, emotional and productive well-being.

Roth et al. (1998) pointed out that positive youth development programs are commonly regarded as "programs that provide opportunities and support to help youth gain the competencies and knowledge they need to meet the increasing challenges they will face as they mature" (p. 423). Although many Western programs have been developed to promote positive development in children and adolescents, not all of them are successful in promoting adolescent development. For example, Catalano et al. (2002) reviewed 77 programs on positive youth development. The review showed that only 25 programs were successful. Obviously, evaluation is an important issue to be considered in positive youth development programs.

Program evaluation is not a simple and straightforward task and there are many types and approaches of evaluation. In his discussion of the major strategies of evaluation, Patton (1997) outlined three basic types of evaluation: quantitative evaluation, qualitative evaluation, and utilization-focused evaluation. Ginsberg (2001) summarized the major forms of evaluation, including quantitative and qualitative approaches, cost-benefit analyses, satisfaction studies, needs assessment, single-subjects designs, experimental approaches and models, utilization-focused evaluation, empowerment evaluations, fraud and abuse detection, client satisfaction and journalistic evaluation. Using starting alphabets as the bases of classification, Patton (1987) suggested that there are more than 100 types of evaluation. In a comprehensive evaluation of the major evaluation paradigms, Patton (2002) pointed out that different attributes are associated with different evaluation paradigms.

As pointed out by Patton (1997), there are two main approaches in the field of evaluation. For the quantitative/experimental paradigm, quantitative data are commonly collected through standardized and uniform procedures as well as fixed and controlled designs such as experiments with treatment and control groups. In addition, deductive hypothesis testing involving independent and dependent variables, linear and sequential modeling, pre-post focus on change, probabilistic and random sampling, statistical analysis, as well as generalizations are intrinsic to this paradigm which emphasizes objectivity in program evaluation and detachment of the evaluator from the program. For the qualitative/naturalistic paradigm, qualitative data such as narratives are collected through naturalistic inquiry, case studies, emergent and flexible designs and inductive analysis. In addition, holistic contextual portrayal, systems perspective, interdependencies, dynamic and ongoing view of change, purposeful sampling of relevant cases focusing on uniqueness and diversity, thematic content analysis are intrinsic to this paradigm which emphasizes subjectivity in program evaluation and close relationship between the researcher and the program.

An examination of the evaluation literature shows that although there is a strong preference for the use of quantitative or experimental approach to evaluate the effectiveness of prevention programs for adolescents, the number of qualitative evaluation studies in this area is increasing (Shek 2008). Moreover, regardless of the general impression that quantitative evaluation is the "mainstream" evaluation approach, there is a growing emphasis on the use of qualitative methods in evaluation. For example, Chatterji (2004) criticized the sole reliance on experimental methods and argued for the use of more diverse types of evaluation strategies, particularly in the context of education. Slayton and Llosa (2005) also remarked that "qualitative methods should be an essential part of large-scale program evaluations if program effectiveness is to be determined and understood" (p. 2543).

To understand the program effects of the Project P.A.T.H.S., several complementary program evaluation strategies including both quantitative and qualitative have been adopted. These included objective outcome evaluation, subjective outcome evaluation, process evaluation, interim evaluation, and qualitative evaluation based on focus groups, in-depth interviews and case studies have been employed to evaluate the effectiveness of the project (e.g., Shek 2006; Shek et al. 2006; Shek and Ma 2007; Shek et al. 2007). Through the adoption of different evaluation strategies, there is evidence supporting the effectiveness of the Tier 1 Program of the Project P.A.T.H.S. based on different types of data collected from different participants utilizing different methods (Shek 2008). For example, both quantitative findings based on randomized group trial and qualitative findings based on different studies provide evidence suggesting the Project P.A.T.H.S. is effective in promoting the psychosocial competencies of the program participants (Shek 2008).

To further understand the perceived program effects of the Tier 1 Program, evaluation findings based on weekly diaries written by students are reported in this paper. In the context of social sciences research, diary is commonly used in the clinical and educational contexts to chart human behavior. There are also studies using diaries or reflective journals as an evaluation strategy to examine program effects (e.g., Schmitz and Wiese 2006). Furthermore, it is a common practice for teachers in Hong Kong to ask students to write weekly diaries or reflective journals to document their views on current events and their experiences. With the ease of collecting students' weekly diaries, the studies reported in this paper utilized students' weekly diaries as a research strategy to evaluate the perceived attributes and effectiveness of the P.A.T.H.S. Project. As there are both Experimental Implementation Phase and Full Implementation Phase in the Project P.A.T.H.S., it is reasonable to ask whether the findings are consistent across studies. As such, weekly diaries written by Secondary 1 students in the Experimental Implementation Phase, Secondary 1 students in the Full Implementation Phase, and Secondary 2 students in the Experimental Implementation Phase were collected and analyzed in Study 1, Study 2 and Study 3, respectively.

As a qualitative evaluation strategy, the question of "rigor" in weekly diaries is an important question to be considered. Shek et al. (2005) suggested that 12 principles should be observed in a qualitative evaluation study. The first principle is that an explicit statement of the philosophical stand of the study should be given. The second principle is that the number and nature of the participants of the study should be justified. The third principle is that the data collection procedures should be clearly described. For the fourth and fifth principles, the biases and preoccupations of the researchers should be outlined and the steps taken to guard against biases should be described, respectively. The sixth principle is that measures of reliability, such as inter-rater reliability and intra-rater reliability should be included. For the seventh and eighth principles, measures of triangulation in terms of researchers and data types and checking procedures (such as peer checking and member checking) should be included. The ninth principle is that the researcher should be conscious of the importance and development of audit trails. For the tenth and eleventh principles alternative explanations for the observed findings and explanations for negative evidence should be addressed. Finally, limitations of the study should be clearly stated. In the studies reported in this paper, the above principles were upheld as far as possible. In terms of philosophical orientation of the study, a general qualitative orientation utilizing qualitative principles (e.g., holistic emphasis and reliance on non-numerical raw data) was adopted.

2 Study 1

2.1 Participants and Procedures

Among the 52 schools joining the Tier 1 Program (Secondary 1 Level) in the Experimental Implementation Phase in 2005/2006, four schools were randomly selected to join this research study. The school teachers were asked to randomly invite some Secondary 1 students to write a journal in the form of weekly diary to reveal their perceptions and feelings after joining the Tier 1 Program or randomly select the submitted weekly diaries to the Research Team. The students were informed of the purpose of this study and confidentiality of the data. The consent of the participants was also sought. The total number of students' weekly diaries received was 95, which was about 15% of the total Secondary 1 students in these four schools. As the cases were randomly selected and the response rate was 100%, the recruited sample could be regarded as respectable.

2.2 Data Analyses

The data were analyzed using general qualitative analyses techniques involving three steps (Miles and Huberman 1994). First, relevant raw codes were developed for words, phrases and/or sentences that formed meaningful units at the raw responses level. Second, the codes were further combined to reflect higher-order attributes at the category of codes level. Third, the categories of codes were further analyzed to reveal the broader themes at the thematic level.

In the present qualitative analyses, as the author designed the program in the Project P.A.T.H.S., he was conscious of his own biases and expectations of the program to be effective. As such, the author was not directly involved in the first few steps of the data analyses. In addition, both intra-rater and inter-rater reliabilities on the coding regarding the views on the program and instructors (Table 1) and perceived benefits of the program

Table 1 Views on the program and instructors in Study 1, Study 2 and Study 3

	Reponses	Study 1	Study 2	Study 3
Views on the program				
Overall impression	Positive (e.g., meaningful, excellent, matches with adolescents' needs, better than other programs)	26	116	277
	Negative/neutral (e.g., mixed blessings)	3	1	18
	Total	29	117	295
Program content	Positive (e.g., practical, creative, rich content, easily understood)	27	25	68
	Negative/neutral (e.g., dislike growth puzzles)	6	30	8
	Total	33	55	76
Learning process	Positive (e.g., funny, interesting, happy, active participation)	34	70	107
	Negative/neutral (e.g., boring)	5	18	96
	Total	39	88	203
Other comments	Positive/neutral comments	23	55	104
	Negative comments	0	4	6
Total		124	319	684
Views on the instructor				
Overall impression	Positive (e.g., positive style)	2	8	41
	Negative/neutral (e.g., disgusting)	3	1	3
	Total	5	9	44
Teaching performance	Positive (e.g., excellent, prepared well)	9	28	51
	Negative/neutral	0	3	4
	Total	9	31	55
Teaching attitude	Positive (e.g., enthusiastic)	5	7	40
	Negative/neutral	0	0	0
	Total	5	7	40
Other comments	Non-negative comments	3	3	17
	Negative comments	0	0	3
Total		22	50	159
Grand total		146	369	843

Note Twenty coded raw descriptors were randomly selected for examining consistency in categorization of responses (views on program vs. instructors). Intra-rater reliability = 100% and inter-rater reliability = 85% in Study 1. Intra-rater reliability = 100% and inter-rater reliability = 85% in Study 2. Intra-rater reliability = 100% and inter-rater reliability = 85% in Study 3

(Table 2) were calculated. For intra-rater reliability, the research assistants responsible for the original coding re-coded 20 randomly selected responses and the mean reliability percentage was computed. For inter-rater reliability, another person (e.g., a doctoral student or a research assistant with a master degree) not involved in the original coding re-coded 20 randomly selected responses without knowing the codes finalized by the author at the end of the scoring process.

Table 2 Perceived benefits of the Tier 1 Program in Study 1, Study 2 and Study 3

Psychosocial domains	Sub-domains	Study 1	Study 2	Study 3
Societal domains	Social norms	3	12	3
	Social responsibilities and knowledge about public affairs	11	33	8
	Total	14	45	11
Familial level	Family relationship	5	22	12
Interpersonal level	General interpersonal competence (e.g., making friends, getting along with others)	42	162	147
	Specific interpersonal competence (e.g., respect, empathy)	6	63	28
	Total	48	225	175
Personal level	Cherishing life	2	24	53
	Reflection	8	14	37
	Cognitive competence	12	46	54
	Ways to face adversity	1	17	33
	Positive self-image	32	124	88
	Emotional competence	11	57	28
	Goal setting	6	23	29
	Moral competence and virtues	14	99	47
	Total	86	404	369
Others	Learns much knowledge	14	26	31
	Learns something useful	13	18	0
	Interest in learning	1	4	10
	Others	22	8	27
	Total	50	56	68
Grand total		203	752	635

Note Twenty coded raw descriptors were randomly selected for examining consistency in categorization of responses (i.e., changes on different levels). Intra-rater reliability = 100% and inter-rater reliability = 85% in Study 1. Intra-rater reliability = 100% and inter-rater reliability = 85% in Study 2. Intra-rater reliability = 100% and inter-rater reliability = 85% in Study 3

2.3 Results and Discussion

As shown in Table 1, 146 meaningful units regarding students' perceptions of the Tier 1 Program and the instructor could be categorized into two categories (i.e., views on program and views on instructors). Overall, most of the responses regarding the students' perceptions of the program and instructors were positive. For the responses on the perceived benefits (Table 2), there were a total of 203 meaningful units which were categorized in five categories (i.e., societal, familial, interpersonal, personal levels of competence and others). Most of the respondents reported that they learnt personal competence, following by moral competence and virtues, cognitive competence, and emotional competence.

Several cases illustrate the positive perceptions of the informants:

Case 1 "Although "P.A.T.H.S." is part of the Integrated Humanities subject, I think they are very different. P.A.T.H.S. is very interesting. The instructor always cracked jokes to create a relaxed atmosphere. Students also gave creative responses to make the class feel that it was a relaxed course. In contrast to other subjects where the classroom atmosphere is solemn, I think this course makes the students feel relaxed. As this course is relaxed and I can learn much knowledge from it, I like P.A.T.H.S. very much."

Case 2 "This program enabled me to learn a lot of things which could be applied in my daily life. It helped me develop team spirit, enhance cooperation amongst group members and acquire independence. It was very easy to understand the content of every lesson. Although we were sometimes noisy, the instructors were very patient in teaching us and they would only teach when classmates were quiet. Because of this, I have learned self-discipline."

Case 3 "After joining P.A.T.H.S., I learned how to deal with problems when I face adversity. I also learned much wisdom of life and I have more self-understanding. Before the course, I did not have any dreams and goals. This course helped me develop my goals, understand my dreams and think about how to fulfill my dreams. When I faced difficulty in the past, I only cried. However, it is different now as I have learned different ways to solve my problems in class. Although these methods cannot totally solve my problems, I will not simply cry now."

3 Study 2

3.1 Participants and Procedures

There were 207 schools joining the Secondary 1 Program of the Full Implementation Phase of the P.A.T.H.S. Project. After completion of the Tier 1 Program, six schools were randomly selected to join this research study, with the school teachers randomly invited some Secondary 1 students to write a journal in the form of weekly diary to reveal their perceptions and feelings after joining the Tier 1 Program. The students were informed of the purpose of this study as well as confidentiality and anonymity of the data collected. The students' willingness to join the study was respected and their consent of participation was sought. A total of 216 Secondary 1 students participated in the study. As the cases were randomly selected and the response rate was 100%, the sample characteristics could be regarded as respectable.

In order to ensure consistency of the data collection procedure, a clear guideline on data collection was given to the teachers concerned. The students were asked to write a reflective journal with the title of "Participation in the Tier 1 Program of the Project P.A.T.H.S.: Experiences and Feelings". The weekly diary was expected to be not less than 200 words in Chinese and it should be related to the students' experience, feelings and comments in connection with their participation in the Tier 1 Program. The students could either complete it at home or during class time.

3.2 Results and Discussion

The data analyses procedures and principles were identical to those adopted in Study 1. Basically, the codes emerged from the content of the weekly diaries and they were developed with reference to the coding system devised in Study 1. As shown in Table 1, 369 meaningful units regarding the students' perceptions of the Tier 1 Program and the instructors could be categorized into two categories (i.e., views about program and views about instructors). In the aspect of "views about program", there were 319 responses which could be categorized into "overall impression", "program content", "learning process", and "other comments and suggestions". On the other hand, there were 50 responses of "views about instructors". In total, there were 84.6% positive responses regarding the students' perceptions of the program and instructors.

The perceived benefits of the program to the students are shown in Table 2. There were 752 meaningful units which could be categorized in five categories (i.e., societal, familial, interpersonal, personal levels of competence and others). Most of the respondents reported that they had learnt personal competence, following by "moral competence and virtues", "emotional competence", and "cognitive competence". Next, many respondents reported that they acquired interpersonal competence. Below are three cases illustrations on the perceived benefits of the program:

Student A "When I first joined the program, I thought it was a program that did not make sense and it wasted our time. However, I gradually felt that the program was very useful—it increased my self-confidence and improved my relationships with friends, classmates and family members. As such, I have gradually liked this program. From the transition period from Primary 6 to Secondary 1, we need the concern of our family, friends and teachers. This program can exactly help us how to live. I remember that there is a lesson entitled "I was born with talents". I understand that everybody has talents. The most important point is how we view ourselves and discover our talents. Besides, as time is precious and important, we have to treasure our time."

Student B "In the project, I could learn more about life from mutual sharing. I really learned a lot from the program. The most impressive lesson was "How to interact with other people", such as tolerance and practice which cannot be learned from the books. This program is not boring and I have interest in it. Life is a process. The sad thing is that we cannot live twice. The joyful thing is that we do not have to live twice as we know how to cherish time. After joining the program, I have become more optimistic and cheerful. Not only do I know how to control my emotions but also have more friends now."

Student C "I think the program is very meaningful. I have watched many video clips in the process. I was moved by the situations in the poor countries in Africa. I hope I could send some clothes to them."

4 Study 3

4.1 Participants and Procedures

Among the 49 schools joining the Tier 1 Program (Secondary 2 level) of the Experimental Implementation Phase, four schools were randomly selected to join this research study. The school teachers were asked to randomly invite some Secondary 2 students to write a journal in the form of weekly diary to reveal their perceptions and feelings after joining the Tier 1 Program. The students were informed of the purpose and confidentiality of the research, and their consent of participation was sought. The students were asked to write a reflective journal with the title of "Participating in the Tier 1 Program of the Project P.A.T.H.S: Experiences and feelings". The reflection was expected not less than 200 words in Chinese and it should be related to the students' experiences, feelings and comments after joining the Tier 1 Program, though there were no specific requirements on how to write it. The students could either complete it at home or during class time. The total number of students' weekly diaries received was 260, which was about 36% of the total Secondary 2 students in these four schools. As the cases were randomly selected and the response rate was 100%, the sample characteristics could be regarded as respectable.

4.2 Results and Discussion

The data analyses procedures and principles were identical to those adopted in Study 1 and Study 2. Basically, the codes emerged from the content of the weekly diaries and the coding system was developed with reference to those devised in Study 1 and Study 2. As shown in Table 1, 843 meaningful units regarding the students' perceptions of the Tier 1 Program and the instructors could be categorized into two categories (i.e., views about program and views about instructors). In the aspect of "views about program", there were 684 responses which could be categorized into "overall impression", "program content", "learning process", and "other comments and suggestions". Most of the respondents had positive views on the "overall impression". There were 159 responses of "views about instructors", which were categorized into "overall impression" (e.g., "the instructor was pleasing"), "teaching performance" (e.g., "instructor's performance was excellent"), "teaching attitude" (e.g., "involved"), and "others". In total, there were 83.63% positive responses regarding the students' perceptions of the program and instructors.

The perceived benefits of the program to the students are shown in Table 2. There were a total of 635 meaningful units which could be categorized in five categories (i.e., societal, familial, interpersonal, personal levels of competence and others). Most of the respondents reported that they had learnt personal competence. In addition, many respondents reported that they had acquired interpersonal competence, which could be categorized into "general interpersonal competence" (e.g., "get along with others") and "specific interpersonal competence" (e.g., "respect").

Some narratives based on the informants revealed that the program was perceived positively by the program participants:

Student A "In the process, the instructors were very dedicated in teaching us about the ways of life. I have learned how to respect others. Even though other people are not doing well, we should not blame them. Also, I have learned that none of us is perfect. Through the activities, I have also learned how to solve problems. Besides transmitting knowledge to us, the instructors also encouraged and supported us. In addition, when we encountered difficulties, we could share our problems with them who would then propose some suggestions and solutions for us."

Student B "I am very fortunate to participate in the program as other schools may not have this opportunity. I have learned much knowledge and got valuable experiences from the program. I remember that in one lesson, the instructor asked those quiet students to answer the questions and I was one of them. When I answered the question, I was very nervous. However, when I answered more questions during class, I gained more confidence. The topics are specially designed for students and they are very practical. Most of the activities can raise the self-esteem of the students. Students can really learn much from the program."

Student C "When I first participated in the Project P.A.T.H.S., I really did not want to join as I did not understand the nature of the program. My thought at that time was even you gave me $1 million or $10 million, I still did not want to join it. However, after a few lessons, I began to like the program because the program enabled me to form close friendships with fellow classmates. I could also understand the past history of the instructor. Most important of all, the program has helped me reflect things in the past."

5 General Discussion

Utilizing weekly diaries written by the students, three studies are reported in this paper to give some clues regarding the program effects of the Tier 1 Program of the P.A.T.H.S. Project. As far as the design and data collection of the studies are concerned, these three studies are qualitative studies, sharing the characteristics of naturalistic inquiry, inductive analysis, holistic perspective, qualitative data, unique case orientation and contextual sensitivity (Patton 1990). Regarding data analyses, both qualitative (e.g., coding and categorizing) and quantitative (mainly counting) analyses were used. According to Miles and Huberman (1994), counting is a general tactic for generating meaning in qualitative research. Tashakkori and Teddlie (1998) also pointed out that mixed data analyses methods could be carried out for qualitative studies.

Based on the weekly diaries written by the students, the studies reported in this paper showed that the participants generally had positive perceptions of the Tier 1 Program of the Project P.A.T.H.S. and the instructors. The findings presented in Table 1 suggest that the participants had positive impression of the program and they appreciated the program content and learning process involved. Besides, Table 2 shows that the participants overwhelmingly regarded the program to be beneficial to the emotional, social and productive quality of life of the program participants. For example, a sizable number of responses were related to positive self-image after joining the program. In addition, many participants remarked that their interpersonal competencies were enhanced after joining the program.

The above findings are generally consistent with previous research findings in the Experimental and Full Implementation Phases and they basically concur with both the quantitative and qualitative findings based on objective outcome, subjective outcome, qualitative and process evaluation findings (e.g., Shek 2008). In short, the present findings provide additional support for the effectiveness of the Tier 1 Program of the Project P.A.T.H.S. in Hong Kong. From the perspective of triangulation, the existing evaluation findings suggest that the effectiveness of the Tier 1 Program P.A.T.H.S. is supported by evaluation data collected from different sources and by different strategies.

In the broader context of science, there are views arguing that replication is an important principle that should be used to evaluate scientific findings. For example, in an attempt to highlight the misinterpretations associated with statistical tests of significance, Cohen (1994) argued that social scientists "must finally rely, as has been done in all the older sciences, on replication" (p. 997). Similar view was held by Shaver (1993) who suggested that "the notion of reproducibility leads directly to replication, widely agreed upon as a crucial element of science, but largely missing from reports of social science" (p. 312). Shaver (1993) further argued that "editors should not only actively encourage the reporting of replications, but in many instances demand replication before results can be published" (p. 312). Obviously, the scientific value of the evaluation findings based on weekly diaries written by the students can be substantially enhanced if we can produce evidence to show that the positive findings can be replicated across studies.

The present findings also underscore the utility of using weekly diaries to evaluate positive youth development programs. By asking the program participants to reflect their experiences, subjective perceptions and perceived benefits of the program can be properly understood in a less mechanical and artificial manner. Such an approach can help to capture the dynamic nature of the perceived qualities and effectiveness of the program. In addition to its holistic emphasis and ease of data collection, Maxwell (2004) commented that "qualitative research is a rigorous means of investigating causality" (p. 3). Slayton and Llosa (2005) also remarked that "qualitative methods can confirm that it is actually the program that is responsible for the effect" (p. 2544). Obviously, the use of reflective journals enjoys the strengths of qualitative studies in assessing the changes in quality of life after joining the program.

Of course, credibility is a basic issue in qualitative research and it is no exception to the present studies. Following the principles of qualitative analyses (Shek et al. 2005), the following attributes of the studies reported in this paper are highlighted: (a) a general qualitative orientation was adopted; (b) recruitment process for the participants and justifications for the number of participants are described; (c) details of the data collection are given; (d) the issues of biases and ideological preoccupation are addressed; (e) inter-rater and intra-rater reliabilities information is presented; and (f) the categorized data are kept in a systematic filing system in order to ensure that the findings are auditable.

Nevertheless, with reference to the arguments of Shek et al. (2005) that the authors should discuss the limitations of the qualitative evaluation studies conducted (Principle 12), several limitations of the studies reported in this paper should be noted. First, for students who are sensitive about the issue of "invasion of privacy" (Rothwell and Ghelipter 2003), the use of weekly diary may be regarded as an obtrusive evaluation device. Second, as the diary method is verbal in nature, students who are not good at using words to express their experiences may write little. This problem may be particularly acute in schools admitting students with poor academic performance. This is also a problem in the Chinese culture where Chinese people may lack the language to describe their feelings. Third, as there was only one occasion through which the participants expressed their views, it was not possible to have dialogues with the informants to further understand some of their views. In particular, theoretical sampling approaches could be attempted in future studies.

Fourth, although the present findings are interpreted in terms of the positive program effects and experiences of the program participants, it should be noted that there are several alternative explanations. These alternative explanations should be considered as high proportions of responses were positive responses across the three studies. The first alternative explanation is that the students were afraid that they would be punished by the program implementers if they did not respond in the favorable direction. However, this possibility can be partially dismissed as the teachers did not mark the weekly diaries and the identity of the students was basically anonymous. The second alternative explanation is that the students consciously acted in a "nice" manner to help the workers to illustrate positive program effect. However, this alternative explanation could be partially dismissed because negative comments were recorded and students are normally encouraged to express their views in Hong Kong. The third alternative explanation is that the high proportion of positive responses observed in fact biased responses. However, this alternative explanation can also be dismissed because the schools and students were randomly selected.

Finally, although eleven principles proposed by Shek et al. (2005) were upheld in this study, peer checking and member checking (Principle 8) were not carried out in this study because of time and manpower constraints. Despite these limitations, this study provides pioneering qualitative evaluation findings over time that support the positive nature of the Project P.A.T.H.S. and its effectiveness in promoting holistic youth development and quality of life among Chinese adolescents in Hong Kong.

Acknowledgment The preparation for this paper and the Project P.A.T.H.S. were financially supported by the Hong Kong Jockey Club Charities Trust.

References

Catalano, R. F., Berglund, M. L., Ryan, J. A. M., Lonczak, H. S., & Hawkins, J. D. (2002). Positive youth development in the United States: Research findings on evaluations of positive youth development programs. *Prevention and Treatment, 5*(1).

Chatterji, M. (2004). Evidence on "what works": An argument for extended-term mixed method (ETMM) evaluation designs. *Educational Researcher, 33*, 3–13.

Cohen, J. (1994). The earth is round (p < .05). *American Psychologist, 49*, 997–1003.

Damon, W. (2004). What is positive youth development? *Annals of the American Academy of Political and Social Science, 591*, 13–24.

Felce, D., & Perry, J. (1995). Quality of life: Its definition and measurement. *Research in Developmental Disabilities, 16*, 51–74.

Ginsberg, L. H. (2001). *Social work evaluation: Principles and methods.* Boston: Allyn and Bacon.

Graczyk, P. A., Weissberg, R. P., Payton, J. W., Elias, M. J., Greenberg, M. T., & Zins, J. E. (2000). Criteria for evaluating the quality of school-based social and emotional learning programs. In R. Bar-On & J. D. A. Parker (Eds.), *The handbook of emotional intelligence* (pp. 391–409). San Francisco, CA: Jossey-Bass.

Guerra, N. G., & Williams, K. R. (2003). Implementation of school-based wellness centres. *Psychology in the Schools, 40*, 473–487.

Maxwell, J. A. (2004). Causal explanation, qualitative research, and scientific inquiry in journal item: Education. *Educational Researcher, 33*, 3–11.

Miles, M. B., & Huberman, A. M. (1994). *Qualitative data analysis.* Thousand Oaks, CA: Sage.

Patton, M. Q. (1987). *How to use qualitative methods in evaluation.* Newbury Park, CA.: Sage.

Patton, M. Q. (1990). *Qualitative evaluation and research methods.* Newbury Park, CA: Sage.

Patton, M. Q. (1997). *Utilization-focused evaluation: The new century text.* Thousand Oaks, CA: Sage.

Patton, M. Q. (2002). Two decades of developments in qualitative inquiry: A personal, experiential perspective. *Qualitative Social Work, 1*, 261–283.

Roth, J., Brooks-Gunn, J., Murray, L., & Foster, W. (1998). Promoting healthy adolescents: Synthesis of youth development program evaluations. *Journal of Research on Adolescence, 8*, 423–459.

Rothwell, A., & Ghelipter, S. (2003). The developing manager: Reflective learning in undergraduate management education. *Reflective Practice, 4*, 241–254.

Schmitz, B., & Wiese, B. S. (2006). New perspectives for evaluation of training sessions in self-regulated learning: Time-series analyses of diary data. *Contemporary Educational Psychology, 31*, 64–96.

Shaver, J. P. (1993). What statistical significance testing is, and what it is not. *Journal of Experimental Education, 61*, 293–316.

Shek, D. T. L. (2006). Effectiveness of the Tier 1 program of the project P.A.T.H.S.: Preliminary objective and subjective outcome evaluation findings. *TheScientificWorldJournal, 6*, 1466–1474.

Shek, D. T. L. (2008). Special issue: Evaluation of project P.A.T.H.S. in Hong Kong. *TheScientificWorldJournal, 8*, 1–94.

Shek, D. T. L., & Ma, H. K. (2007). Subjective outcome evaluation of the project P.A.T.H.S.: Findings based on the perspective of the program participants. *TheScientificWorldJournal, 7*, 47–55.

Shek, D. T. L., Ma, H. K., Lui, J. H. Y., & Lung, D. W. M. (2006). Process evaluation of the Tier 1 program of the project P.A.T.H.S. *TheScientificWorldJournal, 1*, 300–309.

Shek, D. T. L., Ma, H. K., & Merrick, J. (Eds.). (2007). *Positive youth development: Development of a pioneering program in a Chinese context.* London: Freund.

Shek, D. T. L., Tang, V., & Han, X. Y. (2005). Quality of qualitative evaluation studies in the social work literature: Evidence that constitutes a wakeup call. *Research on Social Work Practice, 15*, 180–194.

Slayton, J., & Llosa, L. (2005). The use of qualitative methods in large-scale evaluation: Improving the quality of the evaluation and the meaningfulness of the findings. *Teachers College Record, 107*, 2543–2565.

Tashakkori, A., & Teddlie, C. (1998). *Mixed methodology: Combining qualitative and quantitative approaches.* Thousand Oaks, CA: Sage.

Wallander, J. L., Schmitt, M., & Koot, H. M. (2001). Quality of life measurement in children and adolescents: Issues, instruments and applications. *Journal of Clinical Psychology, 57*, 571–585.

Weissberg, R. P., & O'Brien, M. U. (2004). What works in school-based social and emotional learning programs for positive youth development. *Annals of the American Academy of Political and Social Science, 591*, 86–97.

Soc Indic Res (2010) 95:489–502
DOI 10.1007/s11205-009-9533-7

An Exploration of the Burnout Situation on Teachers in Two Schools in Macau

Andrew L. Luk · Bessie P. S. Chan · Selwyne W. Cheong · Stanley K. K. Ko

Accepted: 14 March 2009 / Published online: 2 October 2009

Abstract To explore the burnout situation of teachers in two schools in Macau and to investigate any differences made of demographic characteristics. The relation of burnout on social problem solving and holistic health of teachers is also studied. A self reported questionnaire with the Chinese Maslach Burnout Inventory (C-MBI), Chinese Social Problem Solving Inventory (C-SPSI) and the Body-Mind-Spirit Well-Being Inventory (BMSWBI) were used. Totally 138 teachers participated in the study. With Hong Kong data as a reference, Macau teachers scored in the average range of burnout in emotional exhaustion and depersonalization but scored in the low range of burnout in personal accomplishment. Significance differences were found in some dimensions of burnout in age, marital status, teaching experiences, education background and satisfaction with income. Both C-SPSI and BMSWBI were found to be significantly negative correlated with emotional exhaustion and depersonalization and positive correlated with personal achievement. The findings identified those with greater degree of burnout, to whom more attention should be paid. The study also contributed to the limited literature on the quality of life of teachers in Macau. Finally, the findings added on the data base for comparison internationally among the Chinese population.

Keywords Burnout · Demographic · Macau teachers · MBI · Problem solving · Holistic health

1 Introduction

Macau is a city near Hong Kong and famous for its gaming business. After the government opened the gaming licensure in 2002, both the number of casinos and the revenue generated from the gaming business increase. People working in casinos can usually receive nearly double the pay of those with the same education background but working in other sectors. It attracts quite a number of young people to work there especially those with less

A. L. Luk (✉) · B. P. S. Chan · S. W. Cheong · S. K. K. Ko
Kiang Wu Nursing College of Macau, Macau, SAR China
e-mail: luk@kwnc.edu.mo

motivation to study. The prevailing atmosphere of working in casinos is so great that it affects the traditional Chinese values of studying hard in order to earn more money for a better life. Community voices increasing concerns about schools enhancing teaching of ideals, will power and personal values so that young people can be positively developed and better prepared to resist the temptation of gambling in the city.

In Macau, there is a 15-year free non-tertiary education system with direct promotion from primary to secondary school without any public examination. There is no public examination either but individual admission examination after secondary school education for entry into local universities. The total number of schools is 82 with 5,100 teachers and the overall teacher–student ratio is 1:17.7 (Education and Youth Affairs Bureau 2008a). As a statutory requirement, teachers who are qualified to teach in kindergarten, primary and secondary school must be graduates from the school of education. Those who are not from the teaching background have to complete a teaching course and pass an examination organized by the government in order to obtain professional qualification in teaching (Education and Youth Affairs Bureau 2008b). As a Chinese community, people are expected to behave in line with their social roles. At schools, teachers are expected to be knowledgeable and with high moral standard. Students are to be well-disciplined, self-engaged and reflective in learning. Teachers are dominant and directive in the Eastern pedagogical culture (Zhang 2007). Therefore, teaching has long been a respectable profession in the Chinese culture. However, with the increasing demand from the public to meet the knowledge needed by the changing world and the greater effort for moral education at the same time, teaching is becoming more stressful and teachers are more prone to burnout.

In the prevention of burnout of teachers, a stress reduction program was designed for one primary and one secondary school in Macau as requested from the school principals. These two schools were established in 2002 by a charity organization to receive students, mainly new immigrants from Mainland China. They are non-religious, non-profit making private schools with full tuition sponsored by the government. Since no formal study on burnout was conducted on this group of teachers, it is important to get to know their burnout situation before the implementation of the stress reduction program. This study is to explore the burnout situation of the teachers of these two schools. Furthermore, this study also examines the effect of burnout related to demographic variables, their problem solving ability and general well being.

The term "burnout" was first coined by Freudenberger (1974) to characterize a situation experienced by human service professionals who appear to be exhausted or up to a state of inability to perform their tasks effectively or sometimes even to care for their clients. Maslach (1976) defined burnout as a condition in which one loses all concerns, feeling toward the person one works with and comes to treat them as impersonal objects. Maslach and Jackson (1981) developed a multidimensional model to delineate three aspects of the content of burnout, namely: (1) emotional exhaustion (feeling of drain and tiredness), (2) depersonalization (treating clients as impersonal objects), and (3) lack of personal accomplishment (feeling of inefficiency, ineffectiveness and inadequacy). Since Maslach and Jackson's model has been adopted widely in investigating teachers' burnout syndromes and the Maslach Burnout Inventory (MBI) is also consistently found to be a reliable instrument, this model was adopted in the present study (Lau et al. 2005; Mo 1991; Sarros and Sarros 1990; Xu et al. 2004). Burnout has generally been viewed as a failure to cope with job stress and there is an international concern about stress and burnout among school teachers (Dworkin 1997; Maslach and Jackson 1981). Numerous studies have been conducted to investigate sources of stress of school teachers and its management. Broadly speaking, job nature in terms of overwork, classroom discipline, lack of parental support;

personal factor consisting of blaming oneself, low self-efficacy, neuroticism; and environmental factors such as lack of information about changes, lack of social, organizational and government supports are the major sources of stress.

Besides large volume of studies about the etiology of stress, there were also many studies on demographic data relating to stress. The most common variables for study are sex, teaching classes, marital status, teaching experiences, education, professional and religious backgrounds. These variables together with satisfaction with income were also examined in this study. In the studies of burnout among human service professionals including teachers by Maslach et al. (1996), results showed that female staff had higher emotional exhaustion than male colleagues. Mendes (2003) examined the relationship between emotional intelligence and teacher burnout on 49 credentialed secondary teachers and found that with more experience, teachers were better at identifying emotions. Lau et al. (2005) investigated the relationship between teachers' demographic variables and burnout in Hong Kong using the C-MBI on 1797 respondents from 45 secondary schools. Gender differences were found in all three burnout syndromes, and teachers who were younger, unmarried, without religious beliefs, less experienced, without finishing professional training and of junior rank were more consistently burned-out. Whereas age was the strongest predictor for emotional exhaustion and depersonalization, teachers' rank is the best predictor for personal accomplishment. In addition, Li et al. (2007) explored the relationship between teachers' sense of teaching efficacy and job burnout by using the Teachers' Sense of Teaching Efficacy Scale and the C-MBI which were administered to 247 secondary school teachers. Results indicated that teachers' length of teaching and marital status have significant effects on their personal teaching efficacy, depersonalization and reduced personal accomplishment.

However, there were also some inconsistent findings relating to relationship among the demographic variables and burnout. For instance, Holloman (1999) examined what personal and school-related variables were associated with 383 first-year school teacher burnout. No statically significant differences were found between areas of burnout and the variables of: gender, age and marital status. Likewise, the study by Zhao and Bi (2003) in a sample of 190 secondary school teachers in Chinese Mainland showed that there was no difference between the genders in the three burnout syndromes. A meta-analysis conducted by Weng (2005) in 35 US research studies with K-12 teacher populations concluded that all of the variables of human characteristics included in the demographics of the selected studies did not have very strong predictive correlations with burnout. That means a single factor, such as gender, cannot be used to predict if a person would be more than others susceptible to three dimensions of burnout.

Other studies also showed that burnout was associated with adverse health outcomes (Lee and Ashforth 1996; Maslach and Goldberg 1998). A recent study by Bian and Fan (2006) investigating the status of teacher's stress of 1012 middle school teachers and the relationship between stress and mental health in Chinese Mainland showed that the stress and the total score of Symptom Check List 90 (SCL-90) had positive correlation. It is suggested to improve the teacher's mental health by reducing their stress. Wang and Guo (2007) studied the relationship among occupational stress, teacher burnout and mental health state of 564 primary and middle school teachers in Chinese Mainland. Questionnaires about occupation stress, teacher burnout and SCL-90 Scale were used. Results showed that there were significant correlation among occupational stress, teacher burnout and mental health. There is a high level of occupational stress, teacher burnout and low level of mental health. In managing the burnout situation, social problem solving ability has been viewed as one of the coping strategies to stress in promoting personal well being. Many studies supported that higher social problem solving ability related to higher psychological well-being and general health (Dreer et al. 2005; Paul-Odouard 2006; Siu and Shek 2005a). Problem solving training in the workplace has been conducted to help employees to reduce distress (Ayres and Malouff 2007; Malouff et al. 2007). However, when Huey (2007) examined whether social problem solving ability moderates the effects of occupational stress on burnout, results indicated that though social problem solving ability significantly correlated with all three dimensions of burnout, more effective problem solving may not buffer against burnout under higher levels of occupational stress. Since no previous study regarding these areas is conducted in Macau, one of the aims of this study is to examine the relation of burnout situation to social problem solving and total well being.

With reference to Macau, though there were some studies on teacher stress, most studies adopted a survey approach with self-developed questionnaire which is difficult to be used for international comparison. Furthermore, little is known about the consequences of increasing stress. Education and Youth Affairs Bureau (2001) conducted a telephone survey on 450 school teachers of all primary and secondary education sectors out of 3194. Results showed that 43.0% of respondents felt stressful at work and 47.5% expressed frequent fatigue at school work. Coping strategies recommended included reducing teaching sessions, providing more free time for school teachers and gaining cooperation from parents. Another postal survey conducted by a teacher professional association on 717 school teachers indicated that 61.4% of respondents perceived their work as "exhausted work". The ranking of difficulties at work listed were lack of learning motivation of students, heavy workload and too many students per class (Macau Chinese Education Association 2002). Ng (2002) carried out a comparison study about teacher's time spent on 400 school teachers each on Beijing, Shanghai, Taipei, Hong Kong and Macau. Results showed that both teachers in Hong Kong and Macau were overloaded, working hours were double than those of the teachers of other three cities and time spent mostly were in class teaching, preparation for teaching and marking assignments. A study by Liu (2005) showed that when compared with Shanghai, Macau lacked approximately one-third of school teachers suggesting school teachers in Macau bear the workload of three teachers as compared with the workload of school teachers in Shanghai.

Since there is a paucity of empirical studies of teacher stress locally, and the relation of burnout with problem solving ability and personal well being is never studied in Macau, the present study can contribute to the understanding in these areas which can help design the stress reduction program as a means of coping strategy. Specifically, this study aims to explore the burnout situation of teachers in two schools in Macau and to investigate any differences made of demographic characteristics. The relation of burnout on social problem solving and the total well being of teachers is also examined. In this study, three questions are raised in the attempt to find out the burnout situation among the teachers in these two schools: (1) What is the level of different burnout syndromes of teachers in these two schools? (2) Do demographic characteristics make a difference in burnout situation? (3) Will the burnout situation relate to their social problem solving and total well being?

2 Method

2.1 Participants and Procedures

Ethical approval was obtained from the research review board of the Kiang Wu Nursing College in Macau. All the teachers of one primary and one secondary school were invited to participate in the study. The self administered questionnaires were sent to individual teachers and collected back by the respective school general offices. Voluntary bases and strict confidentiality were ensured. Verbal consents were obtained. Totally 138 teachers participated in the study. Seventy were from the primary school and 64 from the secondary school and four did not indicate. Seventy-six percent of participants were female and 23.19% were male. The age ranged from 21 to over 51 whereas the range from 26 to 30 and over 51 occupied more than 20.00% of the participants respectively. Regarding teaching experiences, 39.86% was under 5 years; however, 26.09% were over 21 years. The majority of them were with professional training status (83.33%). More than half of them 55.80% were married. Nearly seventy percent of participants were mostly satisfied with their salary. Most of them 66.67% were without religious belief.

2.2 Instruments

2.2.1 Chinese Maslach Burnout Inventory (C-MBI)

The MBI was developed by Maslach and Jackson (1981) and the Chinese version was translated by Lau et al. (2005). The MBI consists of three dimensions with 22 items. They are: emotional exhaustion (EE) 9 items, depersonalization (DP) 5 items and reduced personal accomplishment (PA) 8 items. Maslach et al. (1996) reported the reliability coefficients of 0.90 for EE, 0.79 for DP and 0.71 for PA. The alpha coefficients of the present study for the three C-MBI were 0.85 for EE, 0.76 for DP and 0.83 for PA. The participants were asked to rate the items on a 7-point Likert scale ranging from 0(never) to 6(every day). The higher score in emotion exhaustion shows the feeling of drain and tiredness. The higher score in depersonalization indicates treating students as impersonal objects, while lower score in reduced personal accomplishment demonstrates feeling of inefficiency, ineffectiveness and inadequacy. The normative scores provided by Maslach et al. (1996) for teachers were used in assessing the levels of burnout: 27 or higher on EE; 14 or higher on DP; and 30 or lower on PA.

2.2.2 Chinese Social Problem-Solving Inventory Revised (C-SPSI-R)

The 52 item SPSI-R was developed by D'Zurilla et al. (1996) and the Chinese version with its short form was translated and developed by Siu and Shek (2005b). The C-SPSI-R consists of five dimensions with 25 items. They are: Negative problem orientation (NPO) 5 items, Rational problem solving (RPS) 5 items, Positive problem orientation (PPO) 5 items, Avoidance scale (AS) 6 items and Impulsiveness/Careless scale (ICS) 4 items. The Chinese version was found to be internally consistent with Cronbach's alpha for the 5 subscales varied from 0.65 to 0.88 and temporally stable over time with test–retest reliability for the 5 subscales as indicated by Pearson's r varied from 0.48 to 0.79. (Siu and Shek 2005b). The alpha coefficients of the present study for the 5 subscales varied from 0.68 to 0.83. Studies show that SPSI-R is a liable and valid assessment instrument for research and clinical purposes to assess social problem-solving abilities and deficits (Chang and D'Zurilla 1996; D'Zurilla et al. 1996; Siu and Shek 2005a). The participants were asked to rate on a 5-point Likert scale ranging from (0) "Not at all true of me" to (4) "Extremely true of me". The NPO, AS and ICS consist of negative items indicating a dysfunctional or inhibitive orientation toward problem solving, while RPS and PPO consist of positive items indicating a constructive orientation. However the items are presented in a random order. A total score can be obtained by adding up the total positive scales (PPO and RPS) with the reverse scores of negative scales (NPO, AS and ICS). The higher the score indicates the better ability in problem solving.

2.2.3 The Body-Mind-Spirit Well-Being Inventory (BMSWBI)

The 56 item BMSWBI was developed in Chinese by Ng et al. (2005) to assess holistic health and comprised four scales: Physical distress 14 items, Daily functioning 10 items, Affect 19 items and Spirituality 13 items. The four scales have high reliability in their study, with alpha coefficients ranging from 0.87 to 0.92, and concurrent validity. The alpha coefficients of the present study for the four scales ranged from 0.89 to 0.93. The participants were asked to rate on an 11-point (or a 10-point) scale, with scores ranging from 0(or 1) to 10; negative items were scored in reverse direction. The higher score in Physical distress shows the worse condition in health. On the contrary the higher scores in Daily functioning, Affect and Spirituality indicate the better condition in health. The scores of all items can be added up together to form a total score. The higher the total score indicates the better the overall well-being.

3 Results

3.1 MBI Score of Participants

To study the level of different burnout syndromes of the participants, the means and standard deviations of the three burnout syndromes were calculated. The mean scores for emotional exhaustion, depersonalization and personal accomplishment are 22.09 (SD = 10.49), 6.70 (SD = 5.86) and 31.36 (SD = 9.01), respectively. The results are shown in Table 1. According to Maslach et al. (1996), scores of the MBI subscales are considered high if they fall into the upper third portion of the normative distribution, average if they fill into the middle third and low if they fall into the lower third. Overall, participants scored average in emotional exhaustion and personal accomplishment but low in depersonalization subscales. However, when using the normative scores provided in assessing the high level of burnout, some participants were experiencing high level of burnout. Thirty-four percent of the participants suffered from high level of emotional exhaustion with score 27 or higher, while 12.3% of the participants exhibited high level of depersonalization with score 14 or higher. In addition, 44.2% of the participants experienced lack of personal accomplishment with score 30 or lower. Finally, 4.3% (i.e., six persons) met the criteria of "highly burnout" with scores high on emotional exhaustion and depersonalization and low on personal accomplishment. Whereas 18.8% (i.e., 26 persons) suffered from quite serious condition with scores high on emotional exhaustion and low on personal accomplishment.

Table 1 Mean scores and standard deviations of the MBI subscales of Macau teachers

Maslach burnout inventory subcales	*n*	Number of items	Mean	SD
Emotional exhaustion	138	9	22.09	10.49
Depersonalization	138	5	6.70	5.86
Personal accomplishment	138	8	31.36	9.01

Table 2 Comparison of the categorization of MBI scores of Macau school teachers ($n = 138$) with secondary school teachers of Hong Kong ($n = 1797$) and school teachers of US ($n = 4163$)

MBI subscales	Range of experienced burnout		
	Low (lower third)	Average (middle third)	High (upper third)
Macau teachers (Primary and secondary)			
EE	<17	18–26	>27
DP	<4	5–7	>8
PA	>35	34–28	<27
Hong Kong teachers (grades 7–13)			
EE	<17	18–26	>27
DP	<3	4–7	>8
PA	>38	37–31	<30
US teachers (grades K-12)			
EE	<16	17–26	>27
DP	<8	9–13	>14
PA	>37	36–31	<30

EE emotional exhaustion, *DP* depersonalization, *PA* personal accomplishment

In order to help generate more insights into the burnout situation of Macau, data of the present study is compared with data from Hong Kong teachers (Lau et al. 2005) and North American teachers (Maslach et al. 1996). Adopting the method proposed by Maslach et al. (1996) for computing the cut-off points for the high, average and low range of the MBI subscales, the cut-off points for the Macau data were then calculated. When comparing the three MBI scores of Macau teachers with Hong Kong teachers, it is found that the ranges of all scores are similar to each other. When comparing the three MBI scores of Macau teachers with North American teachers, it is found that the ranges for emotional exhaustion scores and personal accomplishment scores from both places are similar to each other while the range of depersonalization scores of Macau teachers is much lower than that of the North American teachers. The results are presented in Table 2.

3.2 Teacher Burnout and Demographic Characteristics

One way ANOVA test was used to study the effects of demographic variables with teacher burnout. The demographic variables including the participants' gender, teaching class level, age, marital status, teaching experience, education background, professional qualification, satisfaction with income and religious belief were regarded as independent variables while the three burnout syndromes as dependent variables. Scheffe's test was conducted to examine group differences for those independent variables with two or more levels. The results are shown in Table 3.

No significant differences were found in all three burnout syndromes in gender, teaching class, professional qualification and religious belief while significant differences were found in some burnout syndromes in age, marital status, teaching experience, education background and satisfaction with income. Age was found to be one of the demographic variables that was related to burnout. Significant differences were found in emotional exhaustion and depersonalization. Younger teachers tended to show greater burnout syndromes than their older colleagues. According to Scheffe's procedure ($p < 0.05$), teachers below the age of 30 were more burned-out than those at the age of more than 31 and teachers at the age between 30 and 50 showed greater burnout syndrome than those above

Table 3 ANOVA of the MBI subscales by the demographic variables of Macau school teachers

Variables	*N*	Emotional exhaustion			Depersonalization			Personal accomplishment		
		M	SD	*F*	*M*	SD	*F*	*M*	SD	*F*
Sex										
Male	31	22.16	12.23	0.002	8.35	7.36	2.49	33.10	9.10	1.02
Female	100	22.07	10.17		6.47	5.28		31.24	8.92	
Class										
Primary	66	22.32	11.42	0.008	7.16	6.01	0.21	31.66	9.36	0.001
Secondary	62	22.48	9.43		6.69	5.58		31.60	8.59	
Age										
Below 30	49	25.57	8.95	4.83**	8.40	5.67	3.54*	30.81	7.81	1.68
30–50	58	20.48	10.8		6.50	6.48		30.95	9.83	
above 50	25	18.68	811.57		4.85	3.87		34.52	9.76	
Marital status										
Single	58	25.40	9.59	10.33**	8.30	6.01	6.03*	32.33	7.55	0.55
Married	73	19.66	10.57		5.82	5.58		31.16	9.74	
Teaching experience										
Below 10 year	66	23.85	9.46	3.84*	7.31	5.73	1.55	31.58	8.10	0.90
10–20	33	22.67	11.35		7.52	6.91		30.10	9.57	
Over 20	33	17.76	10.97		5.35	4.79		33.06	10.06	
Education background										
Diploma	61	20.02	10.58	4.16*	5.74	5.48	4.35*	32.25	9.97	0.63
Degree	71	23.76	10.47		7.83	6.04		31.00	8.08	
Professional qualification										
No	14	25.07	8.80	1.26	7.30	5.03	0.05	32.55	6.86	0.09
Yes	114	21.6	10.92		6.91	6.00		31.72	9.10	
Income										
Satisfied	95	20.81	10.02	5.63*	6.05	4.91	8.92**	32.41	9.17	2.23
Dissatisfied	33	25.82	11.60		9.48	7.59		29.76	7.98	
Religious belief										
No	87	22.85	10.82	0.08	7.38	6.07	1.06	31.08	8.85	1.11
Yes	41	21.05	10.28		6.24	5.38		32.90	9.38	

N number of subjects, *M* mean, *SD* standard deviation, *F* *F*-value

* $p < 0.05$, ** $p < 0.01$

50. Teaching experience was another demographic variable related to burnout. Teachers with less than 10 year experiences were significantly more burn-out in emotional exhaustion than those working with over 20 year of experiences. Furthermore, teachers who were single, with better education background and dissatisfied with income were found consistently more burned-out in emotional exhaustion and depersonalization.

3.3 Relation of Burnout with Problem Solving and Total Well-Being

With the Pearson correlation test, both the C-SPSI and BMSWBI were found to be significantly negative correlated with emotional exhaustion and depersonalization and

Table 4 Correlation of BMSWBI and MBI subscales, Correlation of C-SPSI and MBI subscales

		Emotional exhaustion	Depersonalization	Personal accomplishment
BMSWBI and MBI subscales				
BMSWBI	Pearson correlation Sig. (2-tailed)	−.626*	−.459*	.232*
	N	124	124	124
C-SPSI and MBI subscales				
C-SPSI	Pearson correlation Sig. (2-tailed)	−.463*	−.462*	.492*
	N	138	138	138

N Number of subjects, * $p < 0.05$

positive correlated with personal achievement indicating that the more burned-out participants were the worse their problem solving ability and personal total well being would be. The results are presented in Table 4.

4 Discussion

4.1 The Burnout Situation of Macau School Teachers

It was found that Macau school teachers on the whole experienced moderate levels of emotional exhaustion, low levels of depersonalization, and moderate levels of personal accomplishment. However, many participants did suffer some psychological distress. Beyond six persons were found to be highly burned-out, twenty-six persons were demonstrating high levels of emotional exhaustion coupled with high levels of reduced personal accomplishment which would be problematic to the participants, their clients and the schools. These situations coincide with the findings of some local studies that school teachers in Macau are facing increasing stress (Education and Youth Affairs Bureau 2001; Macau Chinese Education Association 2002). Interventions are needed to assist them to prevent burnout.

When comparing the mean scores of the present study with the normative data of the Hong Kong teachers (Lau et al. 2005), we found that both teachers of Macau and Hong Kong scored in the average range of burnout in emotional exhaustion, depersonalization and personal accomplishment. These findings coincide with other comparison study between Macau and Hong Kong school teachers that both cities are facing the same problems (Ng 2002). When comparing the mean scores of the Macau data with the normative data of the teaching professionals of the North America (Maslach et al. 1996), Macau school teachers scored lower in depersonalization subscales than that of the North American teachers. These results coincided with the findings of Lau's study (Lau et al. 2005). As suggested, the expectation of the teacher role was different between the East and the West. The traditional role of teachers in the Chinese culture to treat their students in a strict and disciplined approach might be one of the reasons why both Macau and Hong Kong school teachers scored in depersonalization much lower than that of the North American teachers (Lau et al. 2005). Teachers in Macau and Hong Kong might not see themselves dehumanizing or indifferent to their students by being severe and controlling.

On the contrary, they might perceive it as an effective way to train their students with a good will.

4.2 Demographic Differences of Teacher Burnout

Regarding gender differences, previous studies yielded inconsistent findings. In some western studies, Byrne (1991, 1999) found that female teachers reported greater burnout than male teachers among elementary and university educators in emotional exhaustion. On the other hand, no significant gender differences were found in emotional exhaustion in other studies (Maslach and Jackson 1986; Mills and Heubner 1998). In some eastern studies, Lau et al. (2005) found gender differences of the three burnout dimensions among teachers in Hong Kong secondary schools. Male teachers reported more depersonalization while female teachers experienced more emotional exhaustion and reduced personal accomplishment. On the other hand, no significant gender differences were found in the three burnout syndromes in a sample of 190 secondary school teachers in China Mainland. The results of the current study found no significant gender differences of each of the three burnout dimensions which provided evidence to support the inconsistent findings. Differences in the local context may be one explanation which requires further study.

Relating to teaching class, the present study found no difference in burnout situation between the primary and secondary school teachers which is inconsistent with previous studies such as the study by Anderson and Iwanicks (1984) that high school teachers were found to be more burned-out than teachers from elementary schools. There may be several possible reasons for this finding. First, Macau has been ruled by Portugal for more than 200 years before it is handed over to Mainland China in 1999. The values of enjoyment of life and living in a non-competitive environment of a small city like Macau are very much emphasized. Since competition is not encouraged, there is no public examination in both primary and secondary schools after graduation for promotion to the senior grade for studying. Therefore, no stress will be exerted to both primary and secondary school teachers to obtain a good performance of their students in the public examinations. Second, education is well supported by the government in Macau. There is a 15-year free education system from kindergarten to secondary schools. Even in local universities, there are quite a number of sponsorships and awards granted to those who are interested in further studying. Pressure to both students and teachers are less when compared with those countries that are short of support from the government. Third, in traditional Chinese culture, teaching is a respectable profession no matter teacher teaches in primary or secondary school.

With respect to professional qualification, the present finding is also inconsistent with the study of Lau et al. (2005) that teachers without professional training status were more burned-out than those with professional status. One possible reason is that 12 out of 14 participants without professional training status are university graduates who are capable to fulfill the requirement of professional training and pass the required examination organized by the government without much difficulty. Another reason may be due to the small number of participants without professional training status which cannot show the differences by statistical means.

With reference to religious belief, the present finding that no difference in burnout situation between teachers with and without religious belief is also found to be inconsistent with the study by Lau et al. (2005) that teachers with religious belief expressed significantly greater scores in personal accomplishment. One possible explanation is that religious commitment is not high in Macau. Data showed that 79.3% of Macau's population professes the religion of Buddhism, over 5.0% are Roman Catholic and more than 1.0% are

Protestants (US Consulate General 2007). Whereas in Hong Kong, only 43.0% of population participates in some form of religious practice and 9.6% are Christians including Catholics and Protestants (US Consulate General 2008). Though more people are with religious belief in Macau, as shown by Lui (2003) in a study of the local religion in Hong Kong and Macau, specifically referring to the folk religion including a mixture of Buddhism, Taoism and Confucianism, people will only seek a deity who can help them most in their particular area of difficulty. Furthermore, study by Luk and Shek (2006) indicated that only high levels of religious involvement (indexed by higher frequencies of church attendance) were generally related to psychological well being.

When the demographic variables with significant differences are concerned, the findings of the present study are in line with other studies that younger teachers have reported more emotional exhaustion and higher depersonalization (Maslach and Jackson 1981; Lau et al. 2005). It is understandable that young teachers are lacking life experiences in managing people including students, parents, colleagues and supervisors and they are more prone to job stress. When considering marital status, single persons were found to be more emotionally exhausted and depersonalizing than married persons, which were consistent with the findings by (De Heus and Diekstra 1999) and Li et al. (2007). Though divorce is not uncommon nowadays, marriage is still expected to be a lifelong commitment for a stable and enduring relationship which helps married persons to be emotionally supported to one and the other and kept healthy when facing life crisis such as job stress (Tischler 2007). Regarding teaching experiences, teachers with less teaching experience showed higher level of burnout in the emotional dimension, which are in line with the studies conducted by Mo (1991) and Lau et al. (2005) in Hong Kong. Study by Mendes (2003) also supported that with more experience, teachers are better at identifying emotions which helps cope with stress. With respect to education background, those with higher education background expressed more emotional exhaustion and higher depersonalization which may be due to their higher expectation to oneself and to their students. Concerning satisfaction with income, those with dissatisfaction felt more emotionally exhausted and depersonalizing. One possible explanation is that the feeling of unfairness in what they contribute to their work will affect their morale which in turn will increase their emotion drainage.

As far as these demographic variables with significant differences are concerned, some burnout syndromes are found in school teachers who are younger, single, with less teaching experience, higher education background and dissatisfied with income. These findings can provide useful information to the school administrators in developing strategies to combat burnout. Beyond organizing induction program and mentor system for those new teachers who are young and green in the teaching profession, a more challenging in-service training program should also be developed to provide continuing education and enhancement to those who are more academically prepared. Furthermore, a caring atmosphere and a strong team spirit have to be cultivated to provide better social support to those who are single and to those dissatisfied with income to be diverted from only monetary incentives.

4.3 Relation of Burnout with Problem Solving and Total Well-Being

A significant correlation between burnout and personal well-being is in line with other studies (Bian and Fan 2006; Wang and Guo 2007) that high level of burnout may affect one's health in terms of low level of holistic health. Likewise, all three dimensions of burnout were found to be significantly correlated with social problem solving ability indicating that burnout may affect one's problem solving ability. Siu and Shek (2005a) studied the relations between social problem solving and emotional well-being and found that high levels of social problem solving were related to better emotional well-being. Study by Huey (2007) also showed that social problem solving ability significantly correlated with all three dimensions of burnout and suggested that evaluating one's social problem solving ability in addition to occupational stress may allow for better identification of those who may be at risk of burnout. Seeing that burnout is related to social problem solving and personal well-being, it is important to design a well structured and evaluative stress reduction program for those who may be more prone to burnout. However, such intervention program is scarce in Macau.

4.4 Limitations of the Study

There are some limitations of the study. First, the sample size was small; therefore the power of analyses was reduced. However, it still met the minimal numbers for meaningful analysis. Second, the samples came from two schools; the results cannot be generalized to the general population. Third, the cutoff scores of the MBI into high, average and low range of subscales are arbitrary. However, it is still an acceptable way for comparison between different samples. Finally, the management culture of the two schools were not explored which might affect the understanding of its influences to the participants in coping with stress and burnout.

5 Conclusion

The study found that teachers of two schools in Macau experienced relatively average burnout which coincided with the findings in Hong Kong. These findings added on the data base for comparison internationally among the Chinese population. The findings identified those with greater degree of burnout, to whom more attention should be paid. Furthermore, it once again supported that level of burnout may affect one's problem solving ability and holistic health. Finally, the study also contributed to the limited literature on the quality of life of teachers in Macau.

References

Anderson, M. B., & Iwanicki, E. F. (1984). Teacher motivation and its relationship to burnout. *Educational Administration Quarterly, 20*, 94–132.

Ayres, J., & Malouff, J. M. (2007). Problem-solving training to help workers increase positive affect, job satisfaction, and life satisfaction. *European Journal of Work and Organizational Psychology, 16*(3), 279–294.

Bian, B. Q., & Fan, F. M. (2006). Teachers stress and mental health in middle school. *Chinese Mental Health Journal, 20*, 48–50.

Byrne, B. M. (1991). Burnout: investigating the impact of background variables for elementary, intermediate, secondary, and university educators: Teaching and teacher education. *An International Journal of Research, 7*, 197–209.

Byrne, B. M. (1999). The nomological network of teacher burnout: A literature review and empirically validated model. In R. Vandenberghe & A. M. Huberman (Eds.), *Understanding and preventing teacher burnout* (pp. 15–37). Cambridge: Cambridge university Press.

Chang, E. C., & D'Zurilla, T. J. (1996). Relations between problem orientation and optimism, pessimism, and trait affectivity: A construct validation study. *Behaviour Research and Therapy, 34*, 185–194.
D'Zurilla, T. J., Nezu, A. M., & Maydeu-Olivares, A. (1996). *Manual for the social problem-solving inventory-revised (SPSI-R)*. NY, Tonawanda: Multi-Health Systems, Inc.
De Heus, P., & Diekstra, R. F. W. (1999). Do teachers burn out more easily? A comparison of teachers with other social professions on work stress and burnout symptoms. In R. Vandenberghe & A. M. Huberman (Eds.), *Understanding and preventing teacher burnout* (pp. 269–284). Cambridge: Cambridge university Press.
Dreer, L. E., Elliott, T. R., Fletcher, D. C., & Swanson, M. (2005). Social problem solving abilities and psychological adjustment of persons in low vision rehabilitation. *Rehabilitation Psychology, 50*(3), 232–238.
Dworkin, A. G. (1997). Coping with reform, the intermix of teacher morale, teacher burnout, and teacher accountability. In B. J. Biddle, T. L. Good, & I. F. Goodson (Eds.), *International handbook of teachers and teaching* (pp. 459–498). Dordrecht/Boston/London: Kluwer Academic Publishers.
Education and Youth Affairs Bureau. (2008a). *The general situation of non-tertiary education in Macau in academic year 2007/2008*. Retrieved February 20, 2009, from Macau Special Administrative Region, Macau Web site: http://www.dsej.gov.mo/~webdsej/www/einter_dsej_page.php.
Education and Youth Affairs Bureau. (2008b). *Academic and professional qualification: Law 15/96/M- the general rules for teaching personnel*. Retrieved March 2, 2009, from Macau Special Administrative Region, Macau Web site: http://www.dsej.gov.mo/~webdsej/www/edulaw/basic/d1596mc.htm.
Education and Youth Affairs Bureau. (2001). *A survey of teacher work stress 2001*. Macau: Macau Special Administrative Region. in Chinese.
Freudenberger, H. J. (1974). Staff burn-out. *Journal of Social Issues, 30*, 159–165.
US Consulate General (2008). *General information: Background note, Hong Kong*. Retrieved September 2, 2008, from http://hongkong.usconsulate.gov/ushk_2008.html.
Holloman, H. L. (1999). *Factors related to burnout in first-year teachers in South Carolina*. Dissertation, University of South Carolina.
Huey, S. T. (2007). *Occupational stress, social problem solving, and burnout among mental health professionals in HIV/AIDS care*. Dissertation, University of Drexel.
Lau, P. S. Y., Yuen, M. T., & Chan, R. M. C. (2005). Do demographic characteristics make a difference to burnout among Hong Kong secondary school teachers? *Social Indicators Research, 71*, 491–516.
Lee, R. T., & Ashforth, B. E. (1996). A meta-analytic examination of the correlates of the three dimensions of job burnout. *Journal of Applied Psychology, 81*, 123–133.
Li, Y. X., Yang, X., & Shen, J. L. (2007). The relationship between teachers' sense of teaching efficacy and job burnout. *Psychological Science (China), 30*, 952–954.
Liu, S. B. (2005). *Teachers' strategies in facing stress*. (Paper presented at the conference on Enhancing Teachers' Professionalism for Chinese Community, Hong Kong). Retrieved September 3, 2008. from http://cpc.emb.org.hk/conference/download/liu.doc.
Lui, T. S. (2003). A nameless but active religion: An anthropologist's view of local religion in Hong Kong and Macau. In D. L. Overmyer (Ed.), *Religion in China today*. New York: Cambridge University Press. 72.
Luk, A. L., & Shek, D. T. L. (2006). Changes in Chinese discharged chronic mental patients attending a psychiatric rehabilitation program with holistic care elements: A quasi-experimental study. *TSW Holistic Health and Medicine, 1*, 71–83. doi:10.1100/tswhhm.2006.26.
Macau Chinese Education Association. (2002). Teaching job make you exhausted. *Macau Education, 2*, 51–63. (in Chinese).
Malouff, J., Thorsteinsson, E., & Schutte, N. (2007). The efficacy of problem solving therapy in reducing mental and physical health problems: A meta-analysis. *Clinical Psychology Review, 27*, 46–57.
Maslach, C. (1976). Burned-out. *Human Behavior, 5*, 7–22.
Maslach, C., & Goldberg, J. (1998). Prevention of burnout: New perspectives. *Applied and Preventive Psychology, 7*, 63–74.
Maslach, C., & Jackson, S. E. (1981). The measurement of experienced burnout. *Journal of Occupational Behavior, 2*, 99–113.
Maslach, C., & Jackson, S. E. (1986). *Maslach burnout inventory manual* (2nd ed.). CA: Consulting Psychologists Press.
Maslach, C., Jackson, S. E., & Leiter, M. (1996). *Maslach burnout inventory manual* (3rd ed.). CA: Consulting Psychologists Press.
Mendes, E. J. (2003). *The relationship between emotional intelligence and occupational burnout in secondary school teachers*. Dissertation, University of Walden.

Mills, L. B., & Heubner, E. S. (1998). A prospective study of personality characteristics, occupational stressors, and burnout among school psychology practitioners. *Journal of School Psychology, 36*, 103–120.

Mo, K. W. (1991). Teacher burnout: Relation with stress, personality, and social support. *Education Journal, 19*, 3–12.

Ng, K. T. (2002). A comparison study on teacher's activity time and characteristics between Macau and Beijing. *Teacher Journal, 5*, 42–49. (in Chinese).

Ng, S. M., Yau, J. K. Y., Chan, C. L. W., Chan, C. H. Y., & Ho, D. Y. F. (2005). The measurement of body-mind-spirit well-being toward multidimensionality and transcultural applicability. *Social Work in Health Care, 41*, 33–52.

Paul-Odouard, R. (2006). *Emotional intelligence, social problem solving, and demographics as predictors of well-being in women with multiple roles*. Dissertation, University of Adelphi.

Sarros, A. M., & Sarros, J. C. (1990). How burned out are our teachers? A cross-cultural study. *Australian Journal of Education, 34*, 145–152.

Siu, A. M. H., & Shek, D. T. L. (2005a). Relations between social problem solving and indicators of interpersonal and family well-being among Chinese adolescents in Hong Kong. *Social Indicators Research, 71*(1), 517–539.

Siu, A. M. H., & Shek, D. T. L. (2005b). The Chinese social problem solving inventory: Some initial results on reliability and validity. *Journal of Clinical Psychology, 61*, 347–360.

Tischler, H. L. (2007). *Introduction to sociology* (9th ed.). CA: Thomson, Wadsworth. p306.

US Consulate General. (2007). *U.S. and Macau, religious demography*. Retrieved September 2, 2008, from http://hongkong.usconsulate.gov/usmo_hr_2007091401.html.

Wang, W. Z., & Guo, L. Y. (2007). An investigation on occupational stress, teacher burnout and mental health state of primary and middle schools teachers and the relations among them. *Chinese Journal of Clinical Psychology, 15*, 146–148. (in Chinese).

Weng, C. H. (2005). *Meta-analysis of teacher burnout in public schools in the United States*. Dissertation, University of South Dakota.

Xu, F., Ji, F., & Chao, Q. (2004). The development of job burnout questionnaire in primary and secondary teachers. *Chinese Journal of Clinical Psychology, 12*, 13–14. (in Chinese).

Zhang, J. (2007). A cultural look at information and communication technologies in Eastern education. *Education Technology Research and Development, 55*, 301–314. doi:10.1007/s114230079040.

Zhao, Y., & Bi, C. (2003). Job burnout and the factors related to it among middle school teachers. *Psychological Development and Education, 1*, 80–84. (in Chinese).

Soc Indic Res (2010) 95:503–517
DOI 10.1007/s11205-009-9523-9

The Influence of Health Promoting Practices on the Quality of Life of Community Adults in Hong Kong

Phoenix K. H. Mo · W. S. Mak Winnie

Accepted: 5 April 2009 / Published online: 13 October 2009

Abstract The importance of a healthy lifestyle is receiving increasing attention due to its impact on health and well-being. However, very few studies have been done on health promoting practices of the general public in Hong Kong. The present study aimed to identify the patterns of health promoting practices of the general public in Hong Kong, to compare health promoting practices across gender and education levels, and to examine the relationship between health promoting practices and quality of life. A total of 941 community adults were recruited using a randomized household survey design. Results revealed that a large proportion of participants reported practicing various types of health promoting behavior related to healthy food choice, engaging in stress management strategies, and refraining from health compromising behavior such as smoking and drinking excessively. Female participants were more likely to choose healthy food, refrain from smoking and drinking alcohol excessively, and take vitamin supplements, whereas male participants were more likely to exercise regularly. Both men and women with higher levels of education were more likely to report not smoking, not drinking alcohol excessively, and participating in social activities. Women with higher levels of education were also more likely to engage in relaxing activities but less likely to report exercising regularly and sleeping sufficiently. Hierarchical regression analyses revealed that stress management and social relations significantly predicted better quality of life for both male and female participants, and types of preventive health behavior were significant predictors of quality of life for female participants only. Results highlighted the importance of advocating health promoting practices among the general public in Hong Kong. Implications for future practice were discussed.

P. K. H. Mo
Institute of Work, Health and Organisations, University Boulevard, 8 William Lee Buildings, Science and Technology Park, Nottingham NG7 2RQ, UK
e-mail: lwxkhm1@nottingham.ac.uk

W. S. M. Winnie (✉)
Department of Psychology, Chinese University of Hong Kong, 3/F Sino Building, Shatin, Hong Kong
e-mail: wwsmak@psy.cuhk.edu.hk

Keywords Health promoting practice · Health practice · Quality of life · Hong Kong

1 Introduction

The importance of a healthy lifestyle is receiving increasing attention due to its effect on health and well-being. During the past decades, growing emphasis has been placed on preventing disability and death through changes in lifestyle. The World Health Organization estimated in 2002 that 50.8% of deaths are attributable to major chronic diseases (cancer, cardiovascular disease, chronic respiratory disease, and diabetes mellitus) that are closely related to an unhealthy lifestyle. The epidemiologic transition from infection to chronic diseases as leading causes of death, together with the aging of the population and rapidly escalating health care costs have called for an urgent need for a shift in public health care systems from acute treatment to the prevention of disease and the promotion of better health-related behavior (Breslow 1999).

1.1 The Importance of Health Promoting Practice

Health promoting practice is a pattern of self-initiated actions individuals take to control, maintain, or enhance their own health (Acton and Malathum 2000; Hoy et al. 2007). It has become increasingly evident that lifestyle patterns have significant effects on long term morbidity and mortality. Previous studies have shown that healthy lifestyles are not only related to perceived health but can also mitigate the negative effects of chronic disease and decrease the incidence of various health conditions (Dean 1989; Holahan and Suzuki 2004; Wagner et al. 1992). Prospective studies have also reported a strong association between healthy behavior and delay or prevention of major causes of premature disability and mortality in the later stages of life (Hu et al. 2000). For example, Khaw et al. (2008) explored the relationship between lifestyles and mortality among 20,244 men and women using a prospective design and found that the combination of four types of healthy behavior (currently non-smoking, not physically inactive, moderate alcohol intake, and vitamin intake) showed a strong effect in terms of decreased mortality, with an estimated impact of 14 years in chronological age. These trends remained consistent after controlling for sex, age group, body mass index, and social class. Positive types of health behavior are crucial, as they have the potential to reduce substantial suffering, premature mortality, and medical costs.

On the other hand, although unhealthy lifestyles may not produce an immediate effect on morbidity or mortality, many of the negative effects of unhealthy lifestyles develop over a lifetime and surface late in life when it is too late to restore health. Research has widely documented that unhealthy behavior such as smoking, lack of exercise, diet, stressful behavior patterns, and excess alcohol use are associated in the long term with a higher incidence of cancer, circulatory, respiratory, neoplastic, and psychological disorders (Doll et al. 2004; Dornelas 2008; Walker and Townsend 1999). Among the more obvious kinds of unhealthy behavior, unhealthy diet, physical inactivity, tobacco consumption, and the harmful use of alcohol, have been identified as key risk factors responsible for a substantial proportion of the leading causes of death and disability (World Health Organization 2002). As unhealthy kinds of behavior are detectable and modifiable, encouraging the practice of health promoting behavior is crucial as it has the potential to prevent the development of chronic diseases, reduce morbidity, improve quality of life, and decrease the health care burden on society.

1.2 Health Promoting Practices in Hong Kong

Hong Kong is a cosmopolitan city and is one of the most urbanized cities in the Southeast Asia. Over the decades, Hong Kong has experienced a drastic transition in economic, political, and social environments due to rapid urbanization. This urbanization has caused a shift towards Western diets, sedentary lifestyles, high density living, and high job demand. This urban lifestyle has tremendously increased the risks for chronic diseases. For example, one study suggested that the urbanization in Hong Kong has caused high emotional strains, which in turn have increased the prevalence of mental illness (Lo 1976). This has important implications for health care costs and can have important effects on productivity, morbidity and mortality, and quality of life.

Although the importance of maintaining a healthy lifestyle is receiving increasing attention, much of the research on health promoting practices in Hong Kong has been limited to specific populations such as nurses, adolescents, university students, or older adults with diabetes (Lee and Yuen Loke 2005; Wong and Tang 2005; Wu et al. 2004). For example, Callaghan and colleagues (1997) studied the health-related practices of 92 nurses (90% female) in Hong Kong and found that most participants reported avoiding food that is high in sed regularly. Although these limited studies have elucidated the behavior of the target groups concerned, very little is known about the pattern of health promoting practices of Hong Kong's population in general. A better understanding of the patterns and trends of health promoting practices of the general public would provide valuable information for the design of health promotion programs for the general public.

1.3 Health Promoting Practices and Quality of Life

Quality of life (QOL) is defined as "individuals' perception of their position in life in the context of the culture and value systems in which they live and in relation to their goals, expectations, standards and concerns" (WHOQOL Group 1995). It is a broad ranging concept which encompasses a person's physical and psychological state, level of independence, and social relationships (Anderson et al. 1999). While the relationships between health behavior and health status, and health status and perceived QOL have been widely examined, the association between health behavior and QOL has been the subject of relatively few studies, which have focused mainly on disease populations. For example, it has been suggested that exercise and healthy diet are associated with better QOL in various health conditions such as multiple sclerosis, depression, and celiac disease (Motl and Gosney 2008; Mustalahti et al. 2002; Petajan et al. 1996; Tsutsumi 1997). Holahan and Suzuki (2004) examined the relationship between health behavior and quality of life and found that positive psychosocial behavior, positive health practices, and exercise and physical recreation were all significantly related to perceived health and well-being. As QOL constitutes a vital part of health outcome appraisals, understanding the relationship between health behavior and QOL would have important implications for the design of health promotion programs to improve the overall QOL of the public.

1.4 Gender and Health Promoting Practices

Previous studies have consistently demonstrated a gender difference in health promoting practices. While women tend to report higher levels of positive health promoting practices on relaxation, food choice, and interpersonal relationships than men, men tend to report a higher level of exercise than women (Acton and Malathum 2000; Felton et al. 1997;

Hubbard et al. 1984; Lee and Yuen Loke 2005). Some studies have also reported a higher rate of unhealthy lifestyle patterns such as smoking and excessive alcohol consumption in men (Nolen-Hoeksema and Hilt 2006; Shiffman and Paton 1999; Stockton et al. 2000).

Such a difference in the patterns in health behavior can be explained by the difference in gender role socialization. According to the socialization theory, male socialization focuses on masculinity, self-reliance, aggression, and indulgence, whereas female socialization emphasizes dependence, collaboration, and submission. Consequently, individuals may engage in types of behavior that seem appropriate to their gender roles (Bem 1981). In the present study, gender differences in health promoting practices will be examined.

1.5 Education Level and Health Promoting Practices

There is extensive evidence that socioeconomic status (SES) is linked to health or health-related behavior (Adler et al. 1994; Adler and Ostrove 1999; Schnohr et al. 2004). Individuals with higher SES typically have better health than those lower in the social hierarchy. Such SES differences also exist in rates of mortality and morbidity from most diseases and conditions. One reason for this link may be that individuals with higher SES are more likely to be exposed to environments or resources that promote health-related behaviors. The present study also aims to explore the effect of SES differences, as measured by educational level, on health promoting practices by the general public in Hong Kong. The identification of specific health promotion needs for specific groups should facilitate the development and implementation of health promotion programs tailored towards different populations.

1.6 The Present Study

The present study aims to identify the patterns of health promoting practices, and to compare health promoting practices across gender and education levels in Hong Kong. The relationship between health promoting practices and quality of life will also be examined. A better understanding of health promoting practices and its relationship with quality of life will provide valuable guidance for the design of interventions to encourage people to lead healthier lifestyles.

2 Methods

2.1 Procedure

A randomized household survey was conducted across all 18 districts in Hong Kong. A total of 2,033 residential addresses were randomly drawn by the Hong Kong Census and Statistics Department. If the selected residential address had multiple households, one household was randomly selected using the modified Kish grid. If the selected household had more than one eligible member aged 18–65, one household member was again randomly selected using the modified Kish grid. Selected household members were invited to participate in a one-hour structured interview conducted by trained interviewers. The interview was conducted in Cantonese, the native spoken language in Hong Kong. Ineligible households included those with false addresses ($n = 16$), vacant households ($n = 175$), non-residential buildings ($n = 34$), residences where entry was refused by estate security guards ($n = 55$), households without at least one member aged 18 to 65 ($n = 246$), and households whose selected household members were unavailable due to sickness or travel

($n = 53$) or could not be reached after three attempts ($n = 378$). Participants who completed the interview received a HK$70 (approx. US$9) supermarket voucher as a token of our appreciation for their time. The study was approved by the Survey and Behavioral Research Ethics Committee of the Chinese University of Hong Kong.

2.2 Participants

A total of 941 participants completed the interview. The response rate, calculated by the number of completed interviews divided by the total number of eligible households contacted, was 88%. The demographic characteristics of participants are presented in Table 1. The mean age of the participants was 41.31 (SD = 12.78). About half of them (44.4%) were male. Nearly two-thirds (65.3%) of the participants were married or cohabitating. Close to 30% (29.3%) of the sample had better than high school education. About

Table 1 Demographic characteristics of participants

Variables	Total ($n = 941$)
Gender	
Male	44.6%
Female	55.4%
Age	M = 41.31 SD = 12.78
Education	
Primary school or lower	18.2%
High school	52.5%
College or higher	29.3%
Annual Household Income (in HKD)[a]	
Below $120,000	33.3%
$120,001–$240,000	32.4%
$240,001–$360,000	15.7%
$360,001–$480,000	8.4%
$480,001–$600,000	4.2%
$600,001 or above	5.9%
Marital status	
Single	27.7%
Married or cohabitating	65.3%
Separated/divorced/widowed	7.0%
Current occupational status	
Manager and executive	7.9%
Professional or assistant professional	14.5%
Clerical	15.3%
Service	14.9%
Mechanical operator	6.8%
Non-technical worker	9.3%
Homemaker	17.4%
Student	7.5%
Retired	6.3%
Others	9.7%

[a] HKD and USD exchange rate: 1 USD = 7.82 HKD, 1 HKD = 0.12 USD

two-thirds of the participants had an annual household income lower than HKD$360,000. The demographic characteristics of the participants were very similar to those of the Hong Kong population as a whole (Hong Kong Census and Statistics Department 2005). The demographic characteristics of the participants are shown in Table 1.

2.3 Measures

Health promoting practices. Various types of health promoting behavior were measured by a 16-item self-developed scale. Items from the scale were developed based on the Health-Promoting Lifestyle Profile (HPLP) (Walker et al. 1987) and the Health Behavior Checklist (Vickers et al. 1990). Participants were asked to indicate how well the health promoting habits described their typical practice. Responses were measured on a 6-point Likert Scale (range 1–6), with a higher score indicating a higher level of health promoting behavior. The Cronbach's alpha of the scale was .78. Only participants who scored 4 or above were considered as practicing the particular type of health promoting behavior.

Quality of life. Quality of life was measured by the Quality of Life Scale (QOLS). This is a 16-item instrument that measured five conceptual domains of quality of life: material and physical well-being, relationships with other people, social, community and civic activities, personal development and fulfillment, and recreation (Flanagan 1982). Previous exploratory factor analyses of the 16-item QOLS revealed three distinct factors across different samples: relationships and material well being (5 items), personal, social and community commitment (7 items), and health and functioning (4 items) (Burckhardt et al. 2003; Burckhardt and Anderson 2003). Responses were rated on a 7-point Likert scale and were summed to a total score (range 16–112), with a higher score indicating a better quality of life. The Cronbach's alpha of the scale was .81.

3 Results

3.1 Factor Analysis of Health Promoting Practices

To determine the factor structure of health promoting practices, exploratory factor analysis was conducted on the health promoting practices scale. Using the maximum likelihood estimation method, a 5-factor solution was produced (Table 2). Specifically, limiting intake of food with high cholesterol, fat, salt, sugar, watching weight, and eating roughage/fiber loaded on factor 1 and was labeled "food choice". The second factor included maintaining a pleasant mood, sleeping sufficiently, enjoying relaxing activities regularly, and controlling stress, and was labeled "stress management." Not smoking and not drinking alcohol excessively loaded on factor 3, and was labeled "health compromising behavior." Factor 4 included participating in social activities and exercising routinely, and was labeled "social relations." Finally, taking vitamin supplements and checking blood pressure regularly loaded on factor 5, and was labeled "preventive health behavior". The factor structure of health promoting practices is presented in Table 2.

3.2 Health Promoting Practices of the General Public

The number of participants who reported practicing health promoting behavior, and a comparison between males and females, is presented in Table 3. A large proportion of participants (ranging from 70.2 to 79.7%) reported making healthy food choices, engaging

Table 2 Factor analysis of Health Promoting Practices Scale

Factors	F1	F2	F3	F4	F5
Factor 1—food choice (28.50% of variance)					
10. Limit intake of food with high cholesterol	.78				
5. Limit intake of fats	.74				
12. Limit intake of salts	.72				
13. Limit intake of sugars	.71				
6. Watch weight	.60				
9. Eat roughage/fiber	.59				
Factor 2—stress management (10.34% of variance)					
15. Maintain a pleasant mood		.80			
14. Sleep sufficiently		.70			
16. Have some relaxing activities regularly		.61			
8. Control pressure		.57			
Factor 3—health compromising behavior (9.22% of variance)					
1. Do not smoke			.87		
4. Do not drink alcohol excessively			.86		
Factor 4—social relations (6.93% of variance)					
2. Participate in social activities				.75	
3. Exercise routinely				.67	
Factor 5—Preventive health behavior (6.50% of variance)					
11. Take vitamin pills					.85
7. Have regular blood pressure test					.55

in stress management (ranging from 67.7 to 83.4%), not smoking (77.3%), and not drinking excessively (85.9%). Slightly more than half the participants (57.2%) reported exercising routinely, and two-thirds of participants reported participating in social activities (65.3%). Only slightly more than one-third of participants reported checking their blood pressure regularly (37.3%), and only slightly more than one-fifth of participants reported taking vitamin supplements (23.5%).

Results from chi-square tests showed that significantly more women reported practicing various healthy food choices, not smoking and drinking alcohol excessively, and taking vitamin supplements than men, while significantly more men reported exercising routinely than women. There was no significant gender difference in behavior related to stress management, watching weight, participating in social activities, and checking blood pressure regularly.

3.3 Health Promoting Practices and Education Level

The pattern of health promoting practices by participants' education level is shown in Table 4. Results from chi-square tests showed that both male and female participants with a higher level of education were more likely to report not smoking, not drinking alcohol excessively, and participating in social activities. Female participants with a higher level of education were also more likely to engage in relaxing activities. On the other hand, female participants with a lower level of education were more likely to report exercising regularly and sleeping sufficiently.

Table 3 Patterns of health promoting practices of participants

Factors	Total ($n = 941$) (%)	Male ($n = 420$) (%)	Female ($n = 521$) (%)	Difference between groups $\chi^2(2)$
Factor 1—food choice				
10. Limit intake of food with high cholesterol	72.7	67.5	76.8	10.50**
5. Limit intake of fats	76.3	71.1	80.4	11.56**
12. Limit intake of salts	70.1	65.8	73.5	7.03*
13. Limit intake of sugars	70.2	66.0	73.5	6.64**
6. Watch weight	77.2	77.0	77.4	.31
9. Eat roughage/fiber	79.7	76.3	84.3	6.46*
Factor 2—stress management				
15. Maintain a pleasant mood	83.4	82.8	83.9	.40
14. Sleep sufficiently	67.7	64.4	70.2	4.16
16. Have some relaxing activities regularly	73.4	76.3	71.0	3.70
8. Control pressure	70.5	71.8	69.5	1.00
Factor 3—health compromising behavior				
1. Do not smoke	77.3	69.9	83.3	24.21***
4. Do not drink alcohol excessively	85.9	82.3	88.7	7.93**
Factor 4—social relations				
2. Participate in social activities	65.3	62.0	67.9	4.20
3. Exercise routinely	57.2	61.5	53.7	6.43*
Factor 5—preventive health behaviors				
11. Take vitamin pills	23.5	18.9	27.3	9.31**
7. Have regular blood pressure test	37.3	34.0	39.9	5.19

* $p < .05$, ** $p < .01$, *** $p < .001$

3.4 Health Promoting Practices and Quality of Life

Results from correlation analyses (see Table 5) showed that education level ($r = .26$ for male, .15 for female, $ps < .001$), monthly household income ($r = .23$ for male, .20 for female, $ps < .001$), health promoting practices related to food choice ($r = .26$ for male, .20 for female, $ps < .001$), stress management ($r = .37$ for male, .44 for female, $ps < .001$), social relations ($r = . .42$ for male, 40 for female, $ps < .001$), and preventive health behavior ($r = .13$ for male, 25 for female, $ps < .001$) were significantly correlated with better quality of life for both male and female participants. Health compromising behavior was significantly correlated with quality of life for male but not female participants ($r = .19$ for male, $p < .001$, .03 for female, ns).

Results from hierarchical regression analyses revealed that the overall models for both men ($F(8,399) = 20.4$, $p < .001$), and women ($F(8,489) = 24.67$, $p < .001$) on quality of life were significant. Of the demographic variables, household income was a significant predictor of better quality of life for both men ($\beta = .14$) and women ($\beta = .10$), while education level was a significant predictor of better quality of life for men ($\beta = .14$) only. Of the various types of health promoting behavior, those related to stress management ($\beta = .27$ for men, .33 for women) and social relations ($\beta = .26$ for men, .24 for women)

Table 4 Patterns of health promoting practices of participants by education level

Factors	Male (n = 419)				Female (n = 521)			
	Primary school or less (%)	High school (%)	College or above (%)	Difference between groups $\chi^2(3)$	Primary school or less (%)	High school (%)	College or above (%)	Difference between groups $\chi^2(3)$
F1—Food choice								
10. Limit intake of food with high cholesterol	62.0	66.8	71.8	2.12	84.2	75.5	74.1	3.92
5. Limit intake of fats	60.6	71.9	75.6	5.18	82.2	79.8	80.4	.27
12. Limit intake of salts	63.4	65.9	67.2	.30	75.2	69.0	74.8	4.96
13. Limit intake of sugars	62.0	65.9	68.7	.94	77.2	73.6	70.6	1.33
6. Watch weight	69.0	77.4	80.9	3.72	79.2	75.5	79.7	1.23
9. Eat roughage/fiber	73.2	75.6	79.4	1.12	81.1	78.7	83.2	4.92
F2—Stress management								
15. Maintain a pleasant mood	81.7	81.1	86.3	1.60	80.2	84.8	84.6	1.26
14. Sleep sufficiently	71.8	65.4	58.8	3.62	83.2	68.2	65.0	10.47**
16. Have relaxing activities regularly	69.0	75.1	82.4	4.99	66.3	66.8	82.5	12.67**
8. Control pressure	67.6	70.5	76.3	2.13	67.3	68.6	72.7	1.04
F3—Health compromising behavior								
1. Do not smoke	47.9	71.4	79.4	22.21***	75.2	81.9	91.6	12.17**
4. Do not drink alcohol excessively	71.8	82.0	88.5	8.88*	85.1	86.6	95.1	8.28*
F4—Social relations								
2. Participate in social activities	32.4	59.9	81.7	48.38***	56.4	64.6	82.5	21.49***
3. Exercise routinely	54.9	59.4	68.7	4.55	63.4	47.7	53.7	9.33**
F5—Preventive health behavior								
11. Take vitamin pills	16.9	18.0	21.4	.83	18.8	28.9	30.1	4.57
7. Have regular blood pressure test	46.5	31.3	32.1	5.82	43.6	39.0	39.2	.69

* $p < .05$, ** $p < .01$, *** $p < .001$

were significant predictors of better quality of life for both men and women. Types of preventive health behavior were significant predictors of better quality of life for women only ($\beta = .11$). The overall model explained 29.2% of variance in quality of life for men, and 24.6% for women. The results of the hierarchical regression are presented in Table 6.

4 Discussion

The various kinds of health promoting behavior are important determinants of health and quality of life. Although the relationship between health promoting practices and physical

Table 5 Correlations between variables for male and female participants

Variables	1	2	3	4	5	6	7	8	9
1. Quality of life	–	−.08	.26 ***	.23 ***	.26 ***	.37 ***	.19 ***	.42 ***	.13 **
2. Age	.02	–	−.49 ***	−.12 **	.15 **	.15 **	−.11 *	−.16 ***	.29 ***
3. Education level	.15 ***	−.52 ***	–	.47 ***	.06	−.05	.25 ***	.26 ***	−.02
4. Household Income	.20 ***	−.07	.42 ***	–	.05	−.04	.15 **	.12 **	.03
5. Health promoting practices—food choice	.20 ***	.28 ***	−.05	.05	–	.45 ***	.31 ***	.31 ***	.38 ***
6. Health promoting practices—stress management	.44 ***	.14 ***	.01	.11 **	.47 ***	–	.18 ***	.34 ***	.25 ***
7. Health promoting practices—health compromising behavior	.03	−.02	.17 ***	.11 **	.18 ***	.08 *	–	.23 ***	.02
8. Health promoting practices—social relations	.40 ***	.04	.10 **	.11 **	.29 ***	.39 ***	.06	–	.14 **
9. Health promoting practices—preventive health behavior	.25 ***	.24 ***	−.03	.08 *	.33 ***	.29 ***	.08 *	.29 ***	–

Correlations between variables for female participants are shown in the right and correlations between variables for male participants are shown in the left of the diagonal

* $p < .05$, ** $p < .01$, *** $p < .001$

Table 6 Results of hierarchical regression on quality of life by gender

	Male (n = 420)		Female (n = 521)	
	I β	II β	I β	II β
Age	.05	.02	.08	.02
Education Level	.23***	.14*	.13*	.08
Household income	.13*	.14**	.15**	.10**
Food choice		.03		− .06
Stress management		.27***		.33***
Health compromising behavior		.02		−.04
Social relations		.26***		.24***
Preventive health behavior		.02		.11**
R^2 change	.09	.21	.05	.29
F	12.62***	20.4***	8.61***	24.67***
df	3/404	8/399	3/494	8/489
R^2	.09	.29	.05	.25

* $p < .05$, ** $p < .01$, *** $p < .001$

health has been widely established, relatively less has been done to investigate the pattern of health promoting behavior and its association with quality of life of community adults in Hong Kong. The present study aimed to identify patterns of positive health behavior of individuals in Hong Kong, to explore gender differences in health promoting practice, and to examine its relationship with quality of life. The results of the study should provide useful information for health professionals in the design of health interventions to promote health practice for the general public in Hong Kong.

We found that a large proportion of participants reported practicing various types of health promoting behavior related to healthy food choices, engaging in stress management strategies, and refraining from smoking and drinking excessively. Our results indicate that the importance of healthy diet, stress management, and the negative effects of smoking and excessive drinking seem to be reasonably well appreciated by the general public in Hong Kong. However, rather fewer participants reported engaging in exercise regularly and participating in social activities. This is consistent with previous studies showing that physical and social activities were less widely practiced in Hong Kong (Lee and Yuen Loke 2005).

One possible explanation might be the busy schedule and high job demands in Hong Kong, which leave individuals little time for participating in physical and social activities. Our results also indicated that few participants checked their blood pressure regularly or took vitamin supplements. As the benefits of this kind of monitoring and preventive behavior are less noticeable, it is conceivable that they might be given less priority. There is a need for health promotion to further target exercises, social activities, and monitoring and preventive behavior so to improve the health and quality of life of the public in Hong Kong.

The study also reported some gender differences in the pattern of health promoting practices. Findings revealed that female participants were more likely to report healthy food choices, not smoking and drinking alcohol excessively, and taking vitamin supplements than male participants, whereas male participants were more likely to exercise regularly than females. Results concurred with previous studies showing that women were more likely to practice health promoting behavior related to relaxation, food choices, and interpersonal relationships, and men were more likely to report higher levels of exercise, smoking, and alcohol consumption (Acton and Malathum 2000; Felton et al. 1997; Hubbard et al. 1984; Lee and Yuen Loke 2005; Nolen-Hoeksema and Hilt 2006; Shiffman and Paton 1999; Stockton et al. 2000). This difference might be explained by the gender role associated with certain types of behavior. For example, research has shown that masculinity is related to health behavior such as regular exercise (Eisler et al. 1988), and smoking and drinking (Evans et al. 1990; Peralta 2007). Therefore, men might be more likely to engage in such behavior to emphasize their masculine gender role. In addition, in Chinese culture, women are often socialized to assume a caregiving role while men expect to receive care. This might partly explain why men were less likely to engage in voluntary health monitoring behavior (Chang 1999; Zhou 2006).

The present study also reported some differences in practicing health promoting practices across education levels. Specifically, participants with higher levels of education were more likely to report not smoking, not drinking alcohol excessively, and participating in social activities for both men and women. Female participants with higher levels of education were also more likely to enjoy relaxing activities. One possible explanation might be that those with lower education levels might be less aware of the benefits of practicing health related behavior, more susceptible to environmental threats, and less able to gain access to resources related to health related behavior (Adler and Ostrove 1999). On the other hand, women with higher education levels were less likely to report exercising regularly and sleeping sufficiently. This finding is intriguing and might be due to the fact that in Hong Kong, such women are likely to enter the work force. Their heavy work, together with family household duties, might leave them little spare time to take exercise or to get enough sleep.

Consistent with previous studies documenting the value of health promoting practices for health and general well-being, the present study showed that adopting positive health behavior in stress management and social relations was related to quality of life for both male and female participants. As quality of life was conceptualized as a perception of health and well-being, it is not surprising that dietary choices and smoking and drinking excessively might be more relevant to an objective but less relevant to a subjective perception of health. Interestingly, taking vitamin supplements and regularly monitoring blood pressure were significant predictors of quality of life for women but not for men, suggesting that in-depth monitoring and preventive behavior might be a more important concept influencing quality of life for women in Hong Kong. As men tend to have higher risk of higher blood pressure and nutritional problems (Burl et al. 1995), it is possible that taking vitamin supplements and having blood pressure test might not predict better quality of life. Our results highlighted the importance of identifying the correlates of quality of life for different sex groups and examining why differences exist between these groups.

4.1 Limitations of the Study

Several limitations of the study should be noted. Firstly, health promoting practices were measured using a self-reported inventory. Responses may well have been prone to self-reporting bias, in which case the level of health promoting practice of individuals in Hong Kong might have been overestimated. Future studies could fruitfully examine the reliability and validity of this self-reported measure on health promoting behavior before it is applied to other populations. Secondly, the study employed a cross-sectional design which precluded the possibility of establishing causal relationship between factors. Therefore, the assertion that health promoting behavior would lead to better quality of life could not be firmly established. Longitudinal studies are required to further explicate the causal linkages between variables and to predict the long term effects of health promoting behavior on quality of life. Although our results demonstrated that various types of health promoting behavior were important predictors of quality of life, the amount of variance accounted for was modest. Consequently, there might be other factors that are important but have not yet been included in the model. Future studies should explore more proximal factors that may be related to health promoting practices.

5 Implications and Conclusion

As health promoting behavior is modifiable and can be targeted in a cost effective way, the relationship between health promoting practices, gender and quality of life has important implications for the design of interventions to encourage the general public in Hong Kong to adopt such practices. Our findings suggest that health promoting practices related to stress management and social relationship might have the potential to improve the quality of life of individuals in Hong Kong. Therefore, health professionals should seek to design health interventions to encourage individuals to improve their stress management skills, take more exercise and foster social relations. Health care professionals should also seek to advocate positive health promoting behavior as an integral part of a sound lifestyle so that individuals could practice it more extensively and effectively.

References

Acton, G. J., & Malathum, P. (2000). Basic need status and health-promoting self-care behavior in adults. *Western Journal of Nursing Research, 22*(7), 796–811.

Adler, N. E., Boyce, T., Chesney, M. A., Cohen, S., Folkman, S., Kahn, R. L., et al. (1994). Socioeconomic status and health. The challenge of the gradient. *American Psychologist, 49*(1), 15–24.

Adler, N. E., & Ostrove, J. M. (1999). Socioeconomic status and health: what we know and what we don't. *Annals of the New York Academy of Sciences, 896*(1), 3–15.

Anderson, R. B., Hollenberg, N. K., & Williams, G. H. (1999). Physical Symptoms Distress Index: a sensitive tool to evaluate the impact of pharmacological agents on quality of life. *Archives of Internal Medicine, 159*(7), 693–700.

Bem, S. L. (1981). Gender schema theory: A cognitive account of sex typing. *Psychological Review, 88*(4), 354–364.

Breslow, L. (1999). From disease prevention to health promotion. *JAMA, 281*(11), 1030–1033.

Burckhardt, C. S., & Anderson, K. L. (2003). The Quality of Life Scale (QOLS): Reliability, validity, and utilization. *Health and Quality of Life Outcomes, 1*(60). doi:10.1186/1477-7525-1-60.

Burckhardt, C. S., Anderson, K. L., Archenholtz, B., & Hagg, O. (2003). The Flanagan quality of life scale: Evidence of construct validity. *Health and Quality of Life Outcomes, 1*(59). doi:10.1186/1477-7525-1-59.

Burl, V. L., Whelton, P., Roccella, E. J., Brown, C., Cutler, J. A., Higgins, M., et al. (1995). Prevalence of hypertension in the US adult population: Results from the Third National Health and Nutrition Examination Survey, 1988–1991. *Hypertension, 25*(3), 305–313.

Callaghan, P., Ma, K. F., & Fung, C. Y. (1997). Hong Kong nurses' health-related behaviours: Implications for nurses' role in health promotion. *Journal of Advanced Nursing, 25*, 1276–1282.

Chang, L. (1999). Gender role egalitarian attitudes in Beijing, Hong Kong, Florida, and Michigan. *Journal of Cross-Cultural Psychology, 30*(6), 722–741.

Dean, K. (1989). Self-care components of lifestyles: The importance of gender, attitudes and the social situation. *Social Science & Medicine, 29*(2), 137–152.

Doll, R., Peto, R., Boreham, J., & Sutherland, I. (2004). Mortality in relation to smoking: 50 years' observations on male British doctors. *BMJ: British Medical Journal, 328*(7455), 1519–1528.
Dornelas, E. A. (2008). Risk factors and perceptions of risk for cardiovascular disease. In *Psychotherapy with cardiac patients: Behavioral cardiology in practice* (pp. 29–38). Washington, DC: American Psychological Association.
Eisler, R. M., Skidmore, J. R., & Ward, C. H. (1988). Masculine gender-role stress: Predictor of anger, anxiety, and health-risk behaviors. *Journal of Personality Assessment, 52*(1), 133–141.
Evans, R. I., Turner, S. H., Ghee, K. L., & Getz, J. G. (1990). Is androgynous sex role related to cigarette smoking in adolescents? *Journal of Applied Social Psychology, 20*(6), 494–505.
Felton, G. M., Parsons, M. A., & Bartoces, M. G. (1997). Demographic factors: Interaction effects on health-promoting behavior and health related factors. *Public Health Nursing, 14*(6), 361–367.
Flanagan, J. C. (1982). Measurement of quality of life: Current state of the art. *Archives of Physical Medicine and Rehabilitation.*
Holahan, C. K., & Suzuki, R. (2004). Adulthood predictors of health promoting behavior in later aging. *International Journal of Aging & Human Development, 58*(4), 289–313.
Hong Kong Census and Statistics Department. (2005). Hong Kong Statistics. Available from: http://www.censtatd.gov.hk/hong_kong_statistics/statistical_tables/index.jsp?charsetID=1&subjectID=1&tableID ID=002.
Hoy, B., Wagner, L., & Hall, E. O. C. (2007). Self-care as a health resource of elders: an integrative review of the concept. *Scandinavian Journal of Caring Sciences, 21*(4), 456–466.
Hu, F. B., Rimm, E. B., Stampfer, M. J., Ascherio, A., Spiegelman, D., Willett, W. C., et al. (2000). Prospective study of major dietary patterns and risk of coronary heart disease in men. *American Journal of Clinical Nutrition, 72*(4), 912–921.
Hubbard, P., Muhlenkamp, A. F., & Brown, N. (1984). The relationship between social support and self-care practices. *Nursing Research, 33*(5), 266–270.
Khaw, K.-T., Wareham, N., Bingham, S., Welch, A., Luben, R., & Day, N. (2008). Combined impact of health behaviours and mortality in men and women: The EPIC-Norfolk prospective population study. *PLoS Medicine, 5*(1), e12.
Lee, R. L. T., & Yuen Loke, A. J. T. (2005). Health-promoting behaviors and psychosocial well-being of university students in Hong Kong. *Public Health Nursing, 22*(3), 209–220.
Lo, W. H. (1976). Urbanization and psychiatric disorders—the Hong Kong scene. *Acta Psychiatrica Scandinavica, 54*, 174–183.
Motl, R. W., & Gosney, J. L. (2008). Effect of exercise training on quality of life in multiple sclerosis: a meta-analysis. *Multiple Sclerosis, 14*(1), 129–135.
Mustalahti, K., Lohiniemi, S., Collin, P., Vuolteenaho, N., Laippala, P., & Maki, M. (2002). Gluten-free diet and quality of life in patients with screen-detected celiac disease. *Effective Clinical Practice, 5*(3), 105–113.
Nolen-Hoeksema, S., & Hilt, L. (2006). Possible contributors to the gender differences in alcohol use and problems. *Journal of General Psychology, 133*(4), 357–374.
Peralta, R. L. (2007). College alcohol use and the embodiment of hegemonic masculinity among European American men. *Sex Roles, 56*(11–12), 741–756.
Petajan, J. H., Gappmaier, E., White, A. T., Spencer, M. K., et al. (1996). Impact of aerobic training on fitness and quality of life in multiple sclerosis. *Annals of Neurology, 39*(4), 432–441.
Schnohr, C., Hojbjerre, L., Riegels, M., Ledet, L., Larsen, T., Schultz-Larsen, K., et al. (2004). Does educational level influence the effects of smoking, alcohol, physical activity, and obesity on mortality? A prospective population study. *Scandinavian Journal of Public Health, 32*(4), 250–256.
Shiffman, S., & Paton, S. M. (1999). Individual differences in smoking: gender and nicotine addiction. *Nicotine & Tobacco Research, 1*(Suppl 2), S153–S157. discussion S156–165.
Stockton, M. C., McMahon, S. D., & Jason, L. A. (2000). Gender and smoking behavior in a worksite smoking cessation program. *Addictive Behaviors, 25*(3), 347–360.
Tsutsumi, T. (1997). *The effects of strength training on mood, self-efficacy, cardiovascular reactivity and quality of life in older adults*. Dissertation Abstracts International Section A: Humanities and Social Sciences.
Vickers, R. R., Conway, T. L., & Hervig, L. (1990). Demonstration of replicable dimensions of health behavior. *Preventive Medicine, 19*, 377–401.
Wagner, E. H., LaCroix, A. Z., Buchner, D. M., & Larson, E. B. (1992). Effects of physical activity on health status in older adults. I: Observational studies. *Annual Review of Public Health, 13*, 451–468.
Walker, S. N., Sechrist, K. R., & Pender, N. J. (1987). The health-promoting lifestyle profile: Development and psychometric characteristics. *Nursing Research, 36*, 76–81.

Walker, Z. A. K., & Townsend, J. (1999). The role of general practice in promoting teenage health: a review of the literature. *Family Practice, 16*(2), 164–172.

WHOQOL group. (1995). The World Health Organization Quality of Life Assessment (WHOQOL): Position paper from the World Health Organization. *Social Science & Medicine, 41*(10), 1403–1409.

Wong, C.-Y., & Tang, C. S.-K. (2005). Practice of habitual and volitional health behaviors to prevent severe acute respiratory syndrome among Chinese adolescents in Hong Kong. *Journal of Adolescent Health, 36*(3), 193–200.

World Health Organization. (2002). The world health report 2002. Reducing risks, promoting healthy life. Geneva: WHO.

Wu, A. M. S., Tang, C. S.-K., & Kwok, T. C. Y. (2004). Physical and psychosocial factors associated with health-promoting behaviors among elderly Chinese with type-2 diabetes. *Journal of Health Psychology, 9*(6), 731–740.

Zhou, L.-Y. (2006). American and Chinese college students' anticipations of their postgraduate education, career, and future family roles. *Sex Roles, 55*(1–2), 95–110.

Soc Indic Res (2010) 95:519–534
DOI 10.1007/s11205-009-9524-8

"I Wish to be Self-Reliant": Aspiration for Self-Reliance, Need and Life Satisfaction, and Exit Dilemma of Welfare Recipients in Hong Kong

Chack-Kie Wong · Vivian Wei-Qun Lou

Accepted: 21 August 2009 / Published online: 6 October 2009

Abstract This qualitative study explores the welfare recipients' experiences of and attitudes toward the welfare benefit system in Hong Kong. A sample of 19 welfare recipients from six main recipient groups was interviewed, some twice. This study finds that the recipients have strong aspirations to exit the welfare benefit system. The welfare application process is painful; they are strongly stigmatized; they do not have sufficient resources to meet many of their expected needs; and, after all, they have strong ethos for self-reliance. However, they remain in the benefit system. This study looks into this paradox and the challenges facing the welfare benefit system in Hong Kong in terms of providing ontological security on the one hand and promoting self-reliance on the other.

Keywords Self-reliance · Welfare dependence · Ontological security · Social stigma · Life satisfaction

1 Introduction

"I wish to be self-reliant," was echoed by a female welfare recipient who was a single-parent, 41 years old and 7 years on welfare when we conducted the interview in 2007. This statement symbolizes the aspirations of many welfare recipients for self-reliance (Monroe et al. 2007; Scott et al. 2007). In reality, it is quite difficult for her to exit the welfare benefit system. She has a child to care for. In the case that she works, the salary may not be as high as she receives from welfare, and she has to forego, if not all, part of her caring responsibility. The alleged higher compensation from welfare paves the ground for a claim that welfare benefits are too generous and they breed dependency. According to the present

C.-K. Wong (✉)
Social Work Department, The Chinese University of Hong Kong, Hong Kong SAR, People's Republic of China
e-mail: chackkiewong@cuhk.edu.hk

V. W.-Q. Lou
Department of Social Work and Administration, The University of Hong Kong, Hong Kong SAR, People's Republic of China

regulations, she can rely upon welfare until her child reaches 12. In other words, it is perfectly legitimate for her to be a welfare recipient—perhaps a better way of making ends meet; at the same time, it is in the immediate, *albeit* not the best, interest of her child.

In the past two to three decades, there has been an ascendance of a discourse about welfare recipients and public assistance. Welfare recipients are portrayed as dependent due to their adoption of a new culture, and the welfare benefit system is perceived as trapping welfare recipients because benefits are generous. This article looks at these two issues from the reported experiences and attitudes of the welfare recipients toward the welfare benefit system in Hong Kong to see whether and how far the above two claims, a welfare dependency culture and a trapping benefit system, are true from the perspective of welfare recipients.

First, this article looks at the literature to see what the discourse is all about and how it is relevant in the context of a non-Westernized society. A few research questions are generalized for examination at a later stage. Secondly, it examines the welfare benefit system of Hong Kong to see whether benefits are generous and how welfare dependency is tackled. Finally, the article reports the findings of in-depth interviews of welfare recipients to see whether self-reliance ethos is still embraced, if the needs and lives of welfare recipients are satisfied, and how the exit dilemma is addressed by respondents.

2 Literature Review

In the literature, underlying the portrayal of welfare recipients as welfare dependents is about the assumption of a change in the culture of welfare—from self-reliance and work to welfare dependency and work shyness (Cocca 2002; Kittay 1998; Jones 1995; Misra et al. 2003; Niskanen 1996; Scheider and Jacoby 2003). This cultural change has something to do with the alleged generosity of the welfare benefit system which is portrayed as being too generous toward welfare recipients. They are assumed to be rational choice makers, calculative and benefit maximizing, leading to abuse and misuse of the system (Engbersen et al. 1993; Kimenyi 1991). Due to these assumptions, it is necessary to take action, e.g., reforming welfare by cutting benefits, amending active labour market policies by activating employable recipients to employment, and incorporating punitive measures in workforce programmes to push welfare recipients out of the alleged welfare trap (Clasen and Clegg 2003; Hills and Waldfogel 2004).

The above discourse points to two targets for the blame for the ascendance of the welfare dependency phenomenon—welfare recipients, who are rational choice makers, and who no longer embrace the self-reliance ethos and work ethic; and the benefit system that is too generous and inhibits exit from the welfare trap. However, the findings of a literature review on this subject do not provide us with conclusive evidence. Many empirical studies show that welfare recipients have not lost their cultural values or they are totally calculative. For example, Scheider and Jacoby (2003) find that American recipients of public assistance are virtually identical to non-recipients in terms of American core values; in other words, there is no sufficient evidence in their study about the development of a distinctive "culture of dependency."

However, in Kimenyi's study (1991), he finds that welfare recipients with a history of welfare use in the family stay longer in public welfare. This implies that welfare recipients possibly socialize new attitudes and values once they are associated with the benefit system—a cultural adaptation phenomenon. In other words, cultural beliefs and values are not static; they change from time to time. In the case of welfare recipients, once they stay in the system, their behaviour and values as well, may be moderated by their institutional experiences.

We also see another body of literature that points in the other direction of the relationship between culture and public assistance—people who are eligible for public welfare yet opt not to apply for their entitlement. For example, an OECD report estimates that take-up rates of public assistance are in a range between 40 and 80% among the United States, the United Kingdom, France, Germany, and the Netherlands (Hernanz et al. 2004). The low take-up rate of many means-tested welfare programmes reveals the impact of cultural values on welfare behaviour. Researchers often explain the low take-up rate by the strong social stigma associated with the welfare recipient status (Kerr 1983; Hernanz et al. 2004; McGarry 1996).

We also see inconclusive evidence on the effect of benefit generosity on the assumingly "rational and calculative" welfare recipients. Kenworthy (1999: 1121) finds that benefit generosity in the US failed to induce an increase of welfare poor in the period between the mid-1970s and early 1990s. His findings also reveal that states with generous welfare did not attract more welfare poor. The qualitative study of 214 welfare women by Edin and Lein (1998: 63) unveils that the decision between welfare and work was not a rational calculation of benefits; indeed, each woman's choice was set against a back-drop of survival strategy and the threat of serious potential material hardship. Their findings are echoed by East and Bussey (2007) who also found complex situations faced by welfare recipients. They were concerned with survival and coping strategies with personal risks such as substance abuse, learning difficulties, domestic violence, and victimization.

There is, however, empirical evidence which, in contrast, shows welfare recipients have taken the generosity of benefits into consideration. In Kimenyi's (1991) study, long-term welfare dependency is partly explained by the calculation of the expected loss of exiting from welfare; for example, the child care costs plus the expected gain from employment as compared to the benefits of staying. Bailey's study (2005: 134) identifies non-trivial effects of welfare-induced migration between states by poor single mothers. For example, 5 years after increasing benefits by one standard deviation, the simulated effect of welfare migration and spending of one state only—Alabama, would be predicted at US$3.8 million per year on the net in-migration alone (Bailey, ibid.). The study of Hoynes and MaCurdy (1994) reveals that the length of welfare spells varies with demographic backgrounds, generosity of public welfare, and local labour market conditions. The study of welfare reform during the initial period of 1993–1995 by Keng et al. (2002) finds that income from wages and child support were significant factors in reducing welfare dependency.

Now, we come to look at the literature on welfare recipients and public assistance in the Chinese society of Hong Kong. Indeed, there are very few empirical researches on public assistance; but welfare dependency has been at the centre of popular discourse since the handover of the sovereignty in 1997. It started with a review report of the Comprehensive Social Security Assistance scheme (CSSA), i.e., the welfare benefit system for the poor in Hong Kong in 1998. According to the report, there was a 146% increase in the number of CSSA cases from 1993 to1998, with the unemployed cases showed a disproportionate increase due to the increasingly attractive benefit levels versus the relatively low market wages (SWD 1998, pp. 3–6). This highlights the concern of a possible emergence of a dependency culture even though the abuse and fraudulent cases were extremely few (SWD 1998, pp. 9–10). Such a discourse about a cultural change toward welfare dependency has since then fuelled a public outcry especially targeting employable welfare recipients.

The impact is enormous as illustrated by a study conducted in 2000 by gathering all news reports ($N = 202$) over a period of 6 months on CSSA in two popular newspapers

(Choi 2000). The following are some of the findings related to the welfare recipients and the welfare benefit system: 15.8% of all the reports are about crimes, suicide attempts, etc. committed by CSSA recipients; 13.8% are about abuse and fraudulence; 20.3% are about reform measures of the system; 6.9% are about the miserable lives of those on welfare, and 18.8% are about benevolence toward the welfare recipients (ibid.).

The discourse of the media is powerful. Despite the fact that it is not all one-sided, a public image of welfare recipients as the undeserving poor has emerged, and it seemingly affects the attitude of the general public toward the former and the welfare benefit system. A recent telephone survey found that 60% of respondents would not apply for CSSA unless they had exhausted all other possible means (*Takungpao*, July 13, 2007). The reluctance to rely upon public assistance perhaps reflects a self-reliance ethos among the Chinese population in Hong Kong (Chiu and Wong 2005; Chau and Yu 2005; Lau and Kuan 1988; Wong and Wong 1998). In another survey on general social welfare, 70.3% of the respondents were reported to take "own effort" as the best way for satisfying individual needs; only 8.6% of the respondent chose "government provision/policy" (Wong and Chau 2002, p. 299). A news report of a single-parent mother who refused to apply for CSSA, worked 19 h a day, and finally died of exhaustion (*Takungpao,* March 7, 2006) is one case which exemplifies the reluctance to depend upon welfare.

How can we make sense of the above inconclusive and somewhat contradictory evidence about the assumptions underlying the discourse on welfare recipients and the welfare benefit system in the literature and news reports? The body of writing and research on the changing labour markets and its repercussions on social policy in general and public assistance policy in particular (Clasen 1997; Cox 1998) should be helpful. Globalisation and technological change tend to produce greater economic and social inequalities. The low-skilled workers are, in particular, the victims; they are less able to adapt to the change and are exposed to an increasing risk of unemployment, insecure employment, and low-paying jobs. When they are laid off and access their public assistance or unemployment entitlements, they face a welfare benefit system which is generally and increasingly selective and keen on activating them for reemployment for the sake of avoiding the "poverty trap" and the development of a "dependency culture" (Dean and Taylor-Gooby 1992; Halvorsen 1998). Of course, one should not deny the fact of higher welfare benefits and lower market wages, as mentioned above in the CSSA review report of the Hong Kong government. Even though public assistance carries a stigma, it still offers ontological security (Ring 2005) to recipients—a secure source of income that is not found in the often flexible, insecure, and marginalized low-end jobs. In general, the three assumptions of cultural change, generosity of benefits, and rational choice underlying the discourse should be contrasted against a more complicated background of a changing global economy and its impact on the poor and low-income groups.

The above review of the literature, both overseas and local, on welfare recipients and public welfare, unveils a complex situation faced by welfare recipients in relation to the benefits provided by the welfare benefit system. Qualitative research is best used to untangle such a complex situation from the perspective of the affected (Sofaer 1999). The studies by East and Bussey (2007), Edin and Lein (1998), Monroe et al. (2007), Scott et al. (2007) and Underlid (2007) are examples which look at a life in the welfare benefit system from the perspective of those affected. But there is a lack of such studies in Chinese societies. For example, a survey of recipients in Hong Kong investigates the effectiveness of various measures for raising the recipients' work motivation and diminishing their welfare dependency (Tang and Cheung 2007); but not with qualitative research design despite its positive finding. Similar studies by quantitative design are also identified on welfare recipients of the newly established social assistance system, namely the Minimal Living Social Security System, in mainland China (Li 2008; Deng and Zhou 2006). For example, a study found that 46.6% of employable recipients did not have the willingness for reemployment (Li 2008, p. 24). One essential feature of the welfare systems of the Chinese societies, including Singapore and Taiwan, are their relatively low social spending and the public hostility towards welfare (Walker and Wong 2005a, b; Mendes 2007; Wijeysingha 2005; Tang 2000). However, the perspective of those affected as revealed by qualitative methodology, are not identified. This study of the welfare recipients' experiences and attitudes toward the welfare benefit system in Hong Kong should contribute to the literature about the relationship between welfare recipients and public welfare in the Chinese societies where work ethic and self-reliance are strongly embraced (Walker and Wong 2005a; Chau and Yu 2005; Mendes 2007).

On these bases, the following three questions are formulated:

Question 1: Do welfare recipients still embrace a self-reliance ethos?
Question 2: Are their needs and lives being satisfied?
Question 3: How do welfare recipients tackle the exit dilemma, i.e., the stay or exit decision?

Question 1 aims to see whether welfare recipients still hold the self-reliance ethos. Perhaps the welfare experiences or the worsening labour markets may moderate their attitudes and beliefs about supporting oneself and one's family.

Question 2 aims to see whether the welfare benefit system is able to meet the various needs of the recipients. However, carrying the recipient status may mean holding a stigma that implies a negative meaning to one's subjective well-being. In this regard, we add a life satisfactory measure (Diener et al. 1985; Hagerty 1999; Wong et al. 2006) for revealing the subjective cognitive assessment of welfare recipients toward their welfare recipient status. Satisfaction with life not only deals with people's command over their resources, but also the efforts they put into securing their well-being. On this basis, life satisfaction looks promising as a global measure for indicating whether and how far CSSA recipients successfully manage their surroundings without losing sight of the efforts they make. In other words, despite the welfare benefit system in Hong Kong being primarily designed to meet basic needs, individual efforts and reflection may make a difference in terms of how the Hong Kong Chinese appreciate their life. For example, in cases where welfare recipients stay longer in the system, they may culturally adapt to the new environment despite a poor quality of life and a low level of need satisfaction.

Question 3 aims to see how welfare recipients deal with the stay-exit decision. This should elicit whether they are rational, calculative choice makers or simply victims of complex situations whose responses are concerned with survival, as suggested by Edin and Lein (1998) and East and Bussey (2007).

3 The Welfare Benefit System and Its Larger Context

Now we look at the welfare benefit system against the larger context in Hong Kong to see whether it fits with the literature on the changing labour market and its repercussions on public assistance.

The present welfare benefit system of Hong Kong, the CSSA scheme, was started in the early 1970s as a temporary relief system for those who could not be self-reliant. In January

2007, there were 294,963 cases or 520,858 persons on welfare, equivalent to approximately 13% of total households and 7.5% of the general population.[1] The six major recipient groups are elderly, single-parents, unemployed, ill health, permanently disabled, and low-income. In January 2007, their shares were respectively at 51.8, 13, 12.7, 8.2, 6.1, and 6.2%.

The benefit system is periodically revised to keep pace with consumer price changes, but not wages. The components of legitimate consumption include food, fuel and light, drinks, clothing and footwear, durable goods, miscellaneous goods, transportation, and miscellaneous services, covering the needs for income, housing, health care, and education. In general, the benefit system is comprehensive and deliberately maintains relative basic levels of living, compared with standards enjoyed by the general public.

However, the benefit system is generally harsh toward the unemployed because of the fear of engendering welfare dependency. For example, in 2007, an elderly person, age 60 years or above, or a person who was at least 50% disabled, had a *standard* monthly benefit of $2,305 (HK$, HK$7.8 = US$1.0), while an employable recipient only received a standard monthly benefit of $1,630. That was a difference of 41%. Moreover, the unemployed were excluded from special grants. Apart from that, several activation programmes have been developed in recent years to motivate the unemployed recipients to join the labour market.

Against these policy backgrounds, the welfare benefit system is often criticized on two fronts. On the one hand, it is suggested that the system does not have sufficient resources for meeting many of the needs of the welfare recipients. For example, children on welfare do not have sufficient resources for extra-curricular activities and review classes. The concepts of social participation and comparative need are used to justify claims of unsatisfied needs. In terms of the replacement rate to median monthly employment earnings, the average CSSA payment (comprising standard rates and special grants) was about 35% in the financial year of 2006–2007.[2] In reference to the 60% threshold of defining poverty among European Union countries, welfare benefits equivalent to a 35% replacement rate should encounter difficulties. Bear in mind that economic standards in Hong Kong are better than many European Union countries such as Portugal, Greece, and Spain.

On the other hand, the welfare benefit system is also viewed, ironically, as engendering welfare dependency and fraudulence. A recent survey found that half of the respondents believed that only half or less than half of CSSA recipients actually needed the public assistance, and 60% of them thought that CSSA recipients had personality problems—they were lazy and lacked will (Chinareviewnews.com 4th April 2008). In terms of fraudulence, one striking example is a former magistrate, together with his former barrister wife, who was found guilty of fraudulence by the court for not unveiling assets in their CSSA application (*Ming Pao*, 27th January 2007). But this claim of welfare dependency has to be contextualized into the larger economic situation of Hong Kong. It has a widened income gap and the low-income groups have very low compensation from the labour market. Pre-distribution gini ratios are alarming by international standards, according to the last three census reports; they were 0.518 in 1996, 0.522 in 2001, and 0.533 in 2006 (Census and

[1] According to the Census & Statistics Department, there were 6,925.9 thousand population in mid-2007 and 2,251.5 thousand households in the period 12/2007 and 12/2008 in Hong Kong. Accessed to http://www.censtatd.gov.hk/hong_kong_statistics/statistics_by_subject/index_tc.jsp on 2 June 2008; all figures of CSSA were downloaded from the Social Welfare Department website: http://www.swd.gov.hk/en/index/site_pubsvc/page_socsecu/sub_comprehens/. Accessed on July 7, 2007.

[2] The amount of HK$3,487, being the average CSSA payment in the financial year of 2006–2007 was obtained from the Social Welfare Department; while the median monthly employment earnings in June 2006 were from the Census and Statistics Department.

Statistics Department 2007). In household income terms, the 2006 bi-census informs us that, for example, the lowest two decile groups, on an average, only had median monthly household incomes of HK$4,200. This figure was markedly below the average household income of HK$17,250 in the same period. In terms of per capita income, the respective figure was $2,063 for the lowest two decile groups; however, a single-member household received, on an average, a higher amount of HK$3,487 from the welfare benefit system.

Apparently, the seemingly "generous" benefit system has found its true meaning only if it is set against the wide income gap context. In other words, the contradictory situation facing welfare recipients is generally about a welfare benefit system which is "fortunately" able to guarantee basic living standards for the welfare recipients while income in low-end jobs does not make work pay.

4 The Findings of a Qualitative Research of Welfare Recipients

We adopted the purpose sampling method for selecting the cases for interview. Purpose sampling refers to a procedure that selects a sample on the basis of existing knowledge of the population (Rubin and Babbie 2005). The welfare benefit system has six major recipients groups—elderly, disabled, ill-health, single-parents, low-income earners, and unemployed. From March to July 2007, we conducted 19 cases using two to five people from each group. More respondents from the single-parent and unemployed groups were selected because we wanted to know more about the stay-exit decision and how these respondents felt about it. These two groups, especially the unemployed group, are where social stigma should be strongly felt. We also interviewed new entrants twice, with an interval of 3 months between questioning. We aimed to see if there were any attitudinal changes toward the welfare benefit system due to the temporal dimension of life experiences (Neale and Flowerdew 2003). In total, we had 11 new entrants and 8 old cases. Interviewees were referred from 8 social welfare agencies, including one government district office. It took one half to 3 h for a first-round interview, and half an hour to one and one half hours for a second-round interview.

A semi-structured questionnaire, constructed on the basis of the three above-mentioned questions, was used for both rounds of interviews. In addition, the global measure of life satisfaction—The Chinese version of the Satisfaction with Life scale—was adopted to reflect how far welfare recipients successfully manage their surroundings without losing sight of the efforts they make. It was a five-item Likert scale with satisfactory reliability and validity among Hong Kong Chinese population (Wong et al. 2006). In the second round, questions used during the first round of interviews were modified to focus on changes that had happened since the first interview. We saw insignificant changes in the second series of interviews, which may reflect that adaptation to a new situation takes time. Hence, most of the findings are not reported. Interviews were transcribed by eleven trained university students, and all transcriptions were proofread by a third-party research assistant to ensure the quality of the transcripts. Successive approximation was used as a method for data analysis (Krueger and Neumann 2006). In summary, we followed through the general procedural practice of conducting qualitative research in this study.

4.1 Aspiration for Self-Reliance Ethos

Now we come to see whether the welfare recipients in Hong Kong welfare benefit system still preserve their traditional belief about self-reliance. We start with the employable recipients first. To the young employable recipients, they seemed to have a strong aspiration to exit the welfare benefit system. An unemployed youth with unstable employment experiences said:

> The money (CSSA benefit) is not earned by yourself; you feel unhappy and cannot find peace in your mind (*male, aged 19, new case*).

He wanted to find a full-time job, but mentioned that he was rejected three to four times in the past 2 months, and hoped to spend some time to further his studies, e.g., English and cooking, to enhance his market competitiveness.

Another case, a street-sleeper unemployed youth, was also keen on finding jobs. In the first interview, he told us that he tried to find a job but was rejected twenty times in 2 months before he reluctantly fell into the benefit system. He still had strong aspirations to find a job. He talked about the rationale underlying his strong motivation for job searching:

> If I have a job, I can start saving money for emergency needs in future. I am not as young as I was before (*male, aged 29, unemployment, three months on CSSA*).

Three months later in the second interview, he had found a part-time cleaning job with a daily wage of HK$250 and was satisfied with the employment, but intended to look for a full-time job in Chinese tea restaurants, notably a better paying and more stable position.

A single-parent migrant from mainland China found her aspirations for leaving poverty in the second generation. She told us her aspirations were vested in her child:

> On one hand, I receive help from the government. On the other hand, I will educate my child to study hard. One day, he will contribute to society (*female, aged 34, single-parent, seven years on CSSA*).

Nevertheless, she did not give up working. She had worked part-time in a kindergarten for 7 months in 2004, and later became a full-time cleaner in a volunteer organisation, but found herself with only a meagre one thousand dollars additional income. However, this low-earning, single-parent, welfare recipient said,

> I feel near exiting CSSA; I feel near self-reliance (*female, single-parent/low earner, aged 41, seven years on CSSA*).

Another single-parent welfare recipient was on a full-time low-income job. She could not afford expensive private rent and had to rely upon public assistance. She aspired to two conditions for exiting CSSA—first, public housing (i.e., cheaper rent); and second, a job paying six to seven thousand dollars a month:

> Previously I could not work because my child was young and found myself lazy…having a job gets something to engage (*female, single parent/low earner, aged 34, new case, three months on CSSA*).

Apparently, welfare recipients had a strong sense of work ethic and the ethos of self-reliance. We cannot identify any employable recipient who did not have the aspiration to exit the welfare benefit system. Of course, the elderly, disabled, and ill-health recipients were found somewhat contented with their recipient status and life style. Two quotes exemplify:

> (CSSA) helps me not worry about money for food or the need of borrowing money from others. The government gives me money (food and necessities); I feel really comfortable (*female, aged 79, old age, four months on CSSA*).

It (special grant) helps me pay the rent, which is really helpful. Previously, I only had a disability allowance, which was far less than enough to pay the rent (*female, aged 41, permanent disability, four months on CSSA*).

These findings reflect the sense of ontological security provided by public assistance as a safety-net of last resort. The elderly, disabled, and ill-health recipients did not express their aspiration for self-reliance due to their demographic and health characteristics. They opted for security and basic guarantees which public assistance is supposed to offer. Their aspirations are different as exemplified in the following:

My life expectations are very simple—I want enough money for food and daily necessities (rent, water, electronic, and telephone). I expect no more (*female, aged 44, ill health, five years on CSSA*).

In summary, employable welfare recipients still embraced a strong sense of work ethic and self-reliance ethos; however, the unemployable and deserving poor welfare recipients such as those of old aged and ill-health held a different attitude—they uttered more about the need of ontological security.

4.2 Need and Life Satisfaction

In the earlier section, we provided a brief account of Hong Kong's welfare benefit system against the wider context of the labour market and its repercussions in terms of a widened income gap and low-paying jobs. In this light, welfare benefits may be regarded as generous from the perspective of those in the lowest end of the labour market; while welfare recipients, in fact, receive benefit levels barely sufficient to enjoy their quality of life.

As mentioned above, CSSA benefits are quite comprehensive in regard to essential need fulfilment. Special grants supplement needs for those who have additional special circumstances, such as children's education fees, rent, water charges, telephone installation and monthly fees, eye glasses, etc. More importantly, medical fees and charges for treatment in public hospitals and clinics are totally waived. Hence, the basic needs of welfare recipients should be met. Appreciation of a single-parent recipient of the enormous change brought to her once her family was admitted into the welfare benefit system was expressed:

Due to having these benefits (CSSA money) our lives became more stable… My child has a chance to go to school; we have food and a place to stay… I appreciate the government. Without this, I really don't know how we would live our lives (*female, aged 41, single parent, seven years on CSSA*).

The free medical treatment was hailed by one:

It (medical fee waiver) releases my worries about health concerns. Viewing the worst case scenario, poor people mostly fear contracting an illness. Now, we have a 'golden passport' to protect us (*male, aged 53, single parent, twelve years on CSSA*).

However, the relatively low replacement rate as mentioned above has its toll on need satisfaction of welfare recipients. Single parents frequently reported unmet needs of their children; for example, the cost for their children to join an interest group, buy a computer, participate in school activities, buy an electronic camera, etc. Here are two such felt needs:

> My children wish to have the chance, but I don't have money for my children to participate in extra-curricular activities (*female, aged 37, single parent, two months on CSSA*).

> My daughter had a graduation ceremony for her Form 7 class. She told me that she would like to have a camera to take photos of her classmates. However, we didn't have one (*female, aged 41, single parent, seven years on CSSA*).

There are more on the list who understand poverty from a life-style deprivation perspective, but we would like to shift the discussion to a psychological perspective. We will investigate the social stigma which is deeply felt by welfare recipients before we look at the global measure of subjective well being in life satisfaction. The recipients felt strongly about it:

> The public in general considers CSSA recipients as worse than others, like parasites (*female, aged 27, ill health, four months on CSSA*).

> Each time I went to (the Social Security Field Unit) report, I felt uneasy. A lot of people looked at me. I would lower my head....If I had a job, people would have a different impression of me (*female, aged 18, unemployment, three months on CSSA*).

> I will not disclose my status (on CSSA) to those with whom I am not familiar. They may gossip about this with others. I feel bad about this... (*female, aged 48, permanent disability, 15 years on CSSA*).

There are very negative emotional repercussions felt by welfare recipients. Balancing these negative emotional states with the positive feeling of the compensation provided by the welfare benefit system for meeting the seemingly comprehensive basic needs, a life satisfactory measure should be able to capture these two different emotional states. In addition, this measure will inform us of a global indicator which includes the efforts welfare recipients put into their life. A scale of 0–20 was used to measure life satisfaction in this study. The recipients in total scored a range from 2 to 15, with a mean score of 9.1. The findings are as follows: gender made a difference, male 10.9 and female 7.8; those under the age of 40 scored 7.9 while those above got 11; those staying in the system fewer than 6 months scored 8.8, while those who stayed more than 3 years had 9.6. In the differences between CSSA categories, old aged scored at 8.2, the permanently disabled got the best score of 10.5, followed by the unemployed, 9.5 and single parent/low earning recipients, 9.3, and ill health had a mean of 7.5 (Table 1).

How could these scores of life satisfaction be understood? It needs to be considered that we have very few samples, and the findings cannot be generalized. Apart from this, there are some insights from the findings if we refer to the literature on life satisfaction. According to Diener and Diener (1996: 184), most people have subjective well being above the average; they hypothesize a positive baseline for affects in human beings; and this hypothesis is supported by empirical findings (Diener et al. 1985, 1997). Local empirical studies also identify the Hong Kong Chinese with a somewhat neutral mean score (Cheung 1998; Chan et al. 2003; Wong et al. 2006); hence, the below mean average score of 9.1 (the mean score is 10.0) of all welfare recipients should be regarded as an unsatisfactory subjective assessment of life. This also means that the positive feeling from satisfaction of comprehensive needs plus the sense of ontological security do not elevate life satisfaction of welfare recipients to a level at the mean or in the positive territory in our 0–20 scale.

Table 1 Levels of satisfaction with life of the welfare recipients ($N = 19$)

	Life satisfaction (mean score)[a]
All	9.1
Gender	
Male ($n = 8$)	10.9
Female ($n = 11$)	7.8
Age	
≤40 ($n = 8$)	7.9
≥41 ($n = 11$)	11.0
CSSA categories	
Old age ($n = 3$)	8.2
Permanently disability ($n = 2$)	10.5
Ill health ($n = 2$)	7.5
Single parent/low earning ($n = 7$)	9.3
Unemployed ($n = 5$)	9.5
Duration of stay	
≤6 months ($n = 11$)	8.8
≥3 years ($n = 8$)	9.6

[a] Scale scores range from 0 to 20

According to the literature, not all personal characteristics have an impact on life satisfaction, but the one often cited is the positive relationship in the older age recipient (Campbell and Sawer 1976; Fernandez and Kulik 1981; Hong and Giannakopoulos 1994). Perhaps age is a proxy of culture; and the self-reliance ethos has a cut-throat impact on the old-aged recipients' self-evaluation of life—the three old-aged recipients had a mean of 8.2 (Table 1) despite the positive effect of aging as helping people to appreciate the constraints on life. This seems in line with the observation of Inglehart (2000) from the World Values Survey—personal characteristics are not necessarily independent by themselves; they are moderated by the larger society where they are embedded.

It is noteworthy that those who stayed longer in the system (i.e., more than 3 years) had a mean score above the mean (9.6, $n = 8$ vs. 9.1, $n = 19$) and scored higher than the new entrants (i.e., not more than 6 months, 8.8, $n = 11$). On this basis, it is tempting to suggest that a cultural adaptation process was working in favour of those staying longer in the system. If this is the case, it does not work in favour in an exit decision once one stays longer.

4.3 Exit Dilemma

According to the above findings in this study, it seems that the aspiration for self-reliance and the social stigma associated with the recipient status both work positively for exiting the welfare benefit system. This is especially true in young welfare recipients who were the most employable. Three in this study were such cases in question—one found a job and exited the welfare benefit system, one changed jobs, and one completed an operation which improved her health condition and reported a high motivation for job seeking. The followings two quotes are self-evident:

> After I get the operation, I might not be able to get the medical certification (on ill health for welfare benefits). I am planning to seek a job (*female, aged 27, six months on CSSA*).

I am quite satisfied with my life now, mainly because I have a job and have my own earnings… I am planning to save HK$20,000 to HK$30,000. Then, I will think about my future again" (*male, aged 29, exited CSSA by the second interview*).

Some also found the activation programmes helpful in job seeking.

It (Intensive Employment Assistance Programme, IEAP) provides workshops to explain what is expected from the job market. Then, it matches our competence; for instance, if it would not be realistic for you to be in the construction sector and you would rather be a chef. Also, it teaches some interview skills and how to prepare an appropriate resume (*male, aged 28, unemployment, four years on CSSA*).

I found IEAP helpful. I didn't know where to find jobs, so it (IEAP programme) provided me with newspaper information and helped me make telephone calls, which enhanced my confidence (*female, aged 41, single parent, seven years on CSSA*).

Then, what are the inhibiting factors according to the welfare recipients?

Firstly, it is the unfriendly labour market. The low educated, young and middle-aged, and ill-health are more disadvantaged in the labour market. The following are some of the statements along this line from a few welfare recipients with such personal characteristics:

I tried to seek a job but was rejected twice. Both companies rejected me because I did not have working experience and also had language difficulties (she migrated from China in February 2007) (*female, aged 18, unemployment, four months on CSSA*).

I would read the newspaper and/or advertisement on the street and then call to apply. Many times, I was told that the vacancy was filled. Sometimes, they asked how old I was. They wanted (to employ) young people. I am over fifty. Nobody wanted to employ me (*female, aged 50, unemployment, five years on CSSA*).

It is not difficult for me to find a job. However, it is difficult for me to keep the job. Previously, I found a job after my first operation (retinal detachment). But when I worked until afternoon, my eyes became red. My colleagues asked me what had happened to me. It was difficult (*female, aged 27, ill health, four months on CSSA*).

Second, the low-income job is not promising as compared with the compensation from the welfare benefit system.

I can work. However, there must be somebody who will employ me. If I work as a security-guard, the salary is around HK$5,000; if I work as a cleaner, the salary is around HK$3,000. If I take such jobs, I will not be able to take care of my daughter and I will not be able to pay my current rent. I have to have at least HK$6,000 per month to maintain my family. Hence, I feel really disgraced if I earn less than HK$6,000 a month (*male, aged 50, single parent, four months on CSSA*).

It seems that the wider labour market is to blame for the seemingly disgraceful wage from a low-end job that cannot meet the basic needs of oneself and the family. In this case, the respondent was calculative but that "rational calculation" was not to abuse the system for one's favour, but stemmed from a concern for a reasonable compensation from the labour market to make ends meet.

Third, some welfare recipients also reported that they needed to overcome some institutional barriers in employment. For example, they were required to report to social security officers in regard to any change of employment status by providing supporting documents from the employer.

> I find it very difficult to find a job. It is possible for me to find a part-time job. I don't know how long it will take. But I have to report (to the Social Security Unit) using a supporting document. A supporting document for a part-time job is not easy to obtain. It may lead to complications (in my job searching), which discourage me from finding a job (*female, aged 27, ill health, four months on CSSA*).

> I have heard many times that when a boss notices that you are on CSSA, s/he (boss) becomes quite picky. Sometimes, he or she may even say, 'You can earn a living from several sources (referring to another source from CSSA)', which is really disgusting (*male, aged 28, unemployment, four years on CSSA*).

The motivation from activation measure in the welfare benefit system was considered unattractive, as stated by one.

> The government could provide us with more allowances (disregarded income) so that we could be more motivated (*female, aged 41, single parent, five years on CSSA*).

Of course, the old aged, ill-health, and permanently disabled recipients did not have to consider the stay-exit decision; after all, they were considered as the deserving poor, but they unfortunately belonged to the same welfare benefit system which included the undeserving poor such as the unemployed.

To conclude, it seems that the stay-exit decision is a complex one; social stigma, self-reliance ethos, and activation programmes were positives to employment. However, there were some structural (i.e., labour market) and institutional (rules and regulations and reemployment incentives) barriers that inhibit job seeking.

5 Conclusion

The findings of the study show that the experiences of welfare recipients and their exit motivation were embedded in a complex situation of real life experiences in interaction with the benefits provided by the welfare system. The qualitative methodology is best used to untangle such a complex situation as we did in this study. From the perspective of the affected, welfare recipients hold complicated values and motivations for exit. We cannot identify *significant* evidence supporting the three assumptions—i.e., a welfare dependency culture, generosity of welfare benefits, and rational and calculative welfare recipients—underlying the relationship between welfare recipients and public assistance. "I wish to be self-reliant" seems to be a common belief among Chinese welfare recipients of this qualitative study in Hong Kong; it was particularly the case in employable recipients. The comprehensive benefits provided by CSSA in Hong Kong were not in any sense generous, but, from the perspective of the recipients in this study, it enabled them a sense of ontological security. The claims of a welfare dependency culture and welfare benefit system trapping welfare recipients were not found in this study.

In general, welfare recipients were grateful to the government for what they got from the welfare benefit system—the comprehensive needs, ranging from food and housing to children's education, except some expenses for social participation and educational purposes were barely met. We were not able to reveal any severe material hardship on the part of the recipients; but we could detect a very negative emotional state felt by recipients due to the social stigma associated with the recipient status. The negative emotional state is also indicated in the below mean average score of the life satisfaction scale in this study. However, there is an indicator supporting the cultural change assumption—longer-stayed welfare recipients had a higher score above the mean.

Welfare recipients were also not rational calculators. We could only identify one employable recipient who analyzed different costs in his stay-exit choice; however, that was seemingly about the concern of whether or not the compensation from the labour market was sufficient to make ends meet. The lower compensation from employment, as compared with welfare benefits from public assistance, reflects a dilemma many welfare recipients now face against the background of a global economy which is hostile to jobs in the lower-end labour market. In this light, a solution to the dilemma faced by welfare recipients, not only those indicated in this study but also all lower-end workers in today's globalised economies, should not only work on social policy, but also look at how to make work pay in the labour market.

On policy terms, the design of a welfare benefit system is to set benefits basic levels lower than the standard of minimal adequacy (Veit-Wilson 1998: 4). As such a life on public assistance should encounter hardships. The rationale is to generate work incentive and avoid moral hazards. Having said that, the social stigmatization of the traditional deserving poor—the elderly, disabled, and ill-health—is too strong; it is not fair to them. In other words, there is a strong case on moral grounds to argue that a welfare system should not classify all recipient groups together. To do so, given the different nature in terms of the concept of the deserving poor, creates unnecessary psychological pain; even if it is able to provide ontological security to its recipients.

At last, it is necessary to state that the findings of this study are not based on a representative sample, but on in-depth interviews of 19 recipients and their views about the benefit system in Hong Kong. In addition, because quitting the welfare system carries social desirability, the interviewees might show their intention to be self-reliant for such consideration. This may be another limitation of the study. But the findings of this study contribute to the literature by enriching our understanding of the relationship between welfare recipients and public assistance in a society with strong beliefs about work and self-reliance.

Acknowledgments The paper is partially based on the unpublished report of a consultancy study. We are grateful to our client for giving us permission to cite from the report.

References

Bailey, M. A. (2005). Welfare and multifaceted decision to move. *America Political Science Review, 99*(1), 125–135.

Campbell, A., & Sawer, W. (1976). Life satisfaction in the United States. *Social Forces, 54*(3), 621–631.

Census and Statistics Department. (2007). *Thematic report: Household income distribution in Hong Kong*. Hong Kong: Government Logistics Department, The Special Administrative Region Government of Hong Kong.

Chan,Y. K., Kwan, C. C., & Shek, D. (2003). *Quality of life in Hong Kong—The Chinese University of Hong Kong quality of life index*. Hong Kong: The Chinese University of Hong Kong.

Chau, R. C., & Yu, W. K. (2005). Is welfare unAsian? In A. Walker & C. Wong (Eds.), *East Asian welfare regimes in transition* (pp. 21–45). Bristol: Policy Press.

Cheung, C. K. (1998). Impacts of class on Hong Kong people's well-being. *Human Relations, 51*(1), 89–119.

Chiu, S., & Wong, V. (2005). Hong Kong: From familistic to Confucian welfare. In A. Walker & C. K. Wong (Eds.), *East Asian welfare regimes in transition*. Bristol: Policy Press.

Choi, K. S. (2000). The image of comprehensive social security assistance clients in printed media in Hong Kong. *Hong Kong Social and Cultural Quarterly*, No. 5 (in Chinese).
Clasen, J. (1997). *Social insurance in Europe*. Bristol: The Policy Press.
Clasen, J., & Clegg, D. (2003). Unemployment protection and labour market reform in France and Great Britain in the 1990s: Solidarity versus activation? *Journal of Social Policy, 32*(3), 383–401.
Cocca, C. (2002). From "welfare queen" to "exploited teen: Welfare dependency, statutory rape, and moral panic. *NWSA Journal, 14*(2), 56–79.
Cox, R. H. (1998). The consequences of welfare reform: How conceptions of social rights are changing. *Journal of Social Policy, 21*(1), 1–16.
Dean, H., & Taylor-Gooby, P. (1992). *Dependency culture: The explosion of a myth*. London: Oxford University Press.
Deng, R., & Zhou, C.-x. (2006). The dependence on social welfare in current China and the implementation of the policies to go against such dependency. *Journal of Guizhou University (Social Sciences), 24*(6), 82–86.
Diener, E., & Diener, C. (1996). Most people are happy. *Psychological Science, 7*, 181–185.
Diener, E., Emmons, R. A., Larsen, R. J., & Griffin, S. (1985). The satisfaction with life scale. *Journal of Personality Assessment, 49*, 71–75.
Diener, E., Suh, E. M., & Oishi, S. (1997). Recent findings in subjective well-being. *Indian Journal of Clinical Psychology, 24*(March), 25–41.
East, J. F., & Bussey, M. (2007). "I was scared every day": Surviving in the TANF environment. *Journal of Policy Practice, 6*(3), 45–64.
Edin, K., & Lein, L. (1998). *Making ends meet, how single mothers survive welfare and low-wage work*. New York: Russell Sage Foundation.
Engbersen, G., Schuyt, K., Timmer, J., & van Waarden, F. (1993). *Cultures of unemployment: A comparative look at long-term unemployment and urban poverty*. Boulder, CO: Westview Press.
Fernandez, R., & Kulik, J. (1981). A multilevel model of life satisfaction: effects of individual characteristics and neighborhood composition. *American Sociological Review*, December, 840–850.
Hagerty, M. R. (1999). Unifying liveability and comparison theory: Cross-national time-series analysis of life satisfaction. *Social Indicators Research, 47*, 343–357.
Halvorsen, K. (1998). Symbolic purpose and factual consequences of the concepts of "self-reliance" and "dependency" in contemporary discourses on welfare. *Scandinavian Journal of Social Welfare, 7*, 56–64.
Hernanz, V., Malherbet, F., & Pellizzari, M. (2004) *Take-up of welfare benefits in OECD countries: A review of the evidence, OECD social*. Employment and Migration Working Papers, 17.
Hills, J., & Waldfogel, J. (2004). A "third way" in welfare reform? Evidence from the United Kingdom. *Journal of Policy Analysis and Management, 23*(4), 765–788.
Hong, S. M., & Giannakopoulos, E. (1994). The relationship of satisfaction with life to personality characteristics. *The Journal of Psychology, 128*(5), 1–8.
Hoynes, H., & MaCurdy, T. (1994). Has the decline in benefits shortened welfare spells? *American Economic Review, 84*(2), 43–48.
Inglehart, R. (2000). Globalization and postmodern values. *The Washington Quarterly, 23*(1), 215–228.
Jones, R. M. (1995). The price of welfare dependency: Children pay. *Social Work, 40*(4), 496–505.
Keng, S.-H., Garasky, S., & Jensen, H. H. (2002). Welfare dependence and recidivism in an era of welfare reform. *Applied Economics, 34*, 2311–2323.
Kenworthy, L. (1999). Do welfare policies reduce poverty? A cross-national assessment. *Social Forces, 77*(3), 1119–1139.
Kerr, S. A. (1983). *Making ends meet*. London: Bedford Square Press.
Kimenyi, M. S. (1991). Rational choice, culture of poverty, and the intergenerational transmission of welfare dependency. *Southern Economic Journal, 57*(4), 947–960.
Kittay, E. F. (1998). Welfare, dependency, and a public ethic of care. *Social Justice, 25*(1), 123–145.
Krueger, L. W., & Neumann, W. L. (2006). *Social work research methods: Qualitative and quantitative applications*. Boston: Pearson.
Lau, S. K., & Kuan, H. C. (1988). *The ethos of the Hong Kong Chinese*. Hong Kong: The Chinese University Press.
Li, M.-G. (2008). Municipal minimal living security system and the poor's welfare dependency. *Social Work*, No. 2, 24–27. (in Chinese).
McGarry, K. (1996). Factors determining participation of the elderly in supplementary security. *Journal of Human Resources, 31*(2), 331–358.
Mendes, P. (2007). *An Australian perspective on Singaporean welfare policy*. Retrieved from Monash University, Australia on 23 March 2009 http://www.socwork.net/2007/1/articles/mendes.

Misra, J., Moller, S., & Karides, M. (2003). Envisioning dependency: Changing media depictions of welfare in the 20th century. *Social Problems, 50*(4), 482–504.
Monroe, P. A., Tiller, V. R., O'Neil, C., & Blalock, L. L. (2007). "We make our ends meet good": Coping strategies of former welfare reliant women. *Journal of Loss and Trauma, 12*, 199–221.
Neale, B., & Flowerdew, J. (2003). Time, texture and childhood: the contours of longitudinal qualitative research. *International Journal of Social Research Methodology, 6*(3), 189–199.
Niskanen, W. (1996). Welfare and the culture of poverty. *Cato Journal, 16*(1), 1–15.
Ring, P. J. (2005). Security in pension provision: A critical analysis of UK government policy. *Journal of Social Policy, 34*(3), 343–363.
Rubin, A., & Babbie, E. R. (2005). *Research methods for social work*. Pacific Grove: Brooks/Cole.
Scheider, S. K., & Jacoby, W. G. (2003). A culture of dependence? The relationship between public assistance and public opinion. *British Journal of Political Science, 33*, 213–231.
Scott, E. K., London, A. S., & Gross, G. (2007). "I try not to depend on anyone but me': Welfare reliant women's perspectives on self-sufficiency, work, and marriage. *Sociological Inquiry, 77*(4), 601–625.
Social Welfare Department. (1998). *Support for self-reliance: Report on review of the comprehensive social security scheme*. Hong Kong: Government Printer.
Sofaer, S. (1999). Qualitative methods: What are they and why use them? *Health Service Research, 34*, 1101–1118.
Tang, K. (2000). *Social welfare development in East Asia*. Houndmills: Palgrave.
Tang, K. L., & Cheung, C. K. (2007). Programme effectiveness in activating welfare recipients to work: The case of Hong Kong. *Social Policy and Administration, 41*(7), 747–767.
Underlid, K. (2007). Poverty and experiences of insecurity—a qualitative interview study of 25 long-standing recipients of social security. *International Journal of Social Welfare, 16*, 65–74.
Veit-Wilson, J. (1998). *Setting adequacy standards*. Bristol: Policy Press.
Walker, A., & Wong, C. K. (2005a). Introduction: East Asian welfare regimes. In A. Walker & C. Wong (Eds.), *East Asian welfare regimes in transition* (pp. 3–20). Bristol: Policy Press.
Walker, A., & Wong, C. K. (2005b). Conclusion: from Confucianism to globalisation. In A. Walker & C. Wong (Eds.), *East Asian welfare regimes in transition* (pp. 213–224). Bristol: Policy Press.
Wijeysingha, V. (2005). The welfare regime in Singapore. In A. Walker & C. Wong (Eds.), *East Asian welfare regimes in transition* (pp. 187–211). Bristol: Policy Press.
Wong, C. K., & Chau, K. K. L. (2002). Neither welfare state nor welfare society: The case of Hong Kong. *Social Policy and Society, 1*(4), 293–301.
Wong, C. K., & Wong, K. Y. (1998). *Assessment of social welfare conditions in Hong Kong, challenges facing the "self-reliance for welfare" mentality*. Hong Kong: Hong Kong Institute of Asia–Pacific Studies, Chinese University of Hong Kong, Occasional Paper 86 (in Chinese).
Wong, C. K., Wong, K. Y., & Mok, B. H. (2006). Subjective well-being, societal condition and social policy—the case study of a rich Chinese society. *Social Indicators Research, 78*, 405–428.

Soc Indic Res (2010) 95:535–551
DOI 10.1007/s11205-009-9525-7

Social Development in Hong Kong: Development Issues Identified by Social Development Index (SDI)

Hoi-wai Chua · Anthony K. W. Wong · Daniel T. L. Shek

Accepted: 30 July 2009 / Published online: 16 October 2009

Abstract Surviving the aftermaths of the Asian Financial Crisis and SARS in 2003, Hong Kong's economy has re-gained its momentum and its economic growth has been quite remarkable too in recent few years. Nevertheless, as reflected by the Social Development Index (SDI), economic growth in Hong Kong does not seem to have benefited the people of the city at large as we see social qualities such as cohesion, security, equity, and empowerment are gradually eroded. This paper aims to summarize the current state of social development in Hong Kong based on the SDI-2008 and identify the major social, political and economic challenges that are confronted by Hong Kong. Based on the findings, a range of policy options proposed for promoting a more balanced approach to social and economic development are discussed. The article illustrates the utility of social indicators research such as the SDI in assessing quality of life and assisting related social planning initiatives in Asian communities such as Hong Kong.

Keywords Balanced development · Social development · Social development index · Social indicators · Hong Kong

1 Introduction

Hong Kong's achievement in economic development has been remarkable over the last few decades, with an increase of more than 80% in real GDP from 1981 to 1998. Nevertheless, being one of the top 30 most advanced societies in the world (UNDP 2003), many people in Hong Kong generally do not experience social development as impressive as its economic development. Largely predominated by the economic concern, little room has been

H. Chua (✉) · A. K. W. Wong
The Hong Kong Council of Social Service, 15 Hennessy Road, Kowloon, Hong Kong
e-mail: hw.chua@hkcss.org.hk

D. T. L. Shek
Department of Applied Social Sciences, The Hong Kong Polytechnic University, Kowloon, Hong Kong
e-mail: daniel.shek@polyu.edu.hk

available for Hong Kong to pursue social development in accordance with the principle of making human beings "the centre of concerns" as stated in the Agenda 21 and the assertion of treating economic development, social development and environmental development as interdependent components for development expressed in the Copenhagen Declaration on Social Development (UNCED 1992; United Nations 1995). In the Copenhagen Declaration on Social Development, full participation of all people in a society to promote social progress, justice and the betterment of the human condition and integration of economic, cultural and social policies are emphasized. Besides, it is maintained that family is a basic unit of society and it has a significant role to play in social development.

Of course, the attainment or non-attainment of social development in a society must be objectively assessed. Without proper assessment, it would be difficult, if not impossible to chart social changes and to identify gaps in social policies. This paper reports the role of the Social Development Index (SDI) developed by The Hong Kong Council of Social Service (hereafter referred to as 'the Council') in the process of informing, promoting and guiding social development of Hong Kong (Estes 2005a, b). The SDI is also a tool for assessing quality of life indexed by official statistics in Hong Kong.

Leveraging the opportunity of the World Summit on Social Development convened by the United Nations at Copenhagen in 1995 and its outcome, Copenhagen Declaration, the Council identified a gap of social reporting for the advocacy for social development in Hong Kong. The idea of constructing the SDI for Hong Kong was first proposed in 1999. Before the establishment of the SDI, social development of Hong Kong was usually measured by economic measures such as GDP per capita which failed to account for many other aspects of development of Hong Kong. For example, as an economically advanced city with high GDP ranking among the top in the world, its Gini coefficient (which measures income disparity) has been problematically high in the past decades. Thus, a more holistic approach to assess social development of Hong Kong is necessary. Against this background, a Board of Consultants was appointed by the Council comprising key figures in the Hong Kong SAR government, academics from universities in Hong Kong and other community leaders to develop a measure that can reflect social development in Hong Kong. The Council also invited a Panel of Experts with over 40 local experts in various areas of social development under the Board to give their expert views on the SDI. The research team of the SDI project was led by Richard J. Estes, an internationally renowned scholar in social development index construction, from the University of Pennsylvania.

As agreed by both the Panel of Experts and the Board of Consultants, the SDI included 14 sectors and the development of five disadvantaged population groups which should be regarded as adequate in reflecting the general social development of Hong Kong. In order to maximize the advantages of indicator system and indexing, a composite index (SDI) and an indicators system (Social Development Indicators System) were constructed to measure social development of Hong Kong over a period from 1981 to the present.

Since the first report published in 2000, the SDI report was updated bi-annually. In addition to the SDI-2000 report, four more reports have been published, including SDI-2002 published in 2003, SDI-2004 published in 2005, SDI-2006 published in 2007 and SDI-2008 published in 2009. The first release of the SDI was made in 2000, tracking social progress of Hong Kong from 1981 to 1998. Viewing through the broadest possible social lens, substantial social progress took place in Hong Kong between 1981 and 1998, with a net gain on the SDI of some 75% between 1981 and 1998. From then onward, the SDI recorded a gradual increase of 31.8% from 1998 to 2006 (Fig. 1). However, the overall progress slowed down in the recent years as the SDI showed an increasing trend at a decreasing rate as in Fig. 1.

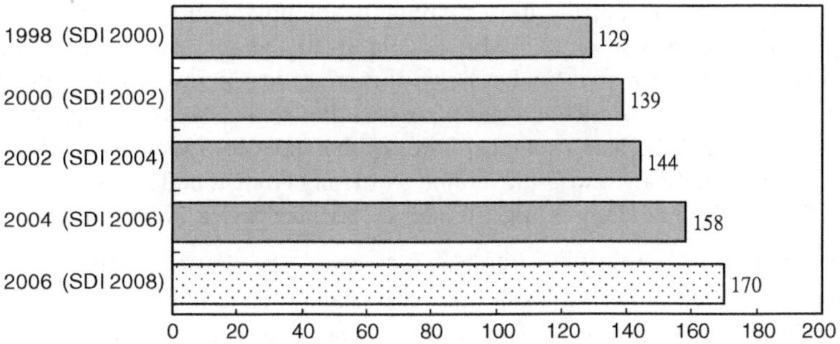

Fig. 1 SDI-2000 to SDI-2008 (base year 1991 = 100)

Despite such positive performance, Hong Kong's pace of social development was not uniform for all time periods studied or across all sectors of development (i.e., patterns more characteristic of *asynchronous* and *asymmetric* development). In addition, considerable variation occurred in the development performances of each of the SDI's 14 sectors, with some of which varied dramatically. For example, in the first release of the SDI, both Science and Technology Sub-index and Education Sub-index made remarkable progress during the period from 1981 to 1998, as measured by the respective sub-index cores (+107 and +102) (The Hong Kong Council of Social Service 2000). However, a very substantial social loss was recorded on the SDI's Family Solidarity Sub-index (−166)—the only basic SDI Sub-index for which substantial net social losses were recorded. The patterns remain unchanged in the ensuing years since the first release of the SDI. In all the previous releases since SDI-2000, some of the Sub-indices (e.g. Family Solidarity Sub-index) consistently appeared to be among the slowest in progress (The Hong Kong Council of Social Service 2007, p. 26). In contrast, other indices such as Science and Technology Sub-index consistently appeared to be among the top (The Hong Kong Council of Social Service 2007, p. 26).

On the other hand, considerable variation existed in the social development performances of Hong Kong's historically vulnerable population groups. As shown in the report *Social Development Index 2006*, although the social trend data showed positive changes for women and the elderly since the first release of the SDI, negative social trend findings for three additional population groups (i.e., low-income households, youth and children) were very disturbing (The Hong Kong Council of Social Service 2007, p. 28). Actually, in all previous releases of the SDI until SDI-2008, trend data for women and the elderly have always been positive and have always been making progress, where trend data for low-income households, youth and children have always been negative. Sub-indices like Children Sub-index have not recorded any gain in any of the previous releases (The Hong Kong Council of Social Service 2007, p. 28).

Subsequent to the first release (SDI-2000), Estes (2005a) reported that there was substantial social progress occurred in Hong Kong between 1981 and 2000 (SDI-2002), with vulnerability in some populations in the society. The situation can be reflected in the following conclusion:

> Hong Kong appears to have already developed into four distinct and unequal societies: 1) the "well off" whose social positions and development status are largely immune from swings in the local economy; 2) the "socially secure" who occupy important positions of influence and who have been able to more or less insulate

themselves against all but the most extreme development shifts occurring in Hong Kong; 3) the "socially insecure" who are employed and are "making it"… but with difficulty; and 4) a growing "underclass" of more or less permanently impoverished persons who possess limited means of extricating themselves from poverty. This study suggests that the harsh social conditions that exist for too many in Hong Kong today could dramatically swell the numbers of Hong Kong's underclass in the decade just unfolding." (The Hong Kong Council of Social Service 2000, pp. 6–7)

As SDI-2002 reported by Estes (2005a) only covered social trends between 1981 and 2000, there is an obvious need to examine social changes up to recent years. Building upon Estes (2005a) findings, the focus of the present paper is to examine the latest social trend data beyond those covered in SDI-2002.

2 Method

The status of social development in Hong Kong was assessed by the SDI developed by the Council. The details of the methodology in developing the SDI and the structure of the database can be seen in Estes (2005a, b). Appendix 1 outlines the steps involved during the construction process of the indicator system and related indices. The SDI is composed of 47 social, political and economic indicators divided across the 14 sectors of development (Appendix 2). An additional 31 indicators are used to assess changes over time in social development patterns among each of the five vulnerable population groups of special concern to the Council (Appendix 3). According to Estes, the project proved to be a successful one in both measuring the performance of Hong Kong in terms of various aspects of social development and drawing people's attention to the importance of social development (Estes 2005a, b).

3 Results

3.1 Current Social Development of Hong Kong Revealed by the SDI-2008

The current social development of Hong Kong can be summarized by the latest SDI figure (SDI-2008) which is 170 for 2006 (Fig. 1). It represents 70% gain as compared to that of base year (Year 1991 = 100), and 7.5% increase as compared to SDI-2006 in our last release. In spite of this overall gain, people's livelihood in terms of their very basic needs fulfillment does not seem to have any relative improvement. Several examples substantiate this conclusion.

The quality of family life, the very basic support as highlighted in the Copenhagen Declaration for Social Development and literature on social capital, is severely jeopardized. Findings in Figs. 2 and 3 as well as Table 1 show that Family Solidarity Sub-index has always been a negative figure since its first release. It has dropped very rapidly in the most recent release of SDI-2008, where we observed −535, which is around 150% drop as compared to the previous release in 2006 (Fig. 3). The figure generally means that it is now 5.35 times worse than that of the base year in 1991. In previous decades, what constituted the poor performance in family solidarity seems to be a gradual drop in the number of marriages while the number of divorces is on the rise. But in recent years, the major factor that accounts for the drop of the Sub-index is domestic violence. From 2004 (measured by

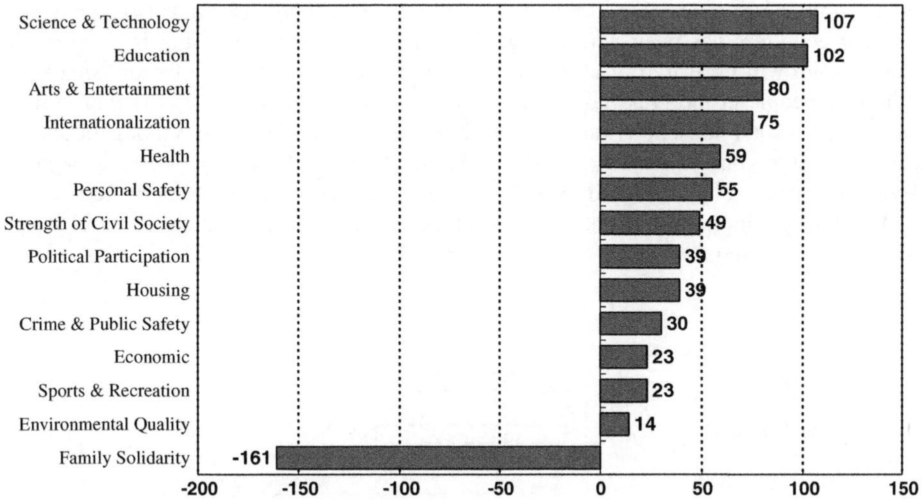

Fig. 2 SDI-2000: Sub-index score (base year 1991 = 100)

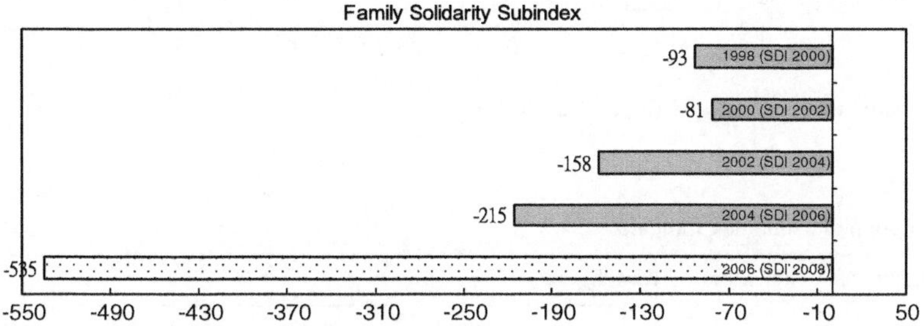

Fig. 3 Family solidarity subindex 2008 (base year 1991 = 100)

Table 1 Family solidarity subindex indicators 2008

Family solidarity subindex Indicators	Raw figures				
	1998 (SDI-2000)	2000 (SDI-2002)	2002 (SDI-2004)	2004 (SDI-2006)	2006 (SDI-2008)
Marriages per 100,000 people aged 15+ (+)	578	552	562	714	849
Divorces as % of marriages (−)	42.2	43.4	40.6	37.8	34.7
Reported domestic violence cases per 100,000 households (−)	58.5	52.6	79.2	105.7	**211.9**

SDI-2006) to 2006 (measured by SDI-2008), the reported cases of domestic violence per 100,000 households had doubled. Figures of spouse abuse, elder abuse and child abuse are all on sharp rise (The Hong Kong Council of Social Service 2009).

Another example is that the material well being of people is also not any better, although Hong Kong's economic achievement is always well acclaimed. A closer look at our Economic Sub-index (Fig. 4 and Table 2) provides a more comprehensive picture of how our economy has been performing. There is a clear indication that in spite of the economic growth measured in terms of GDP, fruits of success have not been adequately shared by people at the grassroots level over the years, as measured by the indicator on percentage of total household income earned by the bottom 50% of households (Table 2). This trend has gone further worse in the latest release (SDI-2008), where a negative development of −11 is recorded (The Hong Kong Council of Social Service 2009).

A further example is that the need for shelter seems not being attended to as it was before. The Housing Sub-index (Fig. 5 and Table 3) has recorded significant improvement

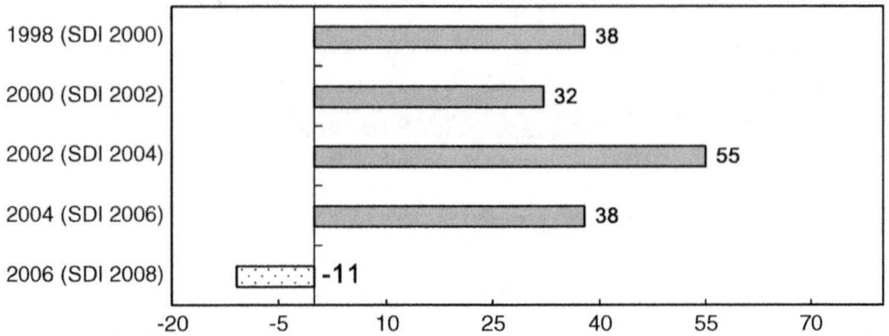

Fig. 4 Economic subindex 2008 (base year 1991 = 100)

Table 2 Economic subindex indicators 2008

Economic subindex indicators	Raw figures				
	1998 (SDI-2000)	2000 (SDI-2002)	2002 (SDI-2004)	2004 (SDI-2006)	2006 (SDI-2008)
Per capita GDP at constant 2000 market prices (+)	197559	197697	189397	190451	215779
Gross international reserves (months of import coverage) (+)	17.1	18.0	22.6	21.1	**18.6**
% of total household income earned by the bottom 50% of households (+)	19.2	18.6	18.0	17.8	**16.0**

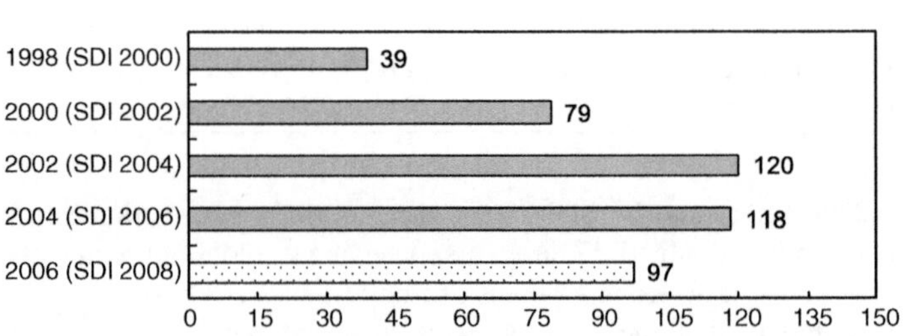

Fig. 5 Housing subindex 2008 (base year 1991 = 100)

Table 3 Housing subindex indicators

Housing subindex indicators	Raw figures				
	1998 (SDI-2000)	2000 (SDI-2002)	2002 (SDI-2004)	2004 (SDI-2006)	2006 (SDI-2008)
No. of waiting list applicants for housing authority rental flats (−)	131160	109633	91578	92556	**106575**
% of expenditure on housing as share of total household expenditure (−)	31.0	32.2	32.2	32.2	30.6

since SDI-2000 till SDI-2004, as compared to the previous observations. The latest trend, however, has been very worrying. Our latest release of SDI-2008 shows an 18% percentage drop in this Sub-index, furthering a slight drop started in the previous release in 2006 (1.7%) (The Hong Kong Council of Social Service 2009). Those most hard hit seem to be, again, the people at the grassroots level when we look into the constituent component of the Sub-index. The waiting list for the public housing has been on the increase. According to the figures supplied by the Housing Authority for 2007, a growing queue of 110,842 applicants waiting for public housing flats was reported.

Finally, the findings based on SDI-2008 showed that there were uneven developments in different sectors in Hong Kong. Although there was positive development in some of those economic-related aspects, some groups in the society were left out of the social progress and economic prosperity being enjoyed by others. Our latest findings showed that although negative values were recorded for Low Income Sub-index (−53) and Youth Sub-index (−19), some improvement has been achieved as compared to that in the previous release (−103 and −50 respectively). The magnitude of loss as compared to the base year of 1991 has reduced by at least half (Table 4 and Fig. 6). The Children Sub-index (Table 4 and Fig. 7) stood at the negative value of −235. This represents a drop by around 46% as compared to the previous release and the figure has been sliding throughout the past decade. Generally speaking, the findings in Table 5 show that (1) the percentage of children living in low-income households has gone up to over 25.3%; (2) number of reported cases per 100,000 of child abuse has increased by 33.3%; (3) more and more children are grown up in single-parent families; and (4) children are more vulnerable to death after being born than they were before (Table 5).

Table 4 Social development trends for Hong Kong's five population groups (1998, 2000, 2002, 2004 and 2006) (base year 1991 = 100)

	Children	Youth	Low income	Women	Elderly
1998 (SDI-2000)	−64	−45	−68	93	21
2000 (SDI-2002)	−82	−58	−80	171	112
2002 (SDI-2004)	−121	−77	−122	237	197
2004 (SDI-2006)	−160	−50	−103	295	269
2006 (SDI-2008)	−235	−19	−53	339	365

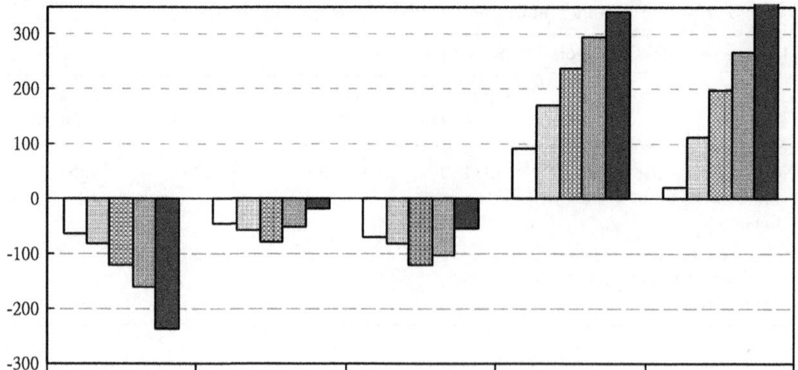

	Child	Youth	Low Income	Women	Elderly
1998 (SDI 2000)	-64	-45	-68	93	21
2000 (SDI 2002)	-82	-58	-80	171	112
2002 (SDI 2004)	-121	-77	-122	237	197
2004 (SDI 2006)	-160	-50	-103	295	269
2006 (SDI 2008)	-235	-19	-53	339	365

Fig. 6 Social development for Hong Kong's five population groups (1998, 2000, 2002, 2004 and 2006) (base year 1991 = 100)

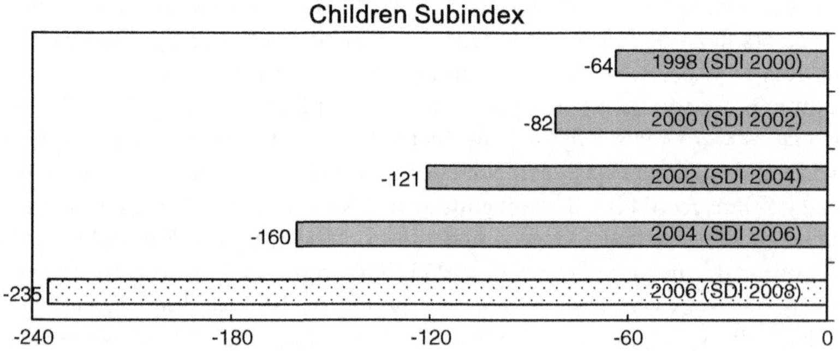

Fig. 7 Children subindex 2008 (base year 1991 = 100)

4 Discussion

4.1 Quality of Life Challenges and the Quest for a Balanced Social Development

Although it is not the main purpose of the SDI to identify factors which contribute to the above-mentioned observations highlighted by SDI-2008, a brief discussion of the key societal conditions contributing to the above-mentioned challenges is in order. In the previous releases of the SDI (e.g., The Hong Kong Council of Social Service 2000, 2002), considerable effort has been devoted to tracing the factors which contributed to the rapid decline of family solidarity in Hong Kong. These factors include the creation of stressful labour market and working environment because of the intense competition due to globalization, acceptance of family unfriendly jobs due to escalated fear of unemployment in the competitive environment, normalization of long working hours, an increased number of

Table 5 Children subindex indicators 2008

Children subindex indicators	Raw figures				
	1998 (SDI-2000)	2000 (SDI-2002)	2002 (SDI-2004)	2004 (SDI-2006)	2006 (SDI-2008)
% of children aged 0–14 in low-income households (−)	26.2	25.9	25.5	24.2	**25.3**
% of children living in single-parent households (−)	5.1	5.5	6.7	7.5	**7.98**
Under-five child mortality per 100,000 (−)	73.6	71.9	57.9	54.6	**72.3**
Children (aged 2–6) enrolled in kindergarten or childcare centers per 100,000 (+)	56,576	60,381	62,718	63,153	**57,722**
Child abuse cases per 100,000 population aged 0–17 (−)	28.5	33.8	36.5	45.2	**62.44**
% of children fully immunized against diphtheria, tetanus and whooping cough (+)	90.7	89.4	85.9	76.1	95
No. of children aged 10–15 arrested per 100,000 (−)	1,090.7	1,164.5	983.4	953.7	907.8

working population leaving the local families for career development in the Mainland due to the increasing social and economic integration between Hong Kong and the Mainland in the past two decades, an elevated tension within individual families because of the social and economic stress, and an increased tolerance for and use of domestic violence (Shek 2005). Likewise, the drop in Housing Sub-index clearly reflects a process of policy fault and its ensuing remedial actions of the Government in the last decade, namely the sudden expansion and abrupt contraction of housing (and land) supply policies (policy faults). The drop was perhaps not a direct result of the policy fault itself, but its impact on the housing market that makes affordable housing less and less accessible to the lower-middle class and the grassroots. As concluded by Chiu (2005), "keeping housing prices at an affordable level despite a recovering or recovered economy is irrefutably a real challenge to the government" (p. 168).

In the first release of SDI-2000, the Council's report concluded that disparities in social development are pronounced among various population groups. Our latest findings have shown that in the last 8 years, since the first release of SDI-2000, our social conditions have swelled the number of Hong Kong underclass. Gains in some area do not seem to be able to offset losses in other areas. While the poor adults at the grassroots are striving to make their ends meet, the future of next generation is jeopardized. Given the size of these disadvantaged populations in Hong Kong and the complexity of their social development requirements, clearly a new agenda must be launched in response to the social development needs. Past initiatives simply have not succeeded in reversing the highly negative conditions in which too many of Hong Kong's low-income households, youth and children find themselves.

Given the development patterns uncovered in the preceding analysis, the Hong Kong society could benefit from a re-examination of the premises used to guide its development—especially the almost exclusive preoccupation with the economic dimensions of development by the Government of the Hong Kong Special Administrative Region. Since the first release of the SDI in Hong Kong, the Council has been advocating for a balanced approach to development. There are several key assertions in the advocacy for a balanced social development in Hong Kong. First, it is argued that social and economic developments are equally important and inter-connected. On the one hand, economic growth provides opportunities for improving people's quality of life. On the other hand, social development, as reflected by better health, education, social protection, sustainable environment, and cultural diversity and so on forms the basis for furthering economic development. Second, it is maintained that excessive focus on any one aspect of development (such as economic development) at the expense of others is detrimental to the development of the society. Finally, the Government should assign equal importance to the social, economic, cultural and environmental development as they are four cornerstones of integrated or balanced social development. While this is the general line to take, a number of policies and measures are suggested to rectify the imbalances that we have identified from the assessment of social development in Hong Kong by SDI-2008.

The first measure is to develop a family-friendly policy such as improvement of the living environment of grassroots families by increasing the construction of public housing and subsidized housing, provision of rental subsidy for those on the waiting list, improvement of community facilities to provide more open space for family activities, and adoption of family impact assessment in all public policy making process and identify impacts of these policies on families. The second measure that should be considered is family-work balance including provision of policy incentive (such as tax reduction measures) to encourage corporations to implement family-friendly measures, such as setting up minimum wage, standardizing working time and providing paternity leave. Empirically, research findings support the benefits of adopting family-friendly policies. In their study of costs, savings and health gains of paternity leave in Sweden based on an examination of paternal leave in 1978–1979 and male mortality during 1981–2001, Mansdotter et al. (2007) found that fathers who took paternity leave had a statistically significant decreased death risk and there were health gains. Grover and Crooker (1995) also showed that employees with greater access to family-responsive human resource policies had higher organizational commitment and lower intention to quit their jobs.

Finally, work and family reconciliation policies and family outcomes were described in the Babies and Bosses reviews of OECD based on data collected in Australia, Denmark and the Netherlands (OECD 2002), Austria, Ireland and Japan (OECD 2003), New Zealand, Portugal and Switzerland (OECD 2004), and Canada, Finland, Sweden and the United Kingdom (OECD 2005). In the press release for the integrative volume on these series of reports (OECD 2008) on the website, it is stated that "getting family-friendly policies right will help reduce poverty, promote child development, enhance equity between men and women and stem the fall in birth-rates".

As the findings in the SDI-2008 suggest that children development in Hong Kong has consistently been deteriorating over the past decade, improvement of child care services to promote healthy growth for children is another policy direction that should be considered. These include shortening the waiting time for residential services for children, providing school social work service in kindergartens and childcare centres, strengthening family life education and marital counselling and enhancing parenting skills for single parents as well as re-married people. For children to grow up and develop in the twenty-first century, it is important to help children acquire multiple intelligences, in addition to providing formal education. As such, implementation of "Head Start" programs to promote language competence, social skills, cultural horizon, self confidence and self-image of children should be developed, particularly for those in the grassroots who can only afford the cost of formal education (Commission on Poverty 2005). Finally, development of economic support measures should be attempted. These include adjustment of the Comprehensive Social Security Assistance, a poverty relief scheme in Hong Kong, such as re-assessment of the level of assistance (especially in terms of food and housing), exploration of the possibility of setting up the child birth allowance, introduction of negative income tax to support low-income families and raise the level of tax exemption for children to help families nurture their children (Commission on Poverty 2007).

4.2 Use of the SDI in Social Reporting and Policy Advocacy: Conceptual and Methodological Considerations

Social development is a broad concept that has to be clearly spelled out in terms of more concrete constructs. However, readily available tool in this regard is rare (Shek and Lee 2007). In Hong Kong, with a few exceptions (e.g., Chan et al. 2005), little effort has been made in conceptualizing social development in a more holistic and systematic way. The Council's SDI is unmistakably a well-acclaimed project that attempts to build a framework to measure social development in a more comprehensive manner. As shown above, the SDI has enabled us to assess how Hong Kong is performing in social development, to identify challenges and critical issues that may hinder a more balanced development, and to propose a consistent set of policy suggestions. The previous releases of the SDI reports have been able to stimulate debates and discussions in the public and they also provide useful pointers for government officials and policy makers.

However, it is noteworthy that a social development index of this kind is bound to be a general measure that may not be able to fully account for the related complex phenomena. Furthermore, although the main purpose of the SDI aims only at reporting the social challenges that Hong Kong faces, it may not be able to describe the particular conditions that give rise to these phenomena. Conceptually and methodologically, the 14-domain structure does not consist of any explanatory factors; only descriptive domains are used to track different aspects of social development of Hong Kong. Even for a general level of description, the lack of empirically verified conceptual model of social development, which specifies the internal relationships among the constructs or domains of development, prevents us from identifying both the sources of any problems highlighted and the effects that these problems may produce. This limitation may reduce precision in the process of policy advocacy and suggestion. However, this should not undermine its power in providing directions for in-depth and detailed policy analysis and policy making. As an NGO in Hong Kong, the Council is concerned with how to involve people from the general public to pay attention to social development. However, as social development is a very broad concept that remains unfamiliar to most of the people, it is very hard to advocate social development without reducing it to the more intelligible constitutive sub-domains of the SDI.

The adequacy of measurement indicator of some Sub-indexes should also be given due consideration. For example, that the Family Solidarity Sub-index consists of only three indicators has been one of the key debates since its inception. While acknowledging the limitations of this Sub-index, in terms of both the number of indicators and the quality of these indicators, it is also noteworthy that indicators such as marriage and divorce rates are very often used in other social development measures, in spite of their limitations. This is more an inherent challenge of social indicator research that researchers have to balance between the principles of parsimony and comprehensiveness of the related measures. Nevertheless, it is noteworthy that the methodology underlying the SDI is commonly used to chart global (Estes 1988, 1998) as well as regional social development (Estes 1996, 1999, 2004) which can appropriately be used in a city like Hong Kong (Estes 2005a, b).

Besides, based solely on official statistics, the SDI may leave out some important but hard to be objectively observable domains for policy advocacy. These domains include what many people talk about in recent years such as social inclusion, trust, harmony and so forth. These are important social qualities that any NGOs or Hong Kong people would like to see in Hong Kong. Without any accurate measures or precise proxies in measuring these qualities, the SDI is unable to provide any insights into whether the government should, for example, put more resources in building more trust among people. With specific reference to this limitation, it is exactly the reason why official statistics, survey data and qualitative data are included in some of the alternative frameworks of social development such as the CUHK Quality of Life Index (Chan et al. 2005). Wong et al. (2006, p. 405) also argued that "social policy needs to pay more attention to the study of subjective well-being".

Although there may be intrinsic limitations in the SDI, the attempt of social reporting with the SDI has so far been quite successful. The study of the SDI in Hong Kong shows that economic growth does not automatically lead to overall development in the social arena. It also shows in general how imbalance Hong Kong's social development is, and thus helps alert people to looking into the people's livelihood and their quality of life behind the common doctrine of economical or material advancement.

Appendix 1: Steps Involved in the Development of the Social Development Index

Step 1: Professor Estes briefly laid down a conceptual framework for understanding social development. As an initial task to kick the project off, this briefing meant to stimulate further discussion on how to conceptualize social development of Hong Kong in more specific terms.

Step 2: A series of methodological decisions was made. In any study of this kind, the following methodological issues must be addressed seriously and carefully. They include:

- Composite Index versus Indicator System: Both were used.
- Objective versus Subjective Indicators: Mainly objective indicators.
- Comparability: Not as important as local relevance.
- Weighting Method: At the beginning, it was thought that statistical factor analysis could be used to assign weighting. As the research evolved, experts' opinions became the basis of weighting.

Step 3: Facilitated by Professor Estes, brainstorming sessions were held among the members of the research team to: (1) identify the major areas of social development as well as the vulnerable population groups to which we would like to give more attention; (2) list the potential indicators for each area of social development identified.

Step 4: Selection of major areas of social development and, more importantly, indicators which were deemed to be highly relevant to Hong Kong according to the following criteria:

- A few minimum scientific criteria: face validity, representativeness, accuracy;
- Availability of data;
- Reflecting development patterns of advanced post-industrial society;
- Outcome measures, instead of investment, input, throughput and process indicators;
- Indicators for which not more than one missing observation point of the five points within the time frame existed.

Step 5: The initial conceptual framework was revised and finalized. It was decided that the SDI-2000 would be concerned with the state/level of development Hong Kong had achieved at one point of time as compared to those at other preceding moments. "Development" would therefore refer to the outcomes at present as compared to those at other preceding times. It was conceptualized as a process in which a given society tried to make progress or to avoid regress as manifested by the outcomes at various points in time. Also, a more concrete specification of the word "social" was laid down given its broad coverage. We did not mean to distinguish "social" from "economic", "political", "cultural", "historical" and the like. We used the word "social" as a more general term covering almost every aspect of life that was deemed to be important for human development and growth. It would therefore include economic development as well as political development. It would cover cultural development as well as ecological development. The project of SDI-2000, therefore, aimed at evaluating the performance of Hong Kong in various areas of concern of social development and identifying areas where progress had been made or regress had been resulted for further actions.

Step 6: Based on the framework, data were collected according to the methodological specifications. Initially, a big database was constructed, called Databank, to record data for over 350 indicators.

Step 7: Led by Professor Estes, we proceeded to index construction. A total of 47 indicators were selected as the core indicators for the construction of the basic SDI-2000 and its components, i.e., the subindexes. These 47 indicators were deemed to be able to represent each area of social development included in our conceptual framework. Indicators were also selected for the construction of five subindexes for five historical vulnerable groups.

Step 8: Statistical analysis was performed, including standardization of measurements, weighting and statistical indexing.

Appendix 2: List of Subindexes and Indicators that Constitutes the SDI

Strength of civil society subindex

No. of charitable institutions and trusts qualifying for tax exemption (+)
Private charitable donations as % of GDP (+)
Ratio of private charitable donations to government subventions (+)
% of work force affiliated with trade unions (+)

Political participation subindex
Turnout rate in most recent District Board elections (+)
Ratio of District Board candidates to District Board offices (+)
% of District Board candidates with political party affiliations (+)

Internationalization subindex
No. of countries to which residents of Hong Kong can travel without visa (+)
No. of registered companies incorporated outside Hong Kong (+)
No. of international conferences held in Hong Kong (+)

Economic subindex
Per capita GDP at constant 2000 market prices (+)
Gross international reserves (months of import coverage) (+)
% of total household income earned by the bottom 50% of households (+)

Environmental quailty subindex
% of gazetted beaches ranked as poor/very poor (−)
Per capita square metres of public open space (+)
Per capita cubic metres of annual fresh water consumption by domestic sector (−)
% of municipal solid waste recycled (+)

Arts & entertainment subindex
No. of buildings and archaeological sites declared as monuments (+)
No. of films produced locally (+)
No. of books and magazines first published in HK (+)
Attendance at museums & cultural venues per 100,000 population (+)

Sports and recreation subindex
No. of public sporting facilities (+)
Average utilization rate of public sports facilities (+)
Size of delegation participating in major games (+)

Science & technology subindex
No. of patents granted to Hong Kong entities (residents + non-residents) (+)
No. of scientific publications in refereed publications (+)

Education subindex
% of people aged 20 + with upper secondary educational attainment (+)
% of people aged 15 + with tertiary education attainment (+)
No. of adults registered in continuing education courses per 100,000 population aged 15+ (+)

Health subindex
Average life expectation at birth (+)
Infant mortality rate per 1,000 live born (−)
Tuberculosis cases per 100,000 population (−)
No. of adults smoking per 100,000 population aged 20+ (−)
No. of deaths from coronary heart diseases per 100,000 population (−)
Adult suicides per 100,000 population aged 20+ (−)

Personal safety subindex
No. of reported food poisoning cases per 100,000 population (−)
No. of occupational fatalities per 100,000 workers (−)
No. of traffic fatalities per 100,000 population (−)

Housing subindex
% of expenditure on housing as share of total household expenditure (−)
No. of waiting list applicants for Housing Authority rental flats (−)

Crime & public safety subindex
No. of reported violent crimes per 100,000 population (−)
No. of reported non-violent crimes per 100,000 population (−)
% of population reporting victimized by violent crimes (−)
No. of corruption crime convictions per 100,000 population (−)

Family solidarity subindex
Marriages per 100,000 people aged 15+ (+)
Divorces as % of marriages (−)
Reported domestic violence cases per 100,000 households (−)

Appendix 3: List of Subindexes for Five Vulnerable Groups and Indicators

Women status subindex
% of women in low income households (−)
Married women labour force participation rate (+)
Median women's wages as a % of median men's wages, all ages (+)
% of female administrators and managers (+)
% of District Board positions occupied by women (+)

Low income subindex
No. of people in low-income domestic households per 100,000 population (−)
% of household expenditure on housing and food for the low-income households (−)
Unemployment rate in low-income households (−)
Real Wage Index of wage workers (+)
Homeless people per 100,000 population (−)

Child status subindex
% of children aged 0-14 in low-income households (−)
% of children living in single-parent households (−)
Under-five child mortality per 100,000 (−)
Children (aged 2-6) enrolled in kindergarten or childcare centers per 100,000 (+)
Child abuse cases per 100,000 population aged 0-17 (−)
% of children fully immunized against diphtheria, tetanus and whopping cough (+)
No. of children aged 10-15 arrested per 100,000 (−)

Youth status subindex
% of youth aged 15-19 in low-income households (−)
% of youth aged 15-19 attaining S4 or above (+)
% of people aged 15-24 studying full-time courses at tertiary education (+)
Youth unemployment rate, aged 15-19 years (−)
No. of youth arrested for violent crimes per 100,000 population 16-20 (−)
Prevalence of drug use among youth aged 15-19 per 100,000 population aged 15-19 (−)
Youth suicide rate, aged 10-19 years (−)

Elderly status subindex
% of people aged 65 + in low-income households (−)
Years of life expectation at age 65 (+)
% of elderly with lower secondary educational attainment (+)
Turnout rate of elderly voting in most recent District Board election(+)
% of elderly as members of social centre or multi-services centre for the elderly (+)
% of elderly aged 65 + living alone (−)
Elderly suicide rate per 100,000 (−)

References

Chan, Y. K., Kwan, C. C. A., & Shek, D. T. L. (2005). Quality of life in Hong Kong: The CUHK Hong Kong quality of life index. *Social Indicators Research, 71*, 259–289.

Chiu, L. H. R. (2005). Housing in the social development perspective. In R. J. Estes (Ed.), *Social development in Hong Kong: The unfinished agenda* (pp. 157–169). Hong Kong: Oxford University Press.

Commission on Poverty. (2005). *Intergenerational poverty*. Hong Kong.

Commission on Poverty. (2007). *Report of the Commission on Poverty*. Hong Kong.

Estes, R. J. (1988). *Trends in world social development: The social progress of nations 1970–1986*. New York: Praeger.

Estes, R. J. (1996). Social development trends in Asia, 1970–1994: The challenges of a new century. *Social Indicators Research, 37*(2), 119–148.

Estes, R. J. (1998). Trends in world social development, 1970–95: Development prospects for a new century. *Journal of Developing Societies, 14*(1), 11–39.

Estes, R. J. (1999). The poverties: Competing definitions and alternative approaches to measurement. *Social Development Issues, 21*(2), 11–21.

Estes, R. J. (2004). Development challenges of the "New Europe". *Social Indicators Research, 69*(2), 123–166.

Estes, R. J. (2005a). Quality of life in Hong Kong: Past accomplishments and future prospects. *Social Indicators Research, 71*, 183–229.

Estes, R. J. (2005b). *Social development in Hong Kong: The unfinished agenda*. Hong Kong: Oxford University Press.

Grover, S. L., & Crooker, K. J. (1995). Who appreciates family-responsive human resource policies: The impact of family-friendly policies on the organizational attachment of parents and non-parents. *Personnel Psychology, 48*(2), 271–288.

Mansdotter, A., Lindholm, L., & Winkvist, A. (2007). Paternity leave in Sweden—Costs, savings and health gains. *Health Policy, 82*, 102–115.

Organization for Economic Co-operation and Development. (2002). *Babies and bosses—Reconciling work and family life volume 1: Australia, Denmark and the Netherlands.* Paris: OECD.

Organization for Economic Co-operation and Development. (2003). *Babies and bosses—Reconciling work and family life volume 2: Austria, Ireland and Japan.* Paris: OECD.

Organization for Economic Co-operation and Development. (2004). *Babies and bosses—Reconciling work and family life volume 3: New Zealand, Portugal and Switzerland.* Paris: OECD.

Organization for Economic Co-operation and Development. (2005). *Babies and bosses—Reconciling work and family life volume 4: Canada, Finland, Sweden and the United Kingdom.* Paris: OECD.

Organization for Economic Co-operation and Development. (2008). *Babies and bosses—A synthesis of findings for OECD volume 5.* Paris: OECD.

Shek, D. T. L. (2005). Social stress in Hong Kong. In R. J. Estes (Ed.), *Social development in Hong Kong: The unfinished agenda* (pp. 213–222). Hong Kong: Oxford University Press.

Shek, D. T. L., & Lee, B. M. (2007). A comprehensive review of quality of life (QOL) research in Hong Kong. *The Scientific World Journal: TSW Holistic Health & Medicine, 7*, 1222–1229.

The Hong Kong Council of Social Service. (2000). *Social development in Hong Kong: The unfinished agenda.* Hong Kong: The Hong Kong Council of Social Service.

The Hong Kong Council of Social Service. (2002). *Social development index 2002 and review of social development 1997–2002.* Hong Kong: The Hong Kong Council of Social Service.

The Hong Kong Council of Social Service. (2007). *Social Development Index 2006.* Hong Kong: The Hong Kong Council of Social Service.

The Hong Kong Council of Social Service. (2009). *Social Development Index 2008.* Hong Kong: The Hong Kong Council of Social Service.

United Nations. (1995). *World summit for social development: The Copenhagen declaration and programme of action.* New York: United Nations.

United Nations Conference on Environment and Development (UNCED). (1992). *Agenda 21: Programme of action for sustainable development.* Rio de Janeiro, Brazil.

United Nations Development Programme. (2003). *Human development report, 2003: Millennium development goals.* New York: Oxford University Press.

Wong, C. K., Wong, K. Y., & Mok, B. H. (2006). Subjective well-being, societal condition and social policy—The case of a rich Chinese society. *Social Indicators Research, 78*, 405–428.

Soc Indic Res (2010) 95:553
DOI 10.1007/s11205-009-9544-4

ERRATUM

Erratum to: The Influence of Health Promoting Practices on the Quality of Life of Community Adults in Hong Kong

Phoenix K. H. Mo · Winnie W. S. Mak

Published online: 3 November 2009

1 Erratum to: Soc Indic Res (2009) DOI 10.1007/s11205-009-9523-9

The name of the second author has been set wrongly. The names of the authors should read:

Phoenix K. H. Mo, Winnie W. S. Mak

The online version of the original chapter can be found under doi:10.1007/978-94-007-0224-0_11.

P. K. H. Mo
Institute of Work, Health and Organisations, University of Nottingham, 8 William Lee Buildings, Science and Technology Park, Nottingham NG7 2RQ, UK
e-mail: lwxkhm1@nottingham.ac.uk

W. W. S. Mak (✉)
Department of Psychology, The Chinese University of Hong Kong, 3/F Sino Building, Shatin, Hong Kong
e-mail: wwsmak@psy.cuhk.edu.hk

GPSR Compliance

The European Union's (EU) General Product Safety Regulation (GPSR) is a set of rules that requires consumer products to be safe and our obligations to ensure this.

If you have any concerns about our products, you can contact us on ProductSafety@springernature.com

In case Publisher is established outside the EU, the EU authorized representative is:

Springer Nature Customer Service Center GmbH
Europaplatz 3
69115 Heidelberg, Germany

Batch number: 10823959

Printed by Printforce, the Netherlands